Case Studies in Sport Communication

EDITED BY ROBERT S. BROWN AND DANIEL J. O'ROURKE III

Westport, Connecticut
London

Library of Congress Cataloging-in-Publication Data

Case studies in sport communication / edited by Robert S. Brown and Daniel J.
O'Rourke III.
    p. cm.
  Includes bibliographical references and index.
  ISBN 0–275–97530–4 (alk. paper)—ISBN 0–275–97531–2 (pbk. : alk. paper)
    1. Mass media and sports—United States—Case studies. I. Brown, Robert S., 1968–
II. O'Rourke, Daniel J.
  GV742.C37   2003
  070.4'49796—dc21   2003045788

British Library Cataloguing in Publication Data is available.

Library of Congress Catalog Card Number: 2003045788
ISBN: 0–275–97530–4
   0–275–97531–2 (pbk.)

First published in 2003

Praeger Publishers, 88 Post Road West, Westport, CT 06881
An imprint of Greenwood Publishing Group, Inc.
www.praeger.com

Printed in the United States of America

The paper used in this book complies with the
Permanent Paper Standard issued by the National
Information Standards Organization (Z39.48–1984).

10 9 8 7 6 5 4 3 2 1

Contents

Preface

Robert S. Brown

Why study sport from a communication approach? It seems that whereas academic areas such as history, sociology, and literature have all discovered the wealth of insightful and socially valuable material produced through and about sport, as Nick Trujillo details in the Introduction to this book, communication-based research has lagged far behind. This is unfortunate, because sport is potentially the most influential, yet understudied, source of messages in society for many reasons.

First, viewers are more open to sport and its messages than to traditional sources where people filter the messages. When exposed to traditional message sources, such as the news media, political outlets, and advertising, people evaluate those messages through a series of attitudinal filters developed through their awareness of particular source-based biases. Receivers develop these critical filters on the basis of perceptions, such as the liberal or conservative reputations of the sources or the amount of favoritism toward a particular product or point of view. These filters then influence the impact of the messages to the point that receivers reject the messages completely. However, these filters are dropped when it comes to sport. Sport is perceived as a source of light entertainment built on physical action for which there is no need for critical evaluation, and thus, message content is accepted without critical evaluation.

Second, people enjoy being a part of the sports world, to the point of going to extreme measures just to be able to witness an event. Unlike the audiences for most other media, people will go out of their way and pay exorbitant amounts of money to view a sport. Fans spend millions of dollars every year to purchase sport-related clothing and merchandise. Voters often allow their taxes to be raised to finance sport facilities. Other message producers in society—think of an advertising agency or a political campaign—can only dream of having audiences go to these lengths just to be exposed to their product.

Third, sport is a collectively shared and reenforced event. Perhaps comparable in society to a music concert or the rare political rally, sport is enjoyed by people in huge gatherings, with large groups even getting together to watch televised events. In these settings, messages are received and shared by all the members of the group and therefore usually elicit some kind of feedback in the form of anything from applause to chants. Fans bond through their sport, a bond that is further developed through postgame discussion and media coverage of the events. Advertisers and politicians would consider themselves fortunate if they could develop the kind of community followings that sport generates.

Fourth, there is an emotional engagement between viewers and sport. The collective passions involved in exposure to sports again is equaled by little else in society. People, particularly fans, do not just listen to or watch sports—they live it. Their emotions are completely tied up in the game they are watching or the team for which they root. During a particularly successful season, these emotions can spread beyond the fan to the public at large, capturing the hearts of entire regions.

Fifth, sport is perceived as real. Politicians are often viewed as fake, and politics is often compared to a circus. The very natures of theater, television, and film demand the suspension of disbelief, and these entertainment forms are often minimized in people's thoughts in terms of the concept of "It was just a movie" or "That only happens on television." Sport, unlike these other areas, is perceived as reality. It is usually live, unscripted, and unpredictable. Even under the current methods of presentation, through which sport has become more a spectacle crafted by public relations and marketing experts, the predominate view that sport represents reality remains.

Sixth, and perhaps most important, is the universal attractiveness of sport. The audience for sport is made up of diverse people who cross all traditional demographic measures. Whereas in the past, sporting audiences might have been predominately male, modern sport audiences—numbering in the millions to hundreds of millions for large-scale events like the Olympics and World Cup—consist of a huge cross-section of the population that is independent of race, religion, gender, economic class, or any other social division.

It is obvious that sport is a major social institution. Look at the money spent and the media dedicated to sport-related coverage. Political leaders try to connect themselves to the sports industry to gain popularity, and in recent years, sport-related issues have led to debate in the highest levels of politics and the judicial system. This book offers a wide array of communication-based studies that attempt to reveal just part of the impact sport might have on society at large. The book by no means represents all the possible approaches and topics related to sport but rather a sample of how we might seek to understand the influence of sport communication.

Introduction

Nick Trujillo

The year was 1987. Leah Vande Berg and I were presenting a paper entitled, "Sports Communication and America's Team: Media, Sports, and Ethics," at the Speech Communication Association convention in Boston. The paper extended some of the ideas we had discussed in a previous publication on sport and values (see Trujillo & Ekdom, 1985). The topic of the panel was something related to mediated sports and ethics, and there seemed to be a better-than-average crowd in the room.

I honestly don't remember how our presentation went that day, but I do remember what happened after the panel. Dozens of colleagues from around the country came up and congratulated members of the panel for "having the courage" to study sport. Many of them said that they also wanted to do research and write about sport but had been discouraged from studying such a "frivolous" topic at their respective institutions. Some of these colleagues wanted to start a Sports Communication Division, while others wanted to keep our mutual interest in sport "underground." After the panel, most of us headed to a bar to celebrate our discovery of such a large group of supportive colleagues and to plot strategies for making sport a serious topic of study in the discipline of communication.

We never did form a Sports Communication Division of the National Communication Association, though there are times I wish we had. Even today, after writing about communication and sport for more than 15 years, some people at conferences still ask me when I am going to get back to doing more "serious" research. I usually respond by saying something like, "What's more serious than sport? It's a billion-dollar industry and an important purveyor of cultural values." Then I ask them why they aren't studying something as important as sport.

Fortunately, fewer and fewer people ask me that question these days. Indeed, many of today's scholars in the communication discipline are treating sport more seriously, as evidenced by this edited volume. But, as I already suggested, this wasn't always the case.

A VERY BRIEF HISTORY OF COMMUNICATION RESEARCH ON SPORT

I do not know the communication scholar who published the first scholarly article on sport. I suppose it depends on your sense of what constitutes a "communication" scholar. For example, there were many early studies about sport writing in *Journalism Quarterly*, which is not surprising because it has long been a topic of study for journalism scholars (for a review, see McChesney, 1989). In their *Index to Journals in Communication Studies*, Matlon and Ortiz (1992) list Ridings's (1934) article entitled, "Use of Slang in Newspaper Sports Writing," as the earliest sport publication in *Journalism Quarterly*. Subsequent articles in *Journalism Quarterly* included Tannenbaum and Noah's (1959) classic analysis of "Sportsugese," Kelley's (1976) reflections on Jackie Robinson's relationship to the press, and many others (e.g., Anderson, 1983; Reid & Soley, 1979; Salwen & Bernstein, 1986).

To find an article published in a communication journal other than *Journalism Quarterly*, Matlon and Ortiz (1992) had to travel all the way to 1975, when the *Journal of Communication* published Real's (1975) timeless piece entitled "Super Bowl: Mythic Spectacle." This article was seminal in the field and generated many subsequent studies of sport, especially televised sport. For whatever reasons, however, only the *Journal of Communication* seemed willing to publish articles on sport in the 1970s (e.g., Poe, 1976; Prisuta, 1979). The most impressive body of work during this decade appeared in a single issue of the *Journal of Communication* in 1977, that featured articles by Bryant, Comisky, and Zillmann; Comisky, Bryant, and Zillmann; Horowitz; Parente; Siegfried and Hinshaw; and Williams. Even though this landmark issue focused on televised sports, it opened a space for further research on communication and sport in the decades to come.

In the 1980s, several journals in the field published articles that dealt with sport, especially mediated sport. The *Journal of Communication* continued to lead the way, with articles by Bryant, Comisky, and Zillmann (1981) on televised football, Hocking (1982) on spectators, Rothenbuhler (1988) on television viewers of the Olympics, and Wanta and Leggett (1988) on sports announcing. The *Journal of Broadcasting* also published articles on mediated sport, including Gantz's (1981) study of the motives and behaviors of fans who watch televised sport and Bellamy's (1988) analysis of the television marketplace and Major League Baseball. A new journal, *Critical Studies in Mass Communication*, published a piece on sport writing and cultural values (Trujillo & Ekdom, 1985). Even the venerable *Quarterly Journal of Speech* published Kruse's (1981) critique of apologia in team sport.

In addition, in 1989, Lawrence Wenner published an edited volume, entitled *Media, Sports, and Society*, which may be the first book on sport published by a communication scholar. Indeed, Wenner described the book as "a maiden voyage for the communication of sport" (p. 8) and outlined a comprehensive research agenda for the study of mediated sport in his introductory chapter that covered media organizations, sport organizations, mediated sport content, and audience experiences. He enlisted the help of scholars such as Bellamy, Bryant, Eastman, Gantz, Jhally, McChesney, Real, Roloff, Trujillo, Vande Berg, and others to illustrate how this research agenda could come to fruition.

In the 1990s, the study of communication and sport continued to grow. Virtually every journal in the discipline of communication published studies of sport, including *Critical Studies in Mass Communication* (Lule, 1995), *Journal of Broadcasting and Electronic Media* (Walker, 1990), *Journal of International Communication* (Emerson & Perse, 1995), *Quarterly Journal of Speech* (Brummett & Duncan, 1990), *Southern Communication Journal* (Rybacki & Rybacki, 1995), *Western Journal of Communication* (Scheibel, 1995), *Women's Studies in Communication* (Daddario, 1992), and others. In addition, communication scholars such as Creedon (1994), Real (1996), Trujillo (1994), Wenner (1998), and others published books that focused on sports. In summary, during the 1990s, communication students and scholars became very serious about studying sport.

THE FUTURE OF COMMUNICATION RESEARCH ON SPORT

The future of communication research about sport is bright. I doubt that we will ever have a journal entitled the *Quarterly Journal of Sports Communication* to complement sport-related journals in other fields, such as sociology (*Sociology of Sport, Journal of Sport and Social Issues*), psychology (*Psychology of Sport*), philosophy (*Philosophy of Sport*), management (*Journal of Sport Management*), and others. Nevertheless, communication scholars interested in studying sport now have more outlets to publish their work than ever before. We can send our work to virtually any journal in our field, depending, as always, on the theoretical and methodological bent of the work, the journal, and its editor. We can also send our work to some of the journals in other fields listed previously. More important, there are more and more courses on sport being offered by communication departments, which indicates that sport has become a legitimate area of study for communication students.

I encourage all readers of this book to pursue their interests in the study of sport and communication. Students can take courses on sport communication proudly, and professors don't need to wait to get tenure to do research on sport. Sport is a legitimate and growing area of study in communication. It's time to play—and study—ball!

REFERENCE LIST

Anderson, D. A. (1983). Sports coverage in daily newspapers. *Journalism Quarterly*, *60*, 497–500.

Bellamy, R. V. (1988). Impact of the television marketplace on the structure of major league baseball. *Journal of Broadcasting and Electronic Media*, *32*, 73–87.

Brummett, B., & Duncan, M. C. (1990). Theorizing without totalizing: Specularity and televised sports. *Quarterly Journal of Speech*, *76*, 227–246.

Bryant, J., Comisky, P., & Zillmann, D. (1977). Drama in sports commentary. *Journal of Communication*, *27*, 140–149.

Bryant, J., Comisky, P., & Zillmann, D. (1981). The appeal of rough-and-tumble play in televised professional football. *Communication Quarterly*, *29*, 256–262.

Comisky, P., Bryant, J., & Zillmann, D. (1977). Commentary as a substitute for action. *Journal of Communication*, *27*, 150–153.

Creedon, P. J. (1994). *Women, media, and sport: Challenging gender values*. Thousand Oaks, CA: Sage.

Daddario, G. (1992). Swimming against the tide: *Sports Illustrated's* imagery of female athletes in a swimsuit world. *Women's Studies in Communication*, *15*, 49–64.

Emerson, M. B., & Perse, E. M. (1995). Media events and sports orientations to the 1992 Winter Olympics. *Journal of International Communication*, *2*, 80–99.

Gantz, W. (1981). An exploration of viewing motives and behaviors associated with television sports. *Journal of Broadcasting*, *25*, 263–275.

Hocking, J. E. (1982). Sports and spectators: Intra-audience effects. *Journal of Communication*, *32*, 100–108.

Horowitz, I. (1977). Sports telecasts: Rights and regulations. *Journal of Communication*, *27*, 160–168.

Kelley, W. G. (1976). Jackie Robinson and the press. *Journalism Quarterly*, *53*, 137–139.

Kruse, N. W. (1981). Apologia in team sport. *Quarterly Journal of Speech*, *57*, 270–283.

Lule, J. (1995). The rape of Mike Tyson: Race, the press, and symbolic stereotypes. *Critical Studies in Mass Communication*, *12*, 176–195.

Matlon, R. J. & Ortiz, S. P. (1992). Index to journals in communication studies through 1990. Annandale, VA: Speech Communication Association.

McChesney, R. W. (1989). Media made sport: A history of sports coverage in the United States. In L. A. Wenner (Ed.), *Media, Sports and Society* (pp. 49–69). Newbury Park, CA: Sage.

Parente, D. E. (1977). The interdependence of sports and television. *Journal of Communication, 27,* 128–132.

Poe, A. (1976). Active women in ads. *Journal of Communication, 26,* 185–192.

Prisuta, R. H. (1979). Televised sports and political values. *Journal of Communication, 29,* 94–102.

Real, M. R. (1975). Super Bowl: Mythic spectacle. *Journal of Communication, 25,* 31–43.

Real, M. R. (1996). *Exploring media culture: A guide.* Thousand Oaks, CA: Sage.

Reid, L. N., & Soley, L. C. (1979). *Sports Illustrated's* coverage of women in sports. *Journalism Quarterly, 56,* 861–862.

Ridings, J. W. (1934). Use of slang in newspaper sports writing. *Journalism Quarterly, 11,* 348–360.

Rothenbuhler, E. W. (1988). The living room celebration of the Olympic Games. *Journal of Communication, 38,* 61–81.

Rybacki, K. C., & Rybacki, D. J. (1995). Competition in the comic frame: A Burkean analysis of vintage sports car racing. *Southern Communication Journal, 61,* 76–90.

Salwen, M. B., & Bernstein, J. M. (1986). Coverage of aftermath of 1984 World Series. *Journalism Quarterly, 63,* 385–389.

Scheibel, D. (1995). "Making waves" with Burke: Surf Nazi culture and the rhetoric of localism. *Western Journal of Communication, 59,* 253–269.

Siegfried, J. H., & Hinshaw, C. E. (1977). Professional football and the anti-blackout law. *Journal of Communication, 27,* 169–174.

Tannenbaum, P. H., & Noah, J. E. (1959). Sportsugese: A study of sports page communication. *Journalism Quarterly, 36,* 163–170.

Trujillo, N. (1994). *The meaning of Nolan Ryan.* College Station: Texas A&M University Press.

Trujillo, N., & Ekdom, L. R. (1985). Sportswriting and American cultural values: The 1984 Chicago Cubs. *Critical Studies in Mass Communication, 2,* 262–281.

Walker, J. R. (1990). Time out: Viewing gratifications and reactions to the 1987 NFL players' strike. *Journal of Broadcasting and Electronic Media, 34,* 335–350.

Wanta, W., & Leggett, D. (1988). "Hitting paydirt": Capacity theory and sport announcers' use of clichés. *Journal of Communication, 38,* 82–89.

Wenner, L. A. (Ed.). (1989). *Media, sport, and society.* Newbury Park, CA: Sage.

Wenner, L. A. (Ed.). (1998). *MediaSport.* London: Routledge.

Williams, B. R. (1977). The structure of televised football. *Journal of Communication, 27,* 133–139.

CHAPTER 1

The Rhetorical Resurgence of Pete Rose: A Second-Chance Apologia

Todd F. McDorman

Jim Gray: Pete, now let me ask you. It seems as though there is an opening, the American public is very forgiving. Are you willing to show contrition, admit that you bet on baseball, and make some sort of apology to that effect?

Pete Rose: Not at all, Jim. I'm not going to admit to something that didn't happen. I know you're getting tired of hearing me say that. ("What they said," 1999)

Banished in 1989 due to allegations that he bet on baseball, Pete Rose, baseball's all-time hits leader, returned to the game for one spectacular evening on October 25, 1999, as baseball honored its "All-Century" team prior to Game 2 of the World Series. Upon his introduction as the final outfielder on the team, Rose received a 55-second standing ovation from the Turner Field crowd in Atlanta—15 seconds longer than the next most appreciative response for hometown hero and all-time home run king Hank Aaron. Immediately following the presentation, Rose conducted a two-and-a-half minute on-field interview with Jim Gray, an investigative sports journalist known for his cutting and sometimes insensitive questions. In the interview, Gray repeatedly pressed Rose to admit that he had gambled on baseball, a charge he had always denied. As Gray aggressively pursued him, Rose became a sympathetic figure. In the media frenzy that followed, Pete Rose became a national topic as people criticized Jim Gray, defended Rose, and seriously questioned why Rose remains banned from baseball. Presented with a redefined rhetorical situation, Rose was able to renew his apologia. This chapter explores the saga of Pete Rose as a critical event in sport communication. Not only does Rose's resurgence provide insight into the immense public appeal of sporting icons, but it enables the exploration of alternative dimensions of the apologia genre. I begin by examining the nature of apologia. Then, I briefly review Rose's failed defense and banishment from baseball in 1989. Finally, I explore how an analysis of the Rose saga offers an expanded understanding of the rhetorical theory of apologia. Specifically, I argue that a new rhetorical situation may create opportunities for the expression of previously ineffective apologia. In addition, the passage of time may alter public memory in ways conducive to the appeal of the renewed apologia. And, finally, the fragmentation of culture may make many contemporary apologia more effective.

THE STUDY OF SPORT APOLOGIA

Although sometimes derided as merely childish extravagance, sport has a great deal to offer society as both a reflection of its conditions and a molding force. The ethos of sport—the virtues of hard work, team play, and, of course, winning—pervade American culture and yet often have remained outside the scope of mainstream academic study (Engen, 1995, p. 142). Jackson B. Miller (1999) argues that sporting events have so much power that they are able "to *create* culturally shared beliefs and values" (p. 189). Because of this, other scholars, such as Noreen Wales Kruse (1981a), argue that "[r]hetorical critics can profit from the recognition that sport constitutes a significant area of study"(p. 283). Gray Matthews (1995) agrees, adding, "The world of sport offers communication scholars an intriguing context in which to study and test theoretical concerns and practical applications. The areas for research are virtually unlimited" (p. 276). One inviting area of research is the study of sports apologia and image restoration. The excesses that seem increasingly to accompany contemporary sport celebrity—domestic turmoil, alcohol and drug addiction, a plethora of legal problems—have made the apology an athletic art form as troubled professionals attempt to hold on to their careers and regain their splendor in the public eye. From Pete Rose's banishment for gambling to Darryl Strawberry's repeated drug problems to John Rocker's apology for his hate-filled diatribe to Bobby Knight's removal as the basketball coach at Indiana University, sporting celebrities have found themselves in need of statements of self-defense. Such episodes caused William L. Benoit and Robert S. Hanczor (1994) to conclude, in their analysis of figure skater Tonya Harding's image restoration efforts, "Thus, sports figures frequently need to defend their images, and the discourse they produce is a legitimate object of study" (p. 428).

First elaborated from a rhetorical perspective by B. L. Ware and Wil A. Linkugel (1973), apologia is a common form of self-defense utilized by rhetors when taking their case to the people. Such efforts, as Benoit (1995a) notes in his exploration of a general theory of image restoration, are "commonplace. Because blame occurs throughout human society and, because face is important for virtually everyone, . . . a felt need to cleanse one's reputation with discourse occurs through our lives, public and private" (p. 5). An expansive body of subsequent scholarship exploring apologia in a variety of social, political, and corporate circumstances has demonstrated the breadth of the apologia genre (Benoit, 1995b, 1997; Benoit & Brinson, 1994; Hearit, 1995; Huxman & Bruce, 1995; Kruse, 1977, 1981a, 1981b). Studies have ranged from analyses of political speeches, such as Richard M. Nixon's "Checkers" address, to corporate apologies, as issued by the likes of Tylenol and Sears, to the image restoration discourse of pop culture figures, such as Hugh Grant.

Ware and Linkugel (1973) develop four modes of defense that remain central to analyses of apologia. Denial, perhaps the most obvious form of defense, consists of the speaker denying any wrongdoing or intent to do wrong. The converse of denial, bolstering, occurs when the rhetor reinforces the audience's identification of the speaker with more positive attributes; it is a repair of the speaker's image. In contrast to the reformative intent of denial and bolstering is the transformative nature of differentiation and transcendence. With differentiation, the speaker explains the legitimacy of his or her choice. Transcendence, the converse of differentiation, moves the audience from the particulars of the present situation to a more abstract view of the speaker's character.[1]

To date, explorations of sport apologia have been infrequent. In addition to Benoit and Haczor's (1994) analysis of Tonya Harding, two analyses relevant to this study are Noreen Wales Kruse's (1981a) exploration of apologia in team sports and Jeffrey Nelson's (1984) treatment of Billie Jean King's response to the revelation of a homosexual affair with her former secretary. Kruse concludes that the "apologetic responses of sport figures do not differ strategically from the character defenses offered by those in the sociopolitical world" (p. 280). She contends that sport figures are likely to say, "I'm sorry," which is notable in light of Rose's explicit refusal to do so. "Regret," according to Kruse, "functions rhetorically as evidence that one has taken the first step in mending one's ways and, thus, serves as temporary proof that one is worthy of being reunited with the community one has offended" (p. 281). The Pete Rose incident is interesting not only because it further demonstrates the utility of studies of sport rhetoric, but also because Rose's strategy, until recently, has challenged Kruse's contention that contrition is the best course of action.

Similarly, Nelson's (1984) analysis foreshadows the potential importance of both the media and sources of apology external to the central rhetor. He argues that expanded media access should encourage critics to consider sources beyond the apologist, noting that "the critic investigating a speaker might gain a richer insight by determining how that speaker's

peers and the media work in concert with or against the principal's rhetorical goals" (p. 100). The multidimensional nature of Rose's renewed
redemptive efforts underscores this observation and provides a rich opportunity to explore its importance for the study of apologia.

Although the perspectives of Ware and Linkugel (1973) and other researchers remain valid, it is my contention that they do not fully capture
the range of considerations and strategies that might be at work in various
sorts of apologia. That is, not only is the nature of apologia changing, but
the Pete Rose controversy also brings to light potential insights into the
evolution of the practice. The case of Pete Rose is interesting on several
counts. First, in his failed 1989 apologia, Rose, one of the most identifiable
figures in the history of baseball, extensively used denial in refusing to
accept any blame. Second, the issue reemerged after 10 years of little media attention, and current explorations of apologia do not address the
potential ramifications of the reintroduction of apologia after an extended
absence. Third, the multiple texts presented in the Rose case evince the
fragmentation of culture. Rather than there being a single, short speech
of self-defense, as is commonly examined in most studies of apologia,
Rose utilized the plethora of formats, ranging from the controversial Gray
interview to press conferences to Web sites, that changes in society have
produced. However, before exploring the implications of such issues for
our understanding of apologia, it is necessary to return briefly to Rose's
1989 exile from baseball.

FALL FROM GRACE: PETE ROSE'S BANISHMENT
FROM BASEBALL

Pete Rose epitomized the American Dream. From his humble begin-
nings, the undersized and modestly talented Cincinnati native became a
baseball icon. Sarcastically derided as "Charlie Hustle" in his rookie season by baseball greats Mickey Mantle and Whitey Ford, Rose came to
embody the label, turning it into high praise. After 23 seasons, Rose held
numerous baseball records, including the all-time hits leader (4,256), most
games played (3,562), and most times at bat (14,053) (Carter, 1999). In 1984,
two years before he retired from playing, he also became the manager of
the Cincinnati Reds, a position he would hold until his banishment from
baseball.

In February 1989, Major League Baseball (MLB) began investigating
Rose because of concerns over gambling allegations. Attorney John Dowd,
hired by MLB as a special investigator in the Rose case, issued a 225-page
summary report (Dowd, 1989), with seven volumes of evidence and testimony, that claimed Rose bet at least $10,000 on 52 different Reds' games
in 1987, among other allegations (Carter, 1999).

As the investigation churned on, the outlook for Rose turned bleak.

Perhaps Thomas Boswell's (1999b) biting critique of Rose—that Rose was a symbol and victim of the greed of the 1980s—is an accurate portrayal. "Sadly for Rose," Boswell writes, "his final act of the decade was a quintessential Eighties turn: the addict in denial. Everybody in America seemed to know what was happening to Rose except Pete himself. He alone didn't get it. Baseball wanted Rose to confess. To everything. Then the game could forgive him. It was that simple. Admit your problem. Get kicked out of the sport for a while. Get yourself fixed. Get reinstated" (p. 248). Although Boswell's advice is consistent with that of rhetorical critics such as Kruse (1981a) and Benoit (1995a), Rose, of course, refused to make such an admission. As one Cincinnati writer following the story puts it, Rose "never cracked," despite the intense scrutiny. He "had the will of a steel door. It was amazing" (Daugherty, 1999). Amazing perhaps, but Rose's was also a strategy that set in motion the chain of events that would place him—potentially permanently—outside baseball's inner sanctum.

On August 24, 1989, just eight days before he would die of a heart attack, Baseball Commissioner A. Bartlett Giamatti closed the investigation by banning Pete Rose from baseball. "The banishment for life of Pete Rose from baseball is the sad end of a sorry episode" said Giamatti (1989, p. 10C). He justified the action by explaining:

One of the game's greatest players has engaged in a variety of acts which have stained the game, and he must now live with the consequences of those acts.

By choosing not to come to a hearing before me, and by choosing not to proffer any testimony or evidence and information contained in the report of the special counsel to the commissioner, Mr. Rose has accepted baseball's ultimate sanction, lifetime ineligibility. (p. 10C)

Cloaking his comments in a defense of the integrity of the game, Giamatti vowed "to use, in short, every lawful and ethical means to defend and protect the game" (p. 10C). He ultimately sought closure while steering baseball into the future: "The matter of Mr. Rose is now closed. It will be debated and discussed. Let no one think it did not hurt baseball. That hurt will pass; however, as the great glory of the game asserts itself and a resilient institution goes forward. Let it also be clear that no individual is superior to the game" (p. 10C).

Writing in the *Southern Communication Journal*, Matthews (1995) argues that Giamatti's statement served as an effective example of epideictic rhetoric that eloquently nurtured community among baseball fans. The success of Giamatti's statement may explain in large measure the ineffectiveness of Rose's 1989 apologia. As for that apologia, Rose continued to stick to his story. In the press conference held at Riverfront Stadium, home of the Reds, on the day of Giamatti's statement, Rose again adamantly denied the charges: "Regardless of what the commissioner said today, I did not bet on baseball" (Groeschen, 1999).

With Giamatti's decision, Rose's days in baseball were over, and it seemed his apologia had failed. A Harris poll, released 10 days after Rose was banished, found that 84 percent of baseball fans believed Rose bet on baseball (Groeschen, 1999). Further tarnishing his image, in 1990 he was found guilty of a petty tax evasion charge and forced to serve five months in jail and three months in a halfway house (Carter, 1999). The conviction was an unfortunate and largely symbolic indignity that capped Rose's descent. Rose had paid 12 times as much in taxes as he had omitted from his tax returns. In all, the income he had avoided paying tax on was only about three percent of his total earnings (Boswell, 1999b, p. 239).

While he was presumably "cleaning up" his life over the next 10 years, Rose's redemptive efforts largely went unnoticed. When he received attention, it generally was for ventures of questionable taste, such as his frequent special appearances at casinos or when he joined Mike Tyson and Gennifer Flowers in the promotion of a Wrestle Mania event in spring 1999. According to Rose, "I told the promoters they could double my pay if one of the wrestlers was going to pick me up and throw me in the stands" (MacGregor, 1999).

During the week marking the tenth anniversary of his ban from baseball, Rose appeared on ESPN's *Up Close* with Gary Miller. In the interview, Rose maintained his innocence and claimed that he had met the conditions set out for reinstatement, primarily "reconfiguring" his life. According to Rose, he no longer participated in any illegal gambling and had disassociated himself from people of questionable character ("I gambled for recreation," 1999). And though Rose indicated he would "absolutely" agree with the ban if "they found I bet on baseball," he employed bolstering in an attempt to "set the record straight" regarding his suspension by noting, "It's amazing to me how many people that report on this story don't really know the facts of this story, but they continue to report on it" ("I gambled for recreation," 1999). That same week, he told the Associated Press that he was being singled out unfairly: "It seems that in our society, 99 out of 100 guys are given another opportunity. I'm the one out of 100 that's not being given another opportunity, which is mind-boggling to me" (MacGregor, 1999).

Writing on the occasion of the 10-year anniversary, Cincinnati sportswriter Tim Sullivan (1999b) noted that Rose had been unable to generate any "real momentum toward reinstatement." "The reality," wrote Sullivan, was "that Pete Rose needs to make the next move. Whatever it is." Boswell (1999b) concurred that Rose had lost his standing in the sport. The author observed that while "most of the legends in sports . . . remain pertinent . . . [w]ith each passing year, Pete Rose makes himself seem more irrelevant. He has not moved on with us but, rather, remains an unevolved prisoner of his past" (p. 249). Rose's opportunity to create new momentum and perhaps escape the past would arrive just over two months later with his appearance at the All-Century team ceremony and the infamous Jim Gray interview.

A SECOND CHANCE: ROSE'S RHETORICAL RESURGENCE

I contend that the All-Century team celebration and the Jim Gray interview created an exigence that provided Pete Rose with an opportunity to rearticulate his apologia. Furthermore, the passage of time, the sympathy evoked by the Gray interview, and the disappearance of many of the scandal's key figures from the public eye made Rose's rhetoric more appealing. Finally, the fragmentation of contemporary culture—seen through the multitude of media outlets broadcasting parts of Rose's message—raised his effectiveness and partially redeemed him in the public eye. All three of these occurrences have relevance for our understanding of apologia.

A (Re)New(ed) Rhetorical Situation

A rhetorical situation, according to Lloyd Bitzer (1974 [1968]) in his influential essay of the same name, is a "complex of persons, events, objects and relations presenting an actual or potential exigency which may be completely or partially removed if discourse, introduced into the situation, can so constrain human decision or action as to bring about the significant modification of the exigency" (p. 252). This concept's relevance to apologia is fairly clear; the rhetor issues a statement in an effort to gain redemption and remove the exigence that has created the need for self-defense. The instance I am interested in here, however, is when the apologia, and the exigence, is removed from the original context. That is, we expect to see an apologia in the immediate wake of a situation—such as Nixon's resignation speech or Edward Kennedy's "Chappaquiddick" address—but does an apologia that occurs in a different frame of time, in response to a new rhetorical situation or renewed attention to a previous situation, present a different set of considerations?

Carole Blair's (1984) analysis of the strategies of apology in the post-Watergate autobiographies of President Richard Nixon's inner circle provides some insight because of its temporal distance from the original controversy and the subsequent apologies. As Blair notes, the rhetorical situation for the autobiographies "was markedly different from that promoting the more immediate public apologias while the crisis was unfolding" (p. 252). Blair comes to an important conclusion: "One cannot judge the actual or potential effectiveness or ineffectiveness of generic rhetoric by analyzing only the particular elements of messages. Rather all of the interactive factors that comprise the rhetorical situation must be considered" (p. 259).

In the case of Pete Rose, a revitalized rhetorical situation was presented, and thus, new interactive factors demanded consideration. First, on the eve of the tenth anniversary of Rose's exile, MLB Commissioner Bud Selig made the surprise announcement that Rose could participate in on-field festivities if fans elected him to the All-Century team. Second, the All-Century announcement renewed Rose's hero status, whereas the Jim Gray interview appeared to make Rose a victim.[2] During the interview, each Rose denial and refusal to apologize was met with another effort to push the issue forward:

Gray: With the overwhelming evidence in that report, why not make that step . . . [to admit you gambled on baseball]?

Rose: No. This is too much of a festive night to worry about that because I don't know what evidence you're talking about. I mean, show it to me.

Gray: The Dowd report says . . . but we don't want to debate that, Pete.

Rose: Well, why not. Why don't we want to hear everything it says?

Gray: Pete, those who will hear this tonight will say you have been your own worst enemy and continue to be. How do you respond to that?

Rose: In what way are you talking about?

Gray: By not acknowledging what seems to be overwhelming evidence.

Rose: Yeah, I'm surprised you're bombarding me like this. I mean I'm doing an interview with you on a great night, a great occasion, a great ovation. Everybody seems to be in a good mood. And you're bringing up something that happened 10 years ago.

Gray: Well, I bring it up because people would like to see you get it on. . . . Pete, we've got to go. We've got a game.

Rose: . . . This is a prosecutor's brief, not an interview, and I'm very surprised at you.

Gray: Some would be surprised that you didn't take the opportunity. ("What they said," 1999, p. 6C)

In five consecutive questions, Gray pushed for a confession. His persistence, along with the immediate lack of evidence and Rose's surprised reaction, put Rose back on the front page. With Rose cast as both hero and victim, a new rhetorical situation that maximized the persuasive appeal of his message was born.

Although some were supportive of Gray, such as legendary baseball writer Murray Chass, who said he thought it "was the best TV interview I've ever seen," the majority of the immediate feedback was quite negative ("Gray says," 1999). For example, NBC's New York television affiliate reported more than 600 complaints about the interview, and the Cincinnati affiliate received two solid hours of calls, with some callers even waiting

30 minutes on hold before they were able to voice their opinion ("Fans flood NBC," 1999). After the game, widely respected Yankees' manager Joe Torre expressed his opinion that the tone of the interview was uncalled for and demonstrated that society has "lost sight of the word 'respect.' We deal too much in shock value" ("Yankees not yet willing," 1999). Oft–scandal-embroiled slugger Darryl Strawberry added: "[W]e were pretty much all disgusted with Jim. It was a night of celebration for Pete Rose. Every player who ever plays cares about Pete Rose. It was embarrassing. It didn't sit too well in this clubhouse" ("Gray says," 1999). Evidence of this displeasure surfaced before Game 3 of the World Series, when Yankees players refused to answer Gray's questions on the field. The disagreement culminated with Gray's efforts to interview Chad Curtis after his game-winning home run. Curtis stood with Gray during a 40-second commercial break only to say hello to his grandmother and announce "Because of what happened with Pete, we decided not to say anything." Curtis turned and walked away from a shocked Gray, who shouted "Don't you want to talk about your home run?" ("Yankees not yet willing," 1999).[3]

An admission by NBC Sports Chairman Dick Ebersol that the interview "probably went too long" ("Yankees not yet willing," 1999) and the demand for an apology from Gray by the corporate sponsor of the All-Century team, MasterCard International, further validated the perception that Rose had been violated and gave him yet more credibility. Through a corporate statement, MasterCard International (1999) said that it shared the fans' "outrage" and "in no way condones or supports Gray's action." "We strongly believe," the statement continued, "that Mr. Gray owes an apology to the millions of fans that tuned in" (MasterCard International, 1999). For his part, Gray issued an apology that stated: "After viewing the videotape, I can understand the reaction of many baseball fans. I thought that it was important to ask Pete Rose if this was the right moment for him to make an apology. If in doing so, the interview went on too long and took out some of the joy of the occasion, then I want to say to baseball fans everywhere that I'm very sorry about this" ("Yankees not yet willing," 1999). Notably absent from Gray's statement is any apology to Rose himself.

Ultimately, Gray's assault made Rose sympathetic and gave many fans justification for looking past Rose's transgressions. As *ESPN.com* contributor Ray Ratto (1999) put it following the Gray interview, "Pete Rose is back, bigger and more sympathetic than ever. He hasn't been this hot for years." Bob Raissman of the *New York Daily News* provided another popularly important perspective that cast Gray as the villain while minimizing Rose's role. To Raissman (1999), "Gray came off as a guy who was looking to enhance his own reputation as an interrogator . . . with[out] any sense of fairness or appreciation for the circumstances surrounding the interview. . . . This was all so pathetic. It was just another case of a guy on TV . . . trying to become the moment and make himself bigger than the game." Not only had a new rhetorical situation given Rose's apologia renewed relevance, but the validation provided by the hundreds of protest calls, the New York Yankees, the president of NBC Sports, and MasterCard International reframed the issue away from the guilt or innocence of Rose to a critique of Gray's tactics. Thus, Gray not only gave Rose's apology more relevance, but also made many audience members more compassionate toward and open to Rose's message. This incident's important contribution to apologia theory is the recognition that the creation of a new rhetorical situation and exigence can redeem the image of a fallen hero while providing the opportunity for a renewed apologia. The disgraced has a new, relevant opportunity to present his or her case and apology, as well as a second chance to regain public favor. And it would seem that by the very nature of the remembrance, that is, a situation that glorifies and humanizes the exiled, a return to the apologia improves the rhetor's chances for possible forgiveness of past transgressions.

Public Memory in Apologia

A second important theoretical connection brought to light by the resurgence of Pete Rose deals with the relationship between apologia and public memory. Recently, communication scholars have sought to explore the process of memory construction and its community-building functions (Browne, 1999; Hasian & Carlson, 2000; Zelizer, 1992). Recognizing that present events create the need to reinvent the past, Louis O. Mink (1987) argues that crises give "each generation . . . its own reason for rewriting its own history" (p. 87). Furthermore, history, as Maurice Halbwachs (1992) explains, "does not impose itself on us" (p. 50), and therefore, "[w]e are free to choose from the past the period into which we wish to immerse ourselves. If certain memories are inconvenient or burden us they can be removed from the view of the present" (p. 222). Whereas renowned baseball author Thomas Boswell's (1999b) harsh treatment of Rose, in which he argues that his "worst punishment . . . is that our appreciation of him as a person and a ballplayer is likely to fade, perhaps even disappear, with time" (p. 239), suggests that Rose is (or at least was) destined to recede into the background, the manner in which history was recalled during the controversy over the Gray interview suggests otherwise. In merging the concerns of public memory with apologia, the case of Pete Rose raises questions as to what happens when an apologia is reintroduced at a time when the public seems amenable to forgetting the past. The vast support of Pete Rose triggered by the All-Century announcement and the Gray interview seems to indicate that the public not only wants to remember Rose the ballplayer, but also may want to forget the possibility that Rose the gambler was guilty—or if he was guilty, to deem it a past event that lacks contemporary relevance.

Adding to the effectiveness of Rose's apology, and I would suggest to the effectiveness of most resurgent apologia, is that most of Rose's significant detractors have left the public scene. Apologias brought about by a new exigence should favor the rhetor because it is their voice, not that of their accusers, that is privileged by the public. Commissioner Giamatti, of course, passed away eight days after banning Rose. Although some, such as Boswell (1999b), claim that "that day Rose's chance [of reinstatement] died too" (p. 249), Giamatti's death also has meant that the spokesperson who may have held the most public influence is not able to campaign against Rose. Fay Vincent, who negotiated much of the Rose agreement and succeeded Giamatti as baseball commissioner, remains opposed to Rose's return to baseball. Writing in the *New York Times*, Vincent (1999) candidly offered: "Sometimes I think Pete Rose will be with me until I die" (p. A23). Vincent also has warned that any commissioner who readmits Rose threatens the sport's current deterrents to gambling. However, he also claims that "[i]f Rose were to fully explain what he did and why, so that kids and other fans could appreciate the consequences, I believe his redemptive efforts would be advanced" (p. A23). Vincent's voice is rather muted, however, in that he was forced out as MLB Commissioner in the early 1990s and is paid little attention by the baseball community.

Likewise, John Dowd, the investigator who compiled the initial report on Rose's gambling, was later dismissed by MLB. Dowd is the only figure who has remained in the spotlight and has sought out occasions to criticize Rose, including the decision to allow his participation in the All-Century festivities. However, MLB has been displeased with Dowd's continued participation and even has filed a failed compliant that would prohibit Dowd from publicly speaking about the matter. Robert DuPuy, baseball's executive vice president of administration and chief legal officer, says, "We do not solicit his [Dowd's] comments nor do we endorse them. We would prefer that Mr. Dowd refrain from commenting on his representation of the office of the commissioner. He is no longer engaged by this office and he has completed his work. We don't look for his guidance in this whatsoever" ("Dowd: Rose," 1999).

Coupled with MLB's rejection of him, early doubts about Dowd's report have grown and attained almost mythic status. Although it was used as the authoritative explanation at the time of Rose's exile, many have subsequently questioned the investigation and the evidence presented. Sam Dash, former chief counsel to the congressional committee that investigated Watergate, charges, "If John Dowd turned in a report like that to me, I'd fire him" (Sullivan, 1999b). Similarly, respected baseball author Bill James contends that Rose has been unfairly convicted. In his *Politics of Glory,* James writes that "John Dowd's investigation of Rose's behavior, which claimed to be fair and impartial, made a mockery of those words.

Dowd leapt to the conclusion that Rose was guilty, and twisted and bent the facts to support that conclusion" (Sullivan, 1999b). Roger Kahn, a long-time baseball author whose books include one that he wrote with Rose entitled *Pete Rose: My Story*, concludes that though the Dowd report is "persuasive in spots . . . overall [it] is an unconvincing mix of allegation and distortion. As I say, I don't know if Rose bet baseball. I do know, however, he was railroaded out of the game" ("How they feel," 1999). Even Rose's continued public statements, which I will review subsequently, have challenged the validity of the report, which means that it is recalled publicly only in a negative light rather than as a fair and thorough investigation.

Finally, most of the persons who provided information to Dowd subsequently spent time in jail due to a variety of offenses. Not only have these sources been criticized for being of questionable character, but their disappearance from the public eye has left a silent void as a counterresponse to Rose's denials. Ron Peters, who was identified as Rose's principle bookie, served two years in prison for tax evasion and cocaine trafficking. Tommy Gioiosa, who allegedly ran bets for Rose to Peters, was sentenced to five years on similar charges. Paul Janszen, who testified that he placed bets for Rose, served time for selling steroids, and Mike Bertolini, who produced the betting slips that allegedly have Rose's fingerprints on them, pleaded guilty to conspiracy to commit tax fraud (Groeschen, 1999). Although none of this disproves their allegations against Rose, it obviously has affected the perceived credibility of their testimony, as well as the credibility of the overall report.

Continued attention to Rose throughout the 2000 baseball season added to Rose's legend and provided more opportunities to reframe the past. Celebrations of the 25th anniversary of the Cincinnati Reds' World Series Championship and the 1980 Philadelphia Phillies' victory, teams that both featured Rose, were notable in part because of Rose's compelled absence. Both organizations requested that Rose be allowed to participate in their celebrations, but MLB Commissioner Selig denied the requests, saying, "as things stand, there's been no change (in Mr. Rose's status). . . . I did make an exception for the All-Century team because fans were voting and I didn't want to do anything to stop that. But we said it was a one-time thing" (Sullivan, 2000c). Predictably, the decision was not well received by either team, Rose's fans, or some local media. Their responses further promote the notion that Rose's actions are considered history that is best forgotten. *Cincinnati Enquirer* columnist Paul Daughtery (2000a), for example, questioned MLB's "integrity" over the incident, saying "so take this personally, fans. Also, take a hike. It's a little kiss-off from Bud [Selig], with love." At the ballpark, there was a massive show of fan support for Rose, with more than a dozen banners and repeated chants of "Pete! Pete! Pete!" during the ceremony. Third base, the position Rose occupied for the 1975 World Champion Reds, was left unoccupied while the other re-tired stars went to their accustomed positions. Then, current Reds' captain Barry Larkin ran onto the field and placed a single red rose on third base. The action sent the crowd into a frenzy ("Rose remembered," 2000).

Despite Selig's resistance, this combination of events seems to suggest that changed circumstances and public memory have given Rose a new opportunity to address the public and MLB. Rose's personal efforts to reshape the meaning of the past are evident in his comments prior to the All-Century celebration. Rose suggested that even the late Bart Giamatti might see things differently today, noting, "I seriously believe that if Bart would have lived, and we all wish he would have, he would have given me a second chance. That's the kind of man he was" (Chastain, 1999). Although it is impossible to predict Giamatti's reaction, public support has swung dramatically toward Rose. A week before the All-Century cere-monies—even prior to the sympathy evoked by the Gray interview—an Associated Press poll found that people felt Rose should be in the Hall of Fame by a 2-to-1 margin (Poll results, 1999). Nine months later, during Hall of Fame ceremonies that included the induction of three figures from Rose's Cincinnati teams, Rose spoke specifically of the changing public perception. Rose cunningly expressed his desire to speak directly to Selig: "I'd just like to sit down and look the guy in the eye and say, 'What do you think the fans want? Isn't baseball for the fans—or did I miss some-thing somewhere? Has my situation changed in the eyes of baseball fans? Is it snowballing my way? I think it is' " (Stark, 2000).

Ultimately, one of the lessons of this exchange and the outpouring of pro-Rose sentiment in the wake of the All-Century and World Champi-onship celebrations is that with the passage of time, a new situation may emerge that creates rhetorical space for the reissuance of the old apology with increased prospects of success. Thus, time and public sentiment are important ingredients to be added to the study of apologia theory, in that they clearly change our understanding of the apologia strategy. As time has passed, Rose's primary use of the reformative techniques of denial and bolstering has created a consistent front that has gained support. However, a slight alteration to the strategy can be found in Rose's in-creased reliance on fan support and a vague admission of "guilt"—though not to betting on baseball. These subtle changes are central to a final ele-ment of Rose's case: how the increased fragmentation of popular culture has combined with a reconstituted public memory and altered popular sentiment to allow for the widespread, though not universal, resurrection of Rose to the realm of baseball immortals.

Apologia in a Fragmented Culture

Finally, I contend that the fragmentary nature of contemporary culture may raise new possibilities for apologia in general and for Pete Rose specifically. Michael Calvin McGee (1990) has suggested that the fragmentation of culture has melded textual interpretation and construction to the point that they are part of an intertwined process. The result, as Sharon Downey (1993) summarizes, is that "[c]oherent, complete discourses characteristic of all preceding periods have been supplanted by 'fragmented,' transient, [and] unfinished" texts (p. 53). Downey argues that the evolution of apologia from classical to contemporary times reflects this cultural fragmentation. Driven primarily by technological innovations, the changing nature of information management during the past century has been "a period of expansion, innovation, ingenuity, and culture shock" (p. 52). Ultimately, I contend that we are seeing such transformation in contemporary apologia in cases in which a single complete text is supplanted by a series of texts that crafts a full defense.

The Pete Rose incident clearly illustrates the development of such changes. At the time of his suspension in 1989, the impact of the Internet was negligible, and 24-hour sports networks and talk shows on cable television news networks were on the periphery. Within 10 years, technological expansion had multiplied the media available for apologia. In the days and weeks following the Gray confrontation, Rose took full advantage of these possibilities by developing a comprehensive and effective public strategy. On an almost weekly basis, Rose capitalized on the media's attention in a variety of forums, ranging from public appearances to numerous interviews to a new series of national television ads for auto-body repair and repainting. For example, Rose used a series of November 1999 public appearances to bolster his character and make his case for reinstatement. These appearances were most noteworthy for Rose's efforts to use humor to deflect attention from the substance of his ban. Appearing on *The Martin Short Show,* Rose played the victim role and claimed he had been misled into doing the Gray interview. According to Rose, "We were told it would be a very positive interview. Everything in the interview was about gambling" ("Rose airs frustration," 1999). Rose subsequently roasted Gray in a sketch in which Rose interviewed Short. That same month, while accepting a "living legend" award from the Philadelphia Sports Writers, Rose was equally jovial. Commenting on the omission of Philadelphia '76ers' basketball star Allen Iverson from the 2000 Olympic team, Rose quipped: "I've got that figured out. Baseball must have selected that team" ("Baseball might meet," 2000). When a cell phone rang later during Rose's remarks, he said, "Quick, answer that. It's probably Bud Selig calling me" ("Baseball might meet," 2000).

A more concerted effort to air his story and gain public support can be found in Rose's use of the Internet, which has been a central feature of Rose's revival. Todd Greanier (1999), a writer for the online *Baseball Archive,* summarizes the strategy: "Pete Rose has recently taken his plight to the Internet. If the response from the users of *The Baseball Archive* is any

indication, he picked a great forum." *Sportcut.com*, that sells sports merchandise and provides sports information, features Rose as a paid endor-
ser. The launch of the Web site on November 30, 1999, was disguised as
a Pete Rose press conference. Subsequently, the site published three extensive pieces on Rose and provided visitors with an opportunity to vote
on whether Rose should be enshrined at Cooperstown. With its varied
forums, the site is indicative of the fragmentary nature of contemporary
culture and the multiple media outlets available. In concluding an interview on the site, Rose defended himself by denying all of MLB's charges:
"We'll present evidence that counters their evidence. We have experts, too,
just like they did. We have fingerprint experts and handwriting experts
too. They're not the only one that has experts. Our experts will tell the
truth and say the opposite of what they say. It's amazing how everybody
believes everything that John Dowd said. Why? It's the same guy that
baseball fired a couple of years ago and tried to get him disbarred about
five months ago" (Twemlow, 1999). The strategy has been well received;
91.7% of the 230,000 votes cast pertaining to Rose's reinstatement supported his admission to the Hall of Fame (Estock, 2000).

Furthermore, private Web sites that were organized in protest of the
Gray interview give the impression that this is a national controversy. The
two most prominent sites defend Pete Rose while calling for boycotts of
NBC and their advertisers (*Pete Rose*, 1999; Rhine, 1999). As the *Pete Rose*
(1999) Web site puts it, "This ill timed attack on Pete Rose and Baseball
Fans should not have happened and it is up to you to tell NBC, Major
League Baseball, and the advertisers about it." The site provides links to
corporate Web sites and a form to send e-mail directly to NBC Sports.
Michael Rhine's (1999) Web site provides 14 pages of links for filing protests, along with links and updates from private individuals all over the
country.

Finally, societal responses have authored a fragmented commentary
that melds into a defense of Rose, as shown in the support offered by the
New York Yankees, as well as the support offered by a variety of figures
ranging from sportswriters to Hall of Fame players to even former President Bill Clinton. Paul Daugherty, who believes Rose bet on baseball, also
agrees that the purpose and rationale of the ban have been increasingly
difficult to support. Daugherty (2000b) points to the numerous travails of
Darryl Strawberry, who since 1987 has been guilty of domestic abuse,
repaid $350,000 in back taxes, been sentenced to six months of home in-
carceration, failed to pay child support, solicited drugs and sex from an
undercover policewoman, and been caught with cocaine on at least three
occasions. Despite all of this, Strawberry was repeatedly welcomed back
to baseball. Writing to Commissioner Selig, Daugherty (2000b) asks: "Does
it get harder to justify Rose's ban every time Strawberry violates your
trust? Who's worse for baseball's image? How does it look to have a

known drug addict and wife abuser in the game, and not Rose? How does it pay to have John Rocker in the game, spewing his hateful nonsense all over the pages of a national magazine, and not Rose?" Respected broadcaster, Hall of Fame member, and former teammate Joe Morgan also defended Rose's participation in the World Championship celebrations. Morgan argued that Rose needed to be a part of the festivities for the 1975 World Champion Reds and charged that the All-Century celebration was just "about money," while "[t]his is about the fans. If the fans aren't the most important thing in the game, what is? I think Pete should be allowed to walk out there with the rest of us" (Sullivan, 2000a). Two days prior to the Cincinnati reunion, Ken Griffey Jr., possibly the most popular baseball player during the 1990s, addressed the media regarding Rose's absence in his usual quiet manner, saying, "Everyone knows that something's missing. And it shouldn't be" (Haft, 2000a). Similarly, Master of Ceremonies Marty Brennamen, a long-time Cincinnati Reds' broadcaster, called attention to Rose's absence during the Cincinnati celebration: "No, we haven't forgotten No. 14 [Rose's uniform number] should be here and isn't" (Erardi, 2000). Finally, President Clinton told *People* magazine for its 1999 year-end issue that he would like to see the redemption of Rose: "I'd like to see it [Rose's suspension] worked out, because he brought a lot of joy to the game, and he gave a lot of joy to people and he's paid his price—God knows, he's paid his price" ("Clinton says," 1999).

These numerous public fragments have coupled with Rose's continuing statements about the issue to weave a tapestry that defends Rose while seeking his forgiveness. In the process, they reinforce Nelson's (1984) suggestion that an apologist's peers and the media are also important for the impact of an apology. These various elements of the apologia have attacked the evidence against Rose, reflected on his contributions to baseball, regarded the passage of time as punishment enough, and embraced fan support. The fragments are united by their common theme—Pete Rose—though a single apologetic text remains absent. Instead, we have a series of public statements by Rose and his defenders that, over the course of several months following the All-Century team controversy, moved from the reformative techniques of denial and bolstering to more transformative efforts of differentiation and transcendence. Rose subsequently apologized and accepted blame for his "mistakes" without specifying exactly what those mistakes entailed. He combines this "admission" with an embrace of fans to argue that it transcends baseball's allegations and punishment. In another *Sportcut.com* interview from February 2000, Rose combines these elements in suggesting that his immense public reception at the All-Century introduction says "that America understands that I made some mistakes and the majority of people are willing to forgive me and let me go on with my life" (Estock, 2000). Adopting a populist approach to the ovation he received, Rose says the reception was "important to me" because "that was America speaking" (Estock, 2000).

Thus, a more reflective and introspective Rose now accepts some blame for the situation. In concluding the *Sportcut.com* interview, Rose offers that "I'm the one that made the mistakes so I can't get mad at anybody else because of the mistakes I made" (Estock, 2000). In March 2000, while visiting his son Pete Rose Jr. at the Philadelphia Phillies' spring camp, Rose reiterated this acceptance of responsibility, offering, "I created the problems I had, but it's kind of sad you can't go down to the [batting] cage to watch your son hit" ("Rose seeks," 2000). He followed this admission with another appeal for his ban to be rescinded: "Everybody in the world will agree that regardless of what you think I did do or didn't do, I've been in the penalty box long enough. It's just the American way to give you a second opportunity" ("Rose seeks," 2000). Months later, at the 2000 Hall of Fame induction ceremonies, Rose again spoke of his remorse, as well as his desire to move on, saying, "I wish those things [presumably the banishment and tax conviction] had never happened. You think I don't wish the last 10 years of my life weren't just a bad dream? I do. But I know I have to live with it" (Stark, 2000). With these statements, Rose has attempted a more transformative approach that says "I'm sorry" yet differentiates between that apology and an admission to gambling on baseball. Instead, he has sought to take advantage of the renewed rhetorical situation and relied on the passage of time to soften public memory. The public reception he has received indicates that, overall, it has been a successful strategy, as Rose has been able to maintain consistency while recapturing public support by portraying himself as both repentant and a victim.

Ultimately, such fragmentation may weaken the ability of truth to compete with sustained fiction. Bombarded with both Rose's denials and public defenses of Rose, the facts become much less important than the public perception. As Adrian Wojnarowski (1999) of the *Hackensack Record* noted, "the truth is losing in a landslide. Somehow, we are a step closer to Rose's return to baseball and the punching of his ticket to the Hall of Fame. He gathered sympathy with his Jim Gray interview, using his sudden stage to sell the same story of innocence again and again until his misinformation starts to sound plausible." Boswell (1999a) concurs, saying, "There's only one rational question remaining about Rose. Why does anybody—let alone so many people—still support him? Are we so gullible and sentimental toward our sports heroes that we join them in their self-delusions and denial?" (p. 12). Ratto (1999) adds that "[t]hus, in the court of public opinion, Pete Rose wins again. In fact, he wins convincingly this time. Were it not for commissioner Bud Selig's unofficial position on Rose's reinstatement ('Over my cold, dead corpse'), he might have been carried to Cooperstown on the backs of his fellow Centurions." Part of the explanation for this turn of events may be discovered in the effects of a fragmented culture in which Rose is afforded multiple outlets. As this analysis demonstrates, Rose's apologia has been seen and discussed across print sources, the Web, and the television dial on channels ranging from the ESPN network to CNN's *Talk Back Live* and CNBC's *Playback*. Those opposing Rose were drowned out as his remarks were broadcast again and again, which created a wall of text that was difficult for the public to either avoid or ignore.

Although the facts remain the same, the presumption of guilt and the anger directed toward Rose largely has lifted. The chorus of voices defending and apologizing for Rose bolsters his image. Although he remains banned from baseball, the situation suggests that in some circumstances time can be an ally to the apologist, and the media age has provided an arsenal of weapons that provide ammunition for an extended defense. And when the apologia can be issued at a later date, after the principle antagonists have left the scene, it is a discourse that is difficult to refute.

CONCLUSIONS

Pete Rose has made significant progress in restoring his image in the court of public opinion; although the one judge he must convince, MLB Commissioner Bud Selig, has yet to be persuaded. Before Game 3 of the 1999 World Series, Selig said the public outcry "certainly can't influence your decision" ("Selig: Rose won't," 1999). However, in late January 2000, Rose's attorneys secured a six-hour meeting with MLB's top lawyer to dispute the findings of the *Dowd Report*. The meeting, a response to Rose's September 26, 1997, request for reinstatement ("Rose's attorneys," 2000), is doubtless a result of Rose's return to the public spotlight. Selig, however, seemed unaffected by the meeting, saying the following month that there "is not a scintilla of give" in terms of the suspension and that "[t]here hasn't been any new evidence since then [1989]. I think just from my answer, you'll understand my depth of feeling on this subject" ("Selig leaves Rose," 2000). And again, in Cincinnati in October 2000 for the groundbreaking of the Reds' new Great American Ball Park, Selig said tersely, "the fact of the matter is that nothing has changed" (Haft, 2000b).

Because Rose's denials have proven ineffective in persuading many within baseball, there has been a push for Rose to fully embrace a transformative strategy. For example, it is clear that those such as Boswell, Morgan, and Vincent believe that an admission of guilt and a show of contrition might pave the way for Rose's return to the game. Jim Caple (1999) agrees with such a strategy and writes that Rose "could get a chance" to be in the Hall of Fame "if he would just express a little remorse for breaking baseball's cardinal rule—as well as some desire to address his gambling problem." In addition, such an admission would demonstrate the type of regret Kruse (1981a) argues is critical for readmission into a sport community.

However, such a full-scale change in approach would cost Rose his most endearing quality during the suspension: his consistency. The prolonged and consistent use of denial, as Benoit (1995a) argues and the Rose case would seem to bear out, can, "if it can be sustained, . . . help to restore a tarnished image" (p. 161). To reverse field (if he indeed is guilty) would force Rose to admit not only that he bet on baseball, but also that his decade of denial was all another lie. Such a shift might assist Rose in gaining reinstatement, but at the cost of the public support he has marshalled. Not only would the ban be proven justified, but, recast as a "liar," Rose would risk losing whatever degree of public trust he has recaptured. As the Cleveland *Plain Dealer*'s Phillip Morris (1999) points out, "To tell the truth now would remove his claim to 'victim' status and make him merely pathetic. We know you did it, Pete. But please, stick to your story" (p. 9B). Thus, with the passage of time, the wounds of Rose's transgressions are healed, and Rose is faced with a painful paradox: The redemption he seeks in the baseball community may only come with the full admission that might simultaneously destroy his redeemed public standing.

The final point that must be considered is Rose's window of opportunity. The rhetorical situation opened by the Gray interview, the All-Century team announcement, and even the World Championship celebrations has a limited life span. Although Rose regained the spotlight while these events captured the public's sports consciousness, there is a substantial risk that the spotlight will soon dim. In this sense, MLB may have the advantage of waiting out Rose and the public. Unless Rose can continue to take advantage of sporadic opportunities, such as the yearly Hall of Fame induction ceremonies, he may win the battle for public opinion while losing the war with Commissioner Selig. The tension and drama may make columnist Tim Sullivan's (2000b) appraisal prophetic: "Maybe Pete Rose works better in absentia, as a martyr to Bud Selig's misguided meanness. Maybe baseball's banished hit king is more attractive as a perpetual victim than as the prodigal son." Ten quiet months later, on the occasion of Rose's 60th birthday, Sullivan (2001) reiterated the dilemma, writing, "With each passing year, Rose improves the odds he will go to his grave unrepentant and unforgiven, excluded by the game he once embodied, and foreclosed from its Hall of Fame. His story is the stuff of epic tragedy, a tale so teeming with irony and hubris that the plot might have been appropriated from Sophocles or Shakespeare."

Regardless of which approach he takes—remaining with his primarily reformative strategy that has incorporated a dose of transformative appeal in his recent "admission" or fully repenting—Pete Rose's rhetorical redemption teaches us much about the nature of apologia as they are projected over time. Rose's rhetorical resurgence suggests that renewed apologias that are sparked by a renewed rhetorical situation may prove more successful, or at least more popular, than their predecessors. This possibility is enhanced by the nature of public memory, as well as the pragmatic effects that time has on the visibility and credibility of witnesses. Finally, the emergence of expanded media in a fragmented culture bodes well for these renewed apologias by providing a multitude of forums and suggests that the nature of apologia—premised on a central speech of self-defense—may need to be reexamined to account for the media age. I hope that the ideas raised in this chapter will encourage increased attention to both the plight of Pete Rose and the nature of apologia in the media age.[4]

NOTES

1. Benoit (1995a) offers both a compelling synthesis of theoretical perspectives on this genre and his own typology. Although I have selected Ware and Linkugel's (1973) seminal piece as my starting point, Benoit's perspective is compatible and offers the strategy of remorse through mortification as an additional rhetorical choice (this is an observation he shares with Kruse [1981a, 1981b]). Similarly, I concur with Benoit in his criticism of the use of the absolutive, vindicative, explanative, and justificative stances as staked out in the original articulation of the theory. I find little rationale for suggesting the four central strategies of apologia can logically be used in only this combination (Benoit, 1995a, pp. 88–89). Not only do I not make use of these stances, but my analysis of Rose's use of a combination of denial, bolstering, differentiation, and transcendence seemingly stands in contradiction to such postures.

2. An alternative, but not necessarily contradictory, approach to the renewed attention to the Pete Rose controversy would be that of issue management. A perspective primarily devoted to issues of public policy and public relations, it examines the lifecycle of an issue in terms of its management, status, and resolution (Crable & Vibbert, 1985). Although not necessarily integrated with apologia, it seems to have implicit connections to Benoit's (1995a) vision of image restoration. Further research exploring the connections between these approaches, which often are artificially divided in different areas of the communication discipline, might raise interesting conclusions.

3. Joe Torre subsequently denied that it was a team decision to refuse to talk to Gray and said that he wished Chad Curtis had indicated it was his personal choice to refuse the interview (Sherman, 1999).

4. Although details of a possible Rose reinstatement remain guarded, additional developments, including a Rose appearance at Game 4 of the 2002 World Series in a ceremony celebrating great moments in baseball history, suggest continued hope for Rose's reinstatement to baseball. Publicly, Commissioner Selig generally has avoided comment while speculation persists that a carefully crafted agreement, likely premised on Rose admitting a degree of guilt, may offer Rose at least probationary reinstatement sometime in the near future (Blum, 2002; Stark, 2003a, 2003b; Erardi, 2003).

REFERENCE LIST

Baseball might meet with Rose's agent. (2000, January 25). *ESPN.com*. Retrieved January 25, 2000, from http://espn.com/mlb/news/2000/0124/311878.html.

Benoit, William L. (1995a). *Accounts, excuses, and apologies: A theory of image restoration strategies*. Albany, NY: State University of New York Press.

Benoit, William L. (1995b). Sears' repair of its auto service image: Image restoration discourse in the corporate sector. *Communication Studies, 46,* 89–105.

Benoit, William L. (1997). Hugh Grant's image restoration discourse: An actor apologizes. *Communication Quarterly, 45,* 251–267.

Benoit, William L., & Brinson, S. L. (1994). AT&T "Apologies are not enough." *Communication Quarterly, 42,* 75–88.

Benoit, William L., & Hanczor, Robert S. (1994). The Tonya Harding controversy: An analysis of image restoration strategies. *Communication Quarterly, 42,* 416–433.

Bitzer, Lloyd. (1974 [1968]). The rhetorical situation. In Walter R. Fisher (Ed.), *Rhetoric: A tradition in transition* (pp. 247–260). Ann Arbor: University of Michigan Press.

Blair, Carole. (1984). From "All the President's Men" to every man for himself: The strategies of post-Watergate apologia. *Central States Speech Journal, 35,* 250–260.

Blum, Ronald. (2002, December 12). "Passage of time" changed Selig's mind. *Enquirer.com*. Retrieved December 12, 2002, from http://reds.enquirer.com/2002/12/12/wwwroseap.html.

Boswell, Thomas. (1999a, December 12). As Fisk enters, Rose should wait outside the Hall. *The Washington Post*, p. 12.

Boswell, Thomas. (1999b). 1980s: Pete Rose. In Michael MacCambridge (Ed.), *ESPN SportsCentury* (pp. 234–249). New York: Hyperion.

Browne, Stephen H. (1999). Remembering Crispus Attucks: Race, rhetoric, and the politics of commemoration. *Quarterly Journal of Speech, 85,* 169–187.

Caple, Jim. (1999, October 26). C'mon, Pete: Admit it and move on. *ESPN.com*. Retrieved October 27, 1999, from http://espn.go.com/premium/mlb/columns/caple_jim/133357.html.

Carter, Bob. (1999, December 17). Hustle made Rose respected, infamous. *ESPN.com*. Retrieved December 17, 1999, from http://espn.go.com/sportcentury/features/00016443.html.

Chastain, Bill. (1999, December 17). History of Pete Rose. *Sportcut.com*. Retrieved December 17, 1999, from http://sportcut.com.

Clinton says Rose should get second chance. (1999, December 17). *ESPN.com*. Retrieved December 17, 1999, from http://espn.go.com/mlb/news/1999/1214/233445.html.

Crable, Richard E., & Vibbert, Steven L. (1985). Managing issues and influencing public policy. *Public Relations Review, 11,* 3–16.

Daugherty, Paul. (1999, August 22). Giamatti's death sealed Rose's fate. *Enquirer.com*. Retrieved December 20, 1999, from http://enquirer.com/columns/daughtery/1999/08/22/pd_pete_cant_hustle.html.

Daugherty, Paul. (2000a, June 2). Ban on Rose hurts Reds' fans the most. *Enquirer.com*. Retrieved November 26, 2000, from http://reds.enquirer. com/2000/06/03/red_big_machine.html.

Daugherty, Paul. (2000b, February 25). If Selig forgives Strawberry, why not Rose? *Enquirer.com*. Retrieved February 25, 2000, from http://enquirer.com/ editons/2000/02/25/spt_if_selig_forgives.html.

Dowd, John. (1989). The Dowd report. *Dowd Report.com*. Retrieved February 14, 2000, from http://dowdreport.com.

Dowd: Rose shouldn't have been invited. (1999, October 25). *ESPN.com*. Retrieved October 27, 1999, from http://espn.go.com/mlb/news/1999/1025/133405. html.

Downey, Sharon D. (1993). The evolution of the rhetorical genre of apologia. *Western Journal of Communication, 57*, 42–62.

Engen, David E. (1995). The making of a people's champion: An analysis of media representations of George Foreman. *Southern Communication Journal, 60*, 141–151.

Erardi, John. (2000, June 4). Big Red Machine brings down the house. *Enquirer.com*. Retrieved June 5, 2000, from http://reds.enquirer.com/2000/06/05/reds_ big_red_machine.html.

Erardi, John. (2003, July 14). Rose decision not likely this year. *Enquirer.com*. Retrieved July 12, 2003, from http://reds.enquirer.com/2003/07/14/ wwwred1rose14.html.

Estock, Debra A. (2000, February 27). Plain talk and baseball with Peter Edward Rose. *Sportcut.com*. Retrieved February 27, 2000, from http://sportcut.com/ dept_magazine/insider_link15.asp.

Fans flood NBC with calls after Rose interview. (1999, October 25). *ESPN.com*. Retrieved October 25, 1999, from http://espn.go.com/mlb/playoffs99/ news/1999/1024/132268.html.

Giamatti, A. B. (1989, August 25). Giamatti: Sad end of sorry story. *USA Today*, p. 10C.

Gray says there's nothing to apologize for. (1999, October 26). *ESPN.com*. Retrieved December 17, 1999, from http://espn.go.com/mlb/news/1999/1025/ 1333839.html.

Greanier, Todd. (1999). Rose vs. baseball. *The Baseball Archive*. Retrieved January 17, 2000, from http://www.baseball1.com.

Groeschen, Tom. (1999, December 20). The who, what, when of Rose's summer of shame. *Enquirer.com*. Retrieved December 29, 1999, from http://reds. enquirer.com/1999/08/22/red _ the _ who _ what _ when_of.html.

Haft, Chris. (2000a, June 2). Griffey: Ceremony hollow without Rose. *Enquirer.com*. Retrieved June 5, 2000, from http://reds.enquirer.com/2000/06/02/red_ griffey_ceremony.html.

Haft, Chris. (2000b, October 5). Selig on Rose: Nothing has changed. *Enquirer.com*. Retrieved October 5, 2000, from http://reds.enquirer.com/2000/10/05/ red_radel_county_reds.html.

Halbwachs, Maurice. (1992). *On collective memory*. (Lewis A. Coser, Ed. and Trans.). Chicago: University of Chicago Press.

Hasian, Marouf, Jr., & Carlson, Cheree. (2000). Revisionism and collective memory:

The struggle for meaning in the *Amistad* affair. *Communication Monographs, 67,* 42–62.

Hearit, Keith Michael. (1995). "Mistakes were made": Organizations, apologia, and crises of social legitimacy. *Communication Studies, 46,* 1–17.

How they feel about Rose. (1999, August 22). *Enquirer.com.* Retrieved December 20, 1999, from http://reds.enquirer.com/1999/08/22/red_how_they_feel_about.html.

Huxman, Susan S., & Bruce, Denise B. (1995). Toward a dynamic generic framework of apologia: A case study of Dow Chemical, Vietnam, and the Napalm controversy. *Communication Studies, 46,* 57–72.

"I gambled for recreation." (1999, September 2). *ESPN.com.* Retrieved December 17, 1999, from http://espn.go.com/mlb/s/rose.html.

Kruse, Noreen Wales. (1977). Motivational factors in non-denial apologia. *Central States Speech Journal, 28,* 13–23.

Kruse, Noreen Wales. (1981a). Apologia in team sports. *Quarterly Journal of Speech, 67,* 270–283.

Kruse, Noreen Wales. (1981b). The scope of apologetic discourse: Establishing generic parameters. *Southern Speech Communication Journal, 46,* 278–291.

MacGregor, Scott. (1999, August 22). Hit king, banned from baseball 10 years ago, still longs to return. *Enquirer.com.* Retrieved December 20, 1999, from http://reds.enquirer.com/1999/08/22/red_rose_in_exile.html.

MasterCard International demands that NBC reporter Jim Gray apologize to America's baseball fans. (1999, October 25). *MasterCard International.* Retrieved November 22, 1999, from http://www.mastercard.com/about/press/991025a.html.

Matthews, Gray. (1995). Epideictic rhetoric and baseball: Nurturing community through controversy. *Southern Communication Journal, 60,* 275–291.

McGee, Michael Calvin. (1990). Text, context, and the fragmentation of contemporary culture. *Western Journal of Speech Communication, 54,* 274–289.

Miller, Jackson B. (1999). "Indians," "Braves," and "Redskins": A performative struggle for control of an image. *Quarterly Journal of Speech, 85,* 188–202.

Mink, Louis O. (1987). On the writing and rewriting of history. In B. Fay, E. O. Golob, & R. T. Vann (Eds.), *Historical understanding* (pp. 89–105). London: Cornell University Press.

Morris, Phillip. (1999, October 26). Rose should stick to his story. *The Plain Dealer* (Cleveland), p. 9B.

Nelson, Jeffrey. (1984). The defense of Billie Jean King. *Western Journal of Speech Communication, 48,* 92–102.

Pete Rose. (1999, December 20). http://www.russellregister.com/pete_rose.html.

Poll results show support for Rose. (1999, October 21). *ESPN.com.* Retrieved December 17, 1999, from http://espn.go.con/mlb/news/1999/1021/126088.html.

Raissman, Bob. (1999, October 25). NBC's Gray wrong to go after Rose. *Daily News* (New York), p. 68.

Ratto, Ray. (1999, October 25). Pete's feat: He's sympathetic again. *ESPN.com.* Retrieved October 27, 1999, from http://espn.go.com/columns/ratto_ray/133178.html.

Rhine, Michael. (1999, December 20). Boycott NBC and Jim Gray until an apology and firing take place! http://www.mawent.com/synergyi/jimgray.html.

Rose airs frustration on television. (1999, November 18). *ESPN.com*. Retrieved November 19, 1999, from http://espn.go.com/mlb/news/1999/1118/179344.html.

Rose remembered along with Big Red Machine. (2000, June 4). *ESPN.com*. Retrieved November 26, 2000, from http://espn.go.com/mlb/s/2000/0604/566679.html.

Rose seeks quick return to baseball. (2000, March 7). *ESPN.com*. Retrieved March 8, 2000, from http://espn.go.com/mlb/news/2000/0307/407070.html.

Rose's attorneys make their case in Dayton. (2000, January 18). *ESPN.com*. Retrieved January 31, 2000, from http://espn.go.com/mlb/news/2000/0128/320779.html.

Selig leaves Rose with little hope. (2000, February 17). *ESPN.com*. Retrieved February 17, 2000, from http://espn.go.com/mlb/news/2000/0216/360850.html.

Selig: Rose won't return during his watch. (1999, October 26). *ESPN.com*. Retrieved October 27, 1999, from http://espn.go.com/mlb/news/1999/1026/135270.html.

Sherman, Ed. (1999, October 28). Angry Rose says Gray misled him. *Chicago Tribune* (online). Retrieved October 28, 1999, from http://www.chicagotribune.com/sports/main/article/0,2669,SAV-9910280246,FF.html.

Stark, Jayson. (2000, July 27). Rose heard from on Big Red weekend. *ESPN.com*. Retrieved November 26, 2000, from http://espn.go.com/mlb/columns/stark/649880.html.

Stark, Jayson. (2003a, August 7). Plenty of big names passing through waivers. *ESPN.com*. Retrieved August 14, 2003, from http://espn.go.com/mlb/columns/stark_jayson/1591973.html.

Stark, Jayson. (2003b, January 17). Rose's reinstatement remains one big mystery. *ESPN.com*. Retrieved January 18, 2003, from http://espn.go.com/mlb/columns/stark_jayson/1494267.html.

Sullivan, Tim. (1999b, August 22). Rose sticks to denials: Baseball sticks to its evidence. *Enquirer.com*. Retrieved December 20, 1999, from http://reds.enquirer.com/1999/08/22/red_rose_sticks_to.html.

Sullivan, Tim. (2000a, April 3). Morgan wants Rose on field with Big Red Machine. *Enquirer.com*. Retrieved April 3, 2000, from http://reds.enquirer.com/2000/04/03/red_morgan_wants_rose_on.html.

Sullivan, Tim. (2000b, June 4). Reds' pick perfect tribute to Rose. *Enquirer.com*. Retrieved June 5, 2000, from http://reds.enquirer.com/2000/06/04/red_reds_pick_perfect.html.

Sullivan, Tim. (2000c, February 8). '75 salute: Stay away, Pete. *Enquirer.com*. Retrieved February 8, 2000, from http://reds.enquirer.com/2000/0208/red_75salute_stay_away.html.

Sullivan, Tim. (2001, April 14). Pete Rose at 60: Older but not wiser. *Enquirer.com*. Retrieved April 14, 2001, from http://reds.enquirer.com/2001/04/14/red_sullivan_pete_rose.html.

Twemlow, Nicholas. (1999, December 2). Pete Rose. *Sportcut.com*. Retrieved December 17, 1999, from http://Sportcut.com.

Vincent, Fay. (1999, December 8). The problem with forgiving Pete Rose. *New York Times*, p. A23.

Ware, B. L., & Linkugel, Wil A. (1973). They spoke in defense of themselves: On the generic criticism of apologia. *Quarterly Journal of Speech, 59,* 273–283.

What they said in interview. (1999, October 26). *USA Today,* p. 6C.

Wojnarowski, Adrian. (1999, December 19). Evidence says Rose did bet on baseball. *The Times-Picayune,* p. 14C.

Yankees not yet willing to forgive Gray. (1999, October 27). *ESPN.com.* Retrieved October 27, 1999, from http://espn.go.com/mlb/news/1999/1026/135290.html.

Zelizer, Barbie (1992). *Covering the body: The Kennedy assassination, the media, and the shaping of collective memory.* Chicago: University of Chicago Press.

CHAPTER 2

Hoop Games: A Narrative Analysis of Television Coverage of Women's and Men's Professional Basketball

Leah R. Vande Berg and Sarah Projansky

We are the stories we tell.
We are the games we yell at, the games we play.
We are the people we choose to be.
We are those who raised us.
We are the obstacles we overcome.
We are the glorious mistakes.
We are the glorious things we do well.
We are the risks we refuse to pass by.
We are the stories we tell.
We are the stories others tell about us, whisper, shout.
We are the stories we tell. (Nike WNBA advertisement, 1997)[1]

1997: A NEW WORLD ORDER IN U.S. PROFESSIONAL SPORTS?

When Leonard (1980) observed that "how we play the game may turn out to be more important than we imagine, for it signifies nothing less than our way of being in the world" (pp. 266–267), he was suggesting that sport is a form of "cultural theatre where the values of the larger society are resonated, dominant social practices are legitimized, and structural inequalities reproduced" (Sabo & Jansen, 1992, p. 173). How Americans play the game of professional basketball changed dramatically in 1996–97, when two newly formed women's professional basketball leagues, the American Basketball League (ABL) and the Women's National Basketball Association (WNBA) played their respective inaugural 44-game and 28-game seasons. As Donna Lopiano of the Women's Sports Foundation explained, "Sports have always been one of boys' most important socio-cultural learning experiences. Now girls and women are having those experiences too" ("Women sports stars," 1996, p. 108). These experiences had seemed impossible until 1996 when, as *People* reporter Cynthia Wang (1997) noted, "The 'impossible' no longer is. Reality for the greatest women players has arrived. . . . A League of Their Own" (p. 6).

TELEVISED SPORT NARRATIVES

"Televised sport," according to Messner, Duncan, and Jensen (1993, p. 132), "is an event that is mediated by the 'framing' of the contest by commentators and technical people . . . thus any meanings that a television viewer constructs from the contest are likely to be profoundly affected by the framing of the contest" (see also Altheide & Snow, 1979; Clarke & Clarke, 1982; Duncan & Brummett, 1987). And in televised sport events, "the ongoing pattern of commentators' discourse takes the form of the narrative; one of the most common strategies of sportscasting is to lay a 'story over story over story' over the visual images of action on a field" and, in so doing, encourage fans to "unify glances at hundreds of brief images into a rapt gaze at a coherent spectacle" (Brummett & Duncan, 1990, p. 233).

This analysis examines how televised sport commentary frames the athletes and actions during women's and men's U.S. professional basketball games in 1996–97. We explore the narrativized identities conveyed through the sport commentary provided during national television coverage of the inaugural seasons of two U.S. women's professional basketball leagues—the 1996–97 ABL season and the 1997 WNBA season—as well as the concurrent 1997 season of the U.S. men's National Basketball Association (NBA).

For this study, we videotaped ten 1996–97 ABL regular-season games and three of the four ABL championship games; ten 1997 WNBA regular-season games, both playoff games, and the championship game; eight 1997 NBA regular-season games, two playoff games, and three of the six championship games. Our critical analysis of these videotapes identified six recurring narrative frames that sport commentators used to describe these sports events and athletes.

The next two sections of the chapter discuss these narrative frames. In the first section, we identify three narrative frames we found in television sports commentary about both women's and men's U.S. professional basketball performances: athletic prowess, agency, and adversity narratives. In the second section, we present three narrative frames we found were used only in televised commentary during women's professional basketball games: discipline narratives, diaspora narratives, and domestic role narratives. In addition, in this second section, we discuss several unique discursive strategies through which sports commentary expressed ambivalence while simultaneously containing the power, agency, and identities of professional female athletes. The concluding section of this chapter discusses some of the implications of such pervasively ambivalent television coverage of women's sports.

SAME STORY, DIFFERENT PLAYERS: TELEVISION SPORTS SUCCESS, ADVERSITY, AND AGENCY NARRATIVES

Historically, sport has provided an arena for reaffirming male hegemony in the face of societal challenges and changes. As Messner et al. (1993) note, "in the 20th century, the institution of sport has provided men with a homosocial sphere of life through which they have bolstered the ideology of male superiority" (p. 121). This hegemony was challenged in 1996–97 with the start of the ABL and the WNBA. Although these were not the first U.S. women's professional basketball leagues, they were the first leagues with sufficient economic power to garner national television coverage. And as the Amateur Athletic Foundation of Los Angeles (Duncan, Messner, Williams, & Jensen, 1990) noted, "the way in which television covers, or fails to cover, women engaged in athletics affects the way in which female athletes are perceived and also tells us something about the status of women in our society" (p. 1).

One of our major analytical conclusions from this analysis of television game coverage of the 1996–97 WNBA, ABL, and NBA seasons is that television coverage indeed included some gender equality: In several respects, the coverage of women's and men's professional basketball was comparable. Specifically, three narrative frames central to televised professional basketball commentary were used in coverage of women's and men's games: success narratives, adversity narratives, and agency narratives. We turn now to a discussion of these shared narratives.

Success Narratives: Athletes as Outstanding Achievers

Among the most pervasive narrative frames that television sports commentators used to describe game events and the actions of female and male athletes were success narratives. These narrative frames included both fully formed stories and paradigmatic narrative fragments.[2] Previous studies have found that media coverage often frames athletes as heroes whose outstanding ability, expertise, courage, perseverance, dedication to goals, creativity, versatility, and spectacular ability to perform under pressure (frequently in the form of coming from behind) enables them to succeed in winning competitions (Csikszentmihalyi & Lyons, 1982; Harris, 1994; Harris & Hills, 1993; "Heroes of young America," 1991; Kahn, 1979;

Smith, 1986; Trujillo, 1991; Trujillo & Vande Berg, 1994; Vande Berg, 1998; Vander Velden, 1986).

Television commentary analyzed in this study of the 1996–97 U.S. professional basketball seasons was no exception: Pregame, game, and halftime commentary repeatedly focused on players' achievements, including their victories, outstanding athletic ability, expertise, strong dedication, ability to win, and willingness to practice long and hard and to endure pain. For example, NBC's Dan Hicks opened the coverage of the WNBA championship game (August 30, 1997) with a brief profile of the achievements and successes of three of the teams' central players: Rebecca Lobo, Sheryl Swoopes, and Cynthia Cooper.

Rebecca Lobo's career may best be described as a fairy tale. She led an unbeaten Connecticut team to a national championship and then won an Olympic gold last summer. The birth of the WNBA brought another new dream to life: She's been the leader of this New York team which showed its mettle in an impressive playoff victory on the road—which is where they find themselves today.

Throughout that same championship game, commentator Hannah Storm repeatedly reminded viewers of Cooper's successes—her National Collegiate Athletic Association (NCAA) titles, her Olympic titles, and her starring role on Italian professional basketball teams—and noted that during this championship game, "Cooper played all 20 minutes of the first half . . . and right now she is carrying the team."

Similarly, NBA game commentary (on NBC, ESPN, and SportsChannel) narrativized NBA team successes and individual athletes' outstanding athletic achievements, framing these victories as a function of the athletes' extraordinary abilities, determination, hard work, and willingness to suffer pain and exhaustion in order to succeed. For example, during a Sacramento Kings versus Philadelphia '76ers game (January 5, 1997), SportsChannel commentator Gary Geroud described the '76ers' Allen Iverson as an especially successful athlete, not because of his size, but because of his athleticism: "The thing about him is, you know, he's only 6 foot and 165, but he doesn't play like that. He plays BIG . . . the guy's an amazing player." Similarly, in commentary prior to the second game (June 4, 1997) of the NBA Championship series between the Utah Jazz and the Chicago Bulls, Marv Albert paid homage to the extraordinary achievements of sports heroes Michael Jordan and Scotty Pippen: "It has been 72 hours since MJ performed the latest in a career full of heroics . . . but the reason the Bulls were able to put themselves into the position to win was because of the all-around magnificent play of Scotty Pippen."

Athletic Adversity Narratives: Heroically Overcoming Pain, Injury, and Physical Limitations

Another frame common to televised ABL, WNBA, and NBA sports commentary was an overcoming physical adversity narrative. In contrast to success narratives, which focus on the final successful outcomes of competition, adversity narratives foreground the pain and physical adversities that athletes had to overcome through endurance, hard work, strength, and determination in order to be among the small, select group of U.S. professional basketball players.

ABL and WNBA basketball commentators recounted heart-warming and inspiring stories about athletes who overcame a plethora of physical illnesses, injuries, and obstacles to achieve their successes. For example, ABL commentators shared stories about the Richmond Rage's Taj McWilliams's ability to successfully overcome sports-induced asthma (March 12, 1997), Jennifer Azzi's rapid recovery from a serious car accident that resulted in 40 stitches in her left knee (October 20, 1996), and center Venus Lacy's Herculean efforts to surmount a childhood in which she wore leg braces and had to be carried piggyback by her brothers (October 20, 1997). These narratives portrayed women basketball professionals as strong, athletically skilled, determined athletes who refused to allow pain, illness, or physical injury to deter them from achieving their dream of playing professional basketball. Tracy Warren, for example, used this "playing through pain" narrative in her description of the Atlanta Glory's E.C. Hill landing on the New England Blizzard's Jennifer Rizotti's ankle and Rizotti's reaction. As the camera tracked the limping Rizotti resuming her point guard position, Warren concluded her narrative with this testimony to Rizotti's determined imperviousness to physical adversity: "But you know Rizotti. Seven stitches in the opener—stitched up during a time-out, came back, and played all 26 minutes after being injured the first 2 minutes of the game" (ABL, October 27, 1996).

Similarly, NBA sports commentators constantly regaled viewers with stories of male athletes playing through pain. For example, they lionized Karl Malone for playing with a huge blister on his hand and Scotty Pippen for playing with an injured left foot during the NBA Championship finals (June 6, 1997). However, arguably the most extraordinary, and certainly the most repeated, Promethean physical adversity narrative of the 1997 NBA season was Michael Jordan's heroic performance in Game 5 of the NBA Finals. Sportscasters repeatedly recounted how Jordan, despite being so ill and dehydrated from the flu that he needed intravenous fluids before and during the game, summoned his extraordinary willpower, endurance, athletic ability, and courage to play 44 minutes and score 38 points—including the game-ending 3-point shot—to lead the Chicago Bulls out of a 16-point deficit to a 90–88 victory.

These physical adversity narratives reaffirm the mythic heroism of athletes by framing them as surmounting injury and pain that would have leveled normal persons and, in doing so, defying "the normal limits of embodiment" (Sabo & Jansen, 1998, p. 203). As Sabo (1994) explains, "the pain principle" is one of the fundamental tenets of patriarchal culture and particularly of a patriarchal sports culture, which believes that "pain is inevitable and that the endurance of pain enhances one's character and moral worth" (p. 3). Enduring pain is the essence of the Promethean myth that undergirds sports adversity narratives, and historically, television media have reified such narratives of the peak performances of the heroic "manly youth" whose effort "transcends, at least for a time, the limits of time, space, duration, resistance, and embodiment" and who display qualities synonymous with those glorified on military as well as sports battlefields (Sabo & Jansen, 1998, p. 203).

Agency Narratives: Athletes as Captains of Their Fates

Agency, Barker (2000) has explained, "is the socially determined capability to act and make a difference" (p. 381). Furthermore, "precisely because agency is socially and differentially produced, some actors have more domains of action than others" (p. 182). Barker also notes that "[t]he concept of agency can be said to be a subject position within discourse. . . . [which] has commonly been associated with notions of freedom, free will action, creativity, originality, and the very possibility of change through the actions of free agents" (pp. 181–182). During the 1996–97 ABL, WNBA, and NBA seasons, agency narratives highlighted the capacity of star athletes to bring about their own individual, as well as their teams', success through the exercise of their individual skill, knowledge, expertise, talent, strength, power, athleticism, hard work, intelligence, and experience. For example, during the ABL Championship game (March 12, 1997), commentator Debbie Antonelli highlighted the Richmond Rage's Dawn Staley's agency: "Dawn Staley will will this team to win. She will put this team on her back, and she will carry it, and she will do whatever she needs to do to get them in a position to be victorious." Similarly, NBC's Dan Hicks addressed the New York Liberty's Rebecca Lobo's agency during the August 30, 1997, WNBA championship game when he reminded viewers that "Rebecca Lobo told Red Auerbach once that she would play for the Celtics some day. Well, now she's getting ready in the inaugural WNBA Championship game."

Sports commentary during NBA games also featured narratives of male athletes' agency. For example, Peter Vecsey's story before Game 2 of the NBA finals (June 4, 1997) included an agency-affirming response from Karl Malone to Vecsey's question about the possibility that Malone's blister caused them to lose Game 1:

Everyone in this business likes to tell you they have an excuse beforehand, so if they don't play up to par and then don't make the free throws, it's because of his hand or something like that. I'm just from an old school that when you suit up, you're ready to play, you know. No excuses. . . . Those two free throws was big. Everybody wants to talk about them. But to me, I cherish the time to do it again. . . . Any time we're in a ballgame and we need the shot, I want it.

Duncan and Messner's (1998) replication of their 1990 Amateur Athletic Foundation Study found that sports commentators for collegiate basketball and professional tennis repeatedly used agency narratives to frame athletes "as active agents, engineering their own successes and their opponents' failures" by attributing success "to their raw talent, power, intelligence, size, quickness, discipline, and risk-taking" and failure "to their opponents' competence" (p. 177). However, both their study and ours found that agency narratives that framed athletic success as a function of individual athletes' talent, enterprise, determination, and hard work were used more often to explain men's than women's athletic performances. As we discuss in the next section, women's athletic successes, unlike men's, were repeatedly attributed to their following the advice of others.

Using similar success, physical adversity, and agency narratives to frame both women and men professional basketball players has important social implications, as Duncan and Hasbrook (1988) note, because "[s]port is not merely a reservoir of social attitudes, norms and values; it also has the potential for actively modifying larger social practice. . . . A more equitable balance of power in sport can lead to a more equitable balance of power in other social spheres" (p. 20).

Nonetheless, the use of these three narratives—success, adversity, and agency—to frame both women's and men's professional basketball games naturalizes the identities and performances of women and men as athletes and invites viewers to regard professional women basketball players as normal, natural, and comparable to men professional basketball players—one of the goals set in motion in 1972 by Title IX. Using these narratives, then, constitutes one challenge to historical masculine hegemony in sports.

ARTEMIS CONTAINED: DISCIPLINE, DIASPORA, AND DOMESTIC ROLE SPORTS NARRATIVES

Despite the challenges to the ideology of male superiority posed by the presence of the three parallel narrative frames of success, adversity, and agency, we found—as did Duncan and Messner (1998)—that sports commentators also repeatedly used three narrative frames that deflected attention away from female athletes' strategic knowledge, skill, expertise, athleticism, and dedication to playing sports. This deflection was conveyed most powerfully through television commentators' repeated use of discipline, diaspora, and domestic role narratives to frame women's but not men's televised professional basketball games. These three gendered sports narratives, in combination with the persistent use of discursive practices that trivialized, marginalized, sexualized, and symbolically annihilated women athletes, provided the overriding message that "female athletes should be recognized and remembered for their stereotypical gender role[s], not for their athletic role" (Kane, 1989, p. 61; see also Duncan, 1986; Duncan & Hasbrook, 1988; Duncan et al., 1994; Halbert & Lattimer, 1995; Messner et al., 1993). In the following sections, we discuss these narratives and several strategic discursive differences in televised sports commentary between women's and men's 1996–97 professional basketball games.

Discipline Narratives: Female Athletes as Subservient Order-Takers

Television commentary during women's professional basketball games repeatedly undermined the agency and competence of professional women basketball players by depicting their victories to be a result of their dependence on and obedient following of the expert advice and orders of others. In contrast to the heroic success and agency narratives that commentators pervasively used to frame male, and sometimes female, professional basketball players and their performances, discipline narratives framed sportswomen as children who needed to be scolded, disciplined, and given orders by expert adults. Such narratives presented women basketball players' and their teams' successes as primarily the result of listening to the strategic advice of (often male) experts, not the result of sportswomen using their own intelligence, knowledge of the game, or competent physical enactment of athletic strength and skill. The following interchange between commentators Ron Barr and Debbie Gore during the Portland versus Seattle game (February 23, 1997), which compares the ABL and NBA, succinctly encapsulates the essence of these discipline narratives:

Ron Barr: Interesting difference between the ABL and the NBA: ABL players LISTEN!

Debbie Gore: You have Scotty Pippen going 1-on-1, Shaquille O'Neal going 1-on-1, I don't know if they need so much strategy.

One particularly powerful illustration of this framing narrative occurred during Lifetime's coverage of the WNBA game between the Sacramento Monarchs and the Houston Comets (July 18, 1997). Commentator Reggie Miller began by telling viewers and his two cocommentators the story of the recent "scolding" that outside consultant John Lucas had given the Houston Comets during practice at the request of their Coach, Van Chancellor. Commentator Meghan Pattyson voiced this objection to Miller's infantilization: "Well, you know, the one thing that I was thinking about was that—Gosh, I'm a player, and I've got a guy coming in who's never been to one of our practices, and he's telling me what I am or am not doing? I don't know, I think I could be pretty fired up." However, her momentary resistance to Miller's expression of male hegemony was

quickly quashed by commentator Michelle Tafoya's testimonial to the efficacy of this paternalistic discipline: "Interestingly, Houston came out at
shooting practice very lethargic, and Van Chancellor, as angry as I've ever
seen him, said 'OK. You know what—forget it. We're going to do this MY
way. We're going to play hard, we're going to play aggressive,' and they
certainly are listening to him today." Later, at the end of the game, Reggie
Miller again reaffirmed the importance of taking orders from expert men
for the Comet's success: "Reiterating what we talked about earlier. I think
the team meeting Coach John Lucas coming in really getting on *the girls*,
really telling them point blank what is going wrong with their organization really have helped two out of the three ballgames" [emphasis added].

These discipline narratives portrayed professional women athletes as
children in need of parental admonishment and, in so doing, undermined
these sportswomen's agency and accomplishments by attributing their
successes not to their own talent and effort, but rather to their following
the orders of others. Furthermore, Miller's "the girls" reference illustrates
a common discursive practice during ABL and WNBA games: infantilization. In contradiction to Duncan and Messner's (1998) finding in their
analysis of televised U.S. Open tennis and NCAA basketball competition
that "the practice of calling women athletes as 'girls' had all but disappeared" (p. 181), we found the practice pervading television coverage of
professional women's basketball. Both female and male commentators
verbally infantilized the professional sportswomen during every game we
analyzed through their use of such descriptors as "young ladies" and
"girls." This repeated infantilization was in sharp contrast to the respectful
descriptors that commentators used to characterize NBA players. Only
once in our study did a commentator refer to a rookie male player as a
"young man," and commentators never referred to these professional
male athletes as "boys" (Daddario, 1994; Eitzen & Baca Zinn, 1989; Halbert
& Latimer, 1994; Messner et al., 1993).

Language, as Messner et al. (1993) note, is never neutral. A possible
reading of the meaning of the recurrent use of discipline narratives and
infantilizing discourse to describe professional sportswomen—and the
concomitant absence of such descriptions of professional men basketball
players—is that men belong on the court, whereas women, though they
have been allowed to enter the arena, clearly are still just girls who are
out of their league.

Diaspora Narratives: Female Athletes as Exiled "Others"

A second recurrent narrative frame that sports commentators used during the inaugural year of the ABL and WNBA was that of diaspora. Diaspora is an exile "characteristically produced by forced dispersal and
reluctant scattering" (Gilroy, 1997, p. 318). As Clifford (1994) has ex-

plained, diaspora links identity, history, and spatial location and explains the oppression and lack of belonging experienced by the subaltern or cultural other.

Historically, U.S. women basketball players have been athletically marginalized "others" unable to pursue professional athletic careers in their home country.[3] In 1996–97, many basketball players in the ABL and WNBA had experienced a career diaspora for more than a decade, and in game after game, commentators recounted diaspora narratives. Their narration traced these professional basketball players' love of the game as children, their outstanding accomplishments and successes as college athletes, and then either their subsequent professional exile to teams in Europe, Australia, Japan, Israel, and Korea or—the only alternative before the WNBA and the ABL—their abandonment of an athletic career.

For example, during the WNBA Championship game (August 30, 1997), Ann Meyers reminded viewers that Tammy Jackson had played 11 seasons overseas, and Hannah Storm noted that when Cynthia Cooper was playing professionally in Italy, she once scored 67 points in a single game. During a regular-season game between the Monarchs and the Comets, commentator Michelle Tafoya explained that Brigette Gordon "had a fan club over in Italy where she played for eight years" (July 19, 1997). And during the final moments of the ABL championship game, as CEO Gary Cavalli prepared to announce the game's most valuable player (MVP) (12-year European sojourner Val Stills), Tracy Warren again recounted the diaspora narrative: "The best athletes in women's professional basketball—all Americans, all stars, stars of their teams. They were looking for an opportunity to play in the United States, to come home to play before the hometown fans!" These diaspora narratives, unique to commentary during women's professional basketball games, reveal the link between women's identity as cultural others and male hegemony in sport (Clifford, 1994; Grossberg, 1996; Hall, 1996; Mercer, 1990).

Women professional basketball players' status as cultural others was further evident in the symbolic annihilation of the inaugural seasons of the two professional women's basketball leagues by the preeminent U.S. sports newsmagazine. Bill Colson, managing editor of *Sports Illustrated*, flatly stated that "At no time did we ever think of doing more than two pages or a 'Scorecard' item on it [the debut of the ABL]. No debate" (quoted in *Women's Sports + Fitness*, 1997, p. 38). Colson's and *Sports Illustrated*'s dismissal of the inauguration of professional women's basketball leagues as not sufficiently newsworthy to warrant substantive coverage reaffirms that, though female professional basketball players' physical exile may have ended with the advent of the WNBA and ABL, female athletes remain exiled to the margins of U.S. sport.

In addition to diaspora narratives, television commentary further marked women professional basketball players as others by repeatedly using masculine standards to describe women players' performances, thus producing symbolic annihilation (i.e., the verbal or visual denial of their existence or visibility).[4] For example, NBC commentator Ann Meyers' description of Cooper's MVP performance during the August 30, 1997, WNBA final as a "Jordanesque ability to take over a basketball game" illustrates commentators' use of male standards to describe female players's athletic performances.

Another typical component of sports narratives was the discursive symbolic annihilation of sportswomen, as illustrated in this Debbie Antonelli commentary during the final moments of the ABL Quest versus Rage game (March 12, 1997): "Now Richmond [is] mixing it up, back in their *man-to-man* defense" (emphasis added). Antonelli could have said "back to their one-on-one defense," but she did not. Instead, she symbolically annihilated all 10 women on the court. Through such symbolic annihilation, as Kane and Greendorfer (1994) note, "[t]he media tell us that sportswomen have little, if any, value in this society, particularly in relation to male athletes" (p. 34).

Domestic Narratives: Female Athletes as Working Parents, Sexual Role Models, Caregivers, and Heterosexual Partners

Another set of narrative frames that television sports commentary used to characterize the performances and identities of women professional basketball players—but not their counterparts in the NBA—focused on these sportswomen's performances of the nonathletic roles of mother, sexual role model, caregiver, and heterosexual romantic partner.

Working Parent Narratives

Narratives that foregrounded professional athletes' identities as mothers occurred during every game we analyzed. Here, for example, was how sportscasters Michele Tafoya and Meghan Pattyson described Pam McGee as she stood at the free throw line during a July 18, 1997, WNBA game:

Tafoya: Pam McGee—another Lady Trojan—at the line. At 34 years old, feeling great. Says she didn't expect to play this well at 34, but says she's going to play until her body says she can't.

Pattyson: And she's the mother of two kids, so I give her all the credit in the world for being out here, playing and staying in what great shape she's in. God knows I could never do that!

Narratives of athletes as mothers also blanketed ABL games, including the ABL Championship final game on March 12, 1997. For example, Debbie Antonelli began her half-time feature on the Columbus Quest's center (and league MVP) Valerie Still not by focusing on Still's athletic accomplishments, but rather on the difficulty Still's dual identity as athlete and working mom posed: "We're here at the half with Valerie Still. . . . Now, Val, you've not only got a lot of priorities on the floor, you've gotta balance a child off the floor and your family life. How does that work out with your travel and everything else that you do?" Later, Antonelli segued into another half-time feature on Taj McWilliams with these words, "Another center, another mom. This time for the Richmond Rage—Taj McWilliams."

Sheryl Swoopes's dual role as mother and professional athlete was referenced scores of times during televised WNBA games; in fact, Swoopes's motherhood became a trope during the inaugural WNBA season. For example, during the Comets versus Monarchs game on July 18, 1997, Maura Driscoll opened the half-time report with a story that began: "Sheryl gave birth to Jordan Eric Jackson . . . and we went to Lubbock, Texas, to check in with Sheryl to see what it takes to move from the maternity room to the locker room." Viewers next saw an image of the spring 1997 *WomenSport* cover photo of the very pregnant Swoopes (accompanied by the headline "A Star is Born: Sheryl Swoopes and the WNBA are both due in June"). This was followed by a series of video clips of Swoopes's then-husband Eric Jackson talking about what a blessing it had been "[t]raveling with Sheryl and watching her grow pretty much from a college player to a professional basketball player, a mature woman giving birth to a baby boy," and then both Jackson and Swoopes cooing over the baby. A voice-over narration then accompanied video highlights of Swoopes's basketball history at Texas Tech University, the 1996 Olympics, and her workouts with a team of male players at her health club. Finally, Swoopes directly addressed the camera, saying "I'm an athlete, and I can be an athlete and a mom at the same time," with her physician (in his office) confirming on camera that she was able to work out and return to athletic competition.

By deflecting the focus away from WNBA and ABL players' athletic accomplishments, sports commentary contains the symbolic threat that competent female athletes pose to the patriarchal status quo. It is only a short step from highlighting sportswomen's nonathletic identities to reasserting the traditional patriarchal notion that these athlete-parents belong not on the court, but at home with their families (see Graydon, 1983). Reggie Miller took this next step during the July 18, 1997, Comets versus Monarchs game when he offered this comment about Swoopes's return to the Comets lineup: "Well, I say why? Why come back? You have a beautiful little baby boy. Uhm, I understand this is the inaugural WNBA season, but—take a year off. Houston's not going to miss you that much, even though they'll all say that they will. Take time to be with your newborn."

As Daddario (1998) notes, "describing female athletes by their 'other' identifying roles, such as wives, mothers, and daughters, is a common strategy in the coverage of women's sports" (p. 98). By locating female athletes' identities within the context of families—as mothers to their daughters and sons—sportscasters define sportswomen "in roles valued by patriarchal society—like wife and mother—that do not threaten masculine sports hegemony" (p. 24) and send the message that what is most valued about these professional basketball players is not their athleticism, but their traditional feminine social roles.

Sexual Role Model Narratives

Closely related to the explicit and repeated narratives that highlighted WNBA and ABL players' identities as working mothers were more subtle narratives that framed the players as sexual role models. One notable, and particularly troubling, example was sports commentary about the Richmond Rage's McWilliams during the ABL Championship final (March 12, 1997). In the half-time feature, commentator Debbie Antonelli used McWilliams's athlete-mom identity as a springboard for discussing the issue of teen pregnancy. Antonelli began the feature like this: "Another center, another mom. This time for the Richmond Rage—Taj McWilliams. . . . Now let's talk a little about how you're able to balance your professional career and life on the floor and balance life of motherhood in this very difficult traveling league." In the interview, McWilliams explained that she hired a nanny who lived with her and her eight-year-old daughter Michelle and took care of Michelle while McWilliams traveled on the road for ABL games. McWilliams also talked about how much more challenging being an athlete had been in college when she had found herself pregnant and then a single mother scholarship athlete. In this and other sexual role model narratives, sports commentators affirmed that ABL and WNBA players accepted the social role of highly visible role models. McWilliams—like other ABL and WNBA players interviewed as part of featured coverage during the inaugural season—took that responsibility seriously:

I try to talk to a lot of at-risk females, teenagers, and in at-risk parts of the city to teach them that having a baby is not as bad as a lot of people make it seem. Even though it's not good for you, you can succeed. Even though you have some problems in your life, you can still succeed. I was told by a lot of people that I should give up on my basketball career and, uh, you know, there was [also] a lot of people who said, "You can do it! You can do it!" And I want to be one of those role models for those young ladies who have dreams and aspirations to do with their child. (March 12, 1997)

Certainly, one can laud this half-time sexual role model narrative feature on McWilliams for the honest, serious way it addressed issues of teen pregnancy and for demonstrating that strong, determined, competent women can overcome all sorts of adversity—including being a single teen parent—and achieve their career dreams. However, one can also read this narrative as a neocolonialist story about African American women. From this perspective, the narrative is seriously problematic, because it focuses solely on McWilliams, without even mentioning other single athlete mothers, her overcoming sports-related asthma, or the dual discrimination—racial and sexual—faced by black women in sport and society. As such, this sexual role model narrative could be read as reinforcing negative stereotypes of black women. As Williams (1994) has noted, though media devote a substantial amount of coverage to elite black male athletes, black female sportswomen receive little coverage, and much of the coverage that exists is in the form of negative images and stereotypes.

Caregiver Narratives

Daddario's (1998) analysis of the 1992 and 1996 televised Olympic coverage found that another strategy through which media marginalize the achievements of female athletes is by highlighting and dramatizing women's interpersonal relationships and their interdependence on significant others. As Daddario explains, "While a man's masculine identity is dependent on the achievement of autonomy or individuation, a woman's feminine identity is dependent on interpersonal relationships" (p. 75). Her analysis demonstrates how "human connections were dramatized and reconstructed rhetorically by the sports media through commentary and camera editing" and how "selflessness as much as athletic achievement is defined as success for female Olympians" (p. 76).

Sports commentary during the inaugural WNBA and ABL seasons also utilized this strategy by regularly framing female athletes as selfless, altercentric caregivers. For example, during every televised Comets game during the inaugural WNBA season, and even during games not involving the Comets, sports commentary about Cooper's athletic success and accomplishments regularly segued quickly into narratives about her role as caregiver for her mother, who was struggling with breast cancer, and the nephews and nieces her mother had been raising. Cooper's caregiving activities became a powerful, recurring trope that almost overshadowed accounts of her extraordinary athletic accomplishments. In turn, this often resulted in accounts of her extraordinary athletic achievements being framed as overcoming interpersonal adversity narratives rather than as success or agency narratives. For example, in Game 1 of the WNBA playoffs between the Houston Comets and the Charlotte Sting, commentator Sandra Neil introduced a relatively lengthy feature story on Cooper with these words: "Cynthia Cooper—the WNBA's brightest star—is shining now at the age of 34, and she is shining in the face of adversity." After briefly summarizing Cooper's professional accomplishments (two national championships at University of Southern California; a gold medal at the 1988 Olympics in Seoul, South Korea; 11 seasons abroad as a professional basketball player in Spain and Italy; and becoming the WNBA's leading scorer and first MVP), Neil segued into the body of the narrative, which again focused on Cooper's caregiving role, not her athletic role: "But Cynthia Cooper's toughest battle, though, is not being fought on the court but at home. Her mother has been diagnosed with breast cancer." Ten minutes after halftime, sportscaster Hannah Storm reiterated the Cooper caregiver narrative: "Cooper not only looking after her mom, but raising nieces and nephews—three of them—at her house and will adopt a three-year-old nephew. Somehow she has juggled it all."

Admirable though Cooper's actions were, narratives about her and other athletes that repeatedly used caregiving roles and responsibilities as the overarching identity narrative within which their professional athletic identities and roles were subsumed invited audiences to read the traditional "feminine" role as paramount. Such depictions undercut and deny the power and significance of women's athletic accomplishments. As Wood (1994) has noted, emphasizing women's roles as "primary caretakers in contemporary Western society serves to perpetuate their already subordinate place within a hegemonic social order that requires but does not reward caregiving" (p. 18). Furthermore, such depictions naturalize the inequitable status quo in which women are expected to work two shifts: "one shift at work outside of the home and a second one in the home" (Wood, 1994, p. 24; see also Hochschild, 1989; Okin, 1989; Sommers & Shields, 1987) and reiterate the patriarchal notion that female athletes' identities are primarily relational, not individual.

These caregiving narratives, like many adversity narratives, illustrate one notable difference we found between the televised adversity narratives used to frame the performances of NBA athletes and those used to frame WNBA and ABL athletes. Adversity stories about male athletes predominantly focused on physical obstacles and adversities they faced as athletes, such as overcoming injuries and pain, and rarely on emotional or psychological obstacles related to their athletic performance (e.g., the crisis in confidence Seattle Supersonic Matt Maloney faced entering the May 9, 1997, game after several games of not scoring). In contrast, though there were many stories about female athletes overcoming physical adversity, there also were stories focused on the relational, emotional, and psychological obstacles female athletes had to overcome as a result of their caregiving relationships with or responsibilities to others (e.g., ill mothers, children).

As Berg (1986) has noted, "Women are told that a great deal has changed, but upon closer look, the scope of change is not what it seems. . . . While women have become a major force in the American workplace, their roles as caregivers remain entrenched in the expectations of society and individual families" (pp. 17, 47). Furthermore, as Wood (1994) has explained, "women are expected to engage in activities that the culture does not value; thus, they are required, or at the very least strongly encouraged to be persons the culture does not value. Inevitably this creates a paradox in which a woman cannot win" (p. 57). By narratively framing WNBA and ABL players' athletic performances in terms of their caregiving roles, televised coverage of women basketball professionals encouraged viewers to continue to regard women as the primary caregivers in contemporary American society and to reinforce women's relational-centered rather than individual achievement-centered roles. In so doing, television coverage of professional basketball reinstantiated women's subordinate place within a hegemonic social order that requires but does not value or reward caregiving (Wood, 1994).

Heteronormative Romance Narratives

Another frame we found frequently used in ABL and WNBA televised sports commentary, but not in NBA coverage, was narratives that highlighted the players' heterosexuality. Both WNBA and ABL commentators repeatedly affirmed the heterosexuality of the women professional basketball players through narratives that referenced the athletes' relationships with their husbands and male fiancés. According to Kane (1995) and Griffin (1992), there are two primary reasons for this focus on heteronormativity in women's sports: sexism and homophobia.

In a sexist and heterosexist society, in which heterosexuality is reified as the only normal, natural, and acceptable orientation, women who defy the accepted feminine role or reject a heterosexual identity threaten to upset the imbalance of power enjoyed by white heterosexual men in a patriarchal society. (Griffin, 1992, p. 252)

Griffin (1993) also has pointed out that "all of the traits of successful athletic performance are defined as masculine. Traditional feminine expectations do not encompass such qualities as physical strength, aggressiveness, independence, tough-mindedness, and muscularity. In a sexist society women who have these qualities are suspect because they challenge social norms that depend on the acceptance of socially constructed differences between men and women as biologically determined" (p. 194). Thus, female athletes threaten male hegemony because female athletes, like some lesbians, "are frequently in groups without men; they are physically active in ways that do not have to do with being sexually appealing to men; and they are engaged in activities that do not enhance their abilities to be good mothers and wives (see Griffin, 1992)" (Kane & Lenskj, 1998, p. 190).

Sports media have responded to this homophobia by presenting women athletes in hyper-heterosexual molds (Kane & Lenskj, 1998, p. 200; see also Kane & Parks, 1992) as wives, heterosexual romantic partners and/ or as overtly feminine. This casting certainly was the case with the television coverage we analyzed during the inaugural WNBA and ABL women's professional basketball seasons. Both WNBA and ABL commentators constantly peppered game commentary with passing references to and narratives about the players' male love interests, engagements, weddings, honeymoons, and romances. For example, during the October 20, 1996, San Jose versus Seattle ABL game, Ron Barr reminded viewers that "Jennifer [Azzi] was a star player at Stanford and her husband was a pretty darn good player as well at the University of San Francisco." During the ABL Championship final (March 12, 1997), Tracy Warren told viewers that the Rage's "Molly Goodenbour [was] really a lesson in persistence. She got married in September to Patrick Scholdo, the coach at Sonoma State University, and for their honeymoon, they spent nine days with the Richmond Rage—in practice!"

CONCLUDING OBSERVATIONS

We tell stories, as Giddens (1991), Hall (1992), Murray (1989), and others explain, in order to answer critical identity questions such as "What should I do?" "How should I act?" "Who should I be?" and "Who can I be?" (Barker, 2000, pp. 166–167). Fejes (2000) has persuasively argued that today, "the realm of media practices constitutes the great definer and enforcer of identity" (p. 115). The narrative frames commentators used during televised U.S. professional basketball games not only constructed narrativized identities for athletes, they also legitimated particular ideological formations because, as Langellier (1989) explains, "in a most profound way, our stories tell us who we are and who we can—or cannot—be, at both surface and deep level meaning . . . a political function obtains for all narratives, whether or not they contain explicit political content" (p. 267).

The narrative frames used by television sportscasters during the 1996–97 U.S. professional basketball season highlighted and legitimated very different aspects of female and male professional athletes' identities and performances. A plethora of ABL and WNBA sports narratives framed female professional athletes as working parents, sexual role models, caregivers, and heterosexual romantic partners. These stories stood in sharp contrast to the total absence of comparable narratives about NBA athletes. Indeed, the only two verbal and visual acknowledgements of males' non-athletic roles in this study were (1) Utah Jazz owner Larry Miller's passing mention to sportscaster Peter Vecsey (June 6, 1997) that he now realized he had had the same unrealistic expectations of perfection for Karl Malone as he had had for his oldest son and (2) the visual sight of several children rushing onto the floor to hug and be lifted into the arms of Jazz players after the Jazz beat the Bulls in Games 3 and 4 of the NBA Finals. In none of the televised NBA games we analyzed for this study did sportscasters verbally mention male athletes' nonathletic roles. Nor did they ever subsume descriptions of male athletes' professional game performances within narratives about them as working parents, caregivers, sexual role models, or romantic partners, as commentators did during WNBA and ABL games. Nor did sports commentators in this study ever question male athletes about the difficulty of simultaneously being professional athletes and fathers or being unmarried fathers. Not until *Sports Illustrated*'s May 1998 "Where's Daddy?" story on the "NBA All-Paternity Team" (consisting of Larry Bird, Patrick Ewing, Juwan Howard, Shawn Kemp, Jason Kidd, Stephon Marbury, Hakeem Olajuwon, Gary Payton, Scottie Pippen, Isaiah Thomas, Kenny Anderson, Allen Iverson, and Latrell Sprewell—all out-of-wedlock and/or deadbeat dads) was this dual role highlighted for male professional basketball players (Wahl & Wertheim, 1998).

Daddario (1998) has argued that deathleticized narrative identities may facilitate some viewers' identification with and acceptance of "successful athletes" as a realistic identity for women. She also has suggested that, in the same way that soap operas may be read as empowering, "feminine" sports coverage may be empowering: "Soap operas empower female characters by focusing on aspects of domestic life, such as parenting, family, romance, career-family conflicts, and female identity crises, which have been marginalized or omitted in other program genres" (Daddario, 1998, p. 101). Although such readings of feminized sports narration as empowering are possible, we argue that the dominant reading invited by the presence of domestic narrative frames in coverage of sportswomen and the absence of such narrative frames in the coverage of sportsmen during the television coverage of professional basketball in 1996–97 was to impose traditional definitions of femininity and sexuality on female athletes and to suggest that "female athletes should be recognized and remembered for their stereotypical gender role, not their athletic role" (Kane, 1989, p. 61). Furthermore, sports commentary that constantly framed WNBA and ABL players during games in terms of their nonathletic domesticity marginalized and trivialized these sportswomen's athletic identities and subverted their sports achievements. As Tudor (1998) has observed,

Sport is about difference. . . . But this is not all. Sport is also about identity, for how else can there be difference if there are no identities to differentiate one from the others? . . . To narrate a sporting event is to articulate the conjunction where difference and identity meet, to render intelligible not just the differential skills on display but also the identities in whose service such skills are harnessed. . . . Whatever it may have been in the past, sport in the age of television has become a spectacle on which is mounted an extraordinary array of naturalized discourses of identity and differences. (p. 147)

Historically, sport has been an institution of male dominance and control. Duncan et al. (1990), for example, found that 92% of television sports airtime was given to men's sports, and only 5% was given to women's sports. In light of this, "women's entry into this arena on such a national scale represents, by definition, a fundamental challenge to male power and prestige" (Kane & Greendorfer, 1994, p. 33). Sports commentators' use of similar success, physical adversity, and agency narratives to frame game events and performances of female and male professional players during 1996–97 WNBA, ABL, and NBA games suggested that some level of gender equity had been achieved. However, those suggestions of equality were consistently and pervasively undercut by narratives and linguistic strategies that framed female athletes as exiled others, working moms, sexual role models, caregivers, and heterosexual romantic partners. Ultimately, television commentary discursively created differential identities for women and men professional basketball players and, in doing so, told television viewers that a frequent WNBA advertisement during the summer of 1997 featuring Rebecca Lobo was wrong: Cinderella still is only welcome at the ball, not to the ball.[5]

The Nike ad is right: We *are* the stories we tell. We *are* the stories others tell about us. So, perhaps one day, the 51% of us who are women *will* have a league of our own where the only barrier is a backboard and we are limited solely by our drive to succeed. However, as this analysis indicates in 1996–97 that day had not yet arrived. Not by a long shot.

NOTES

1. This Nike advertisement appeared in a number of broadcast and print outlets, including during the July 5, 1997, WNBA game between the Los Angeles Sparks and the Charlotte Sting. These words are reprinted here with the permission of Nike.

2. As Boje (2001) has noted, "the crisis of narrative method in modernity is what to do with non-linear, almost living storytelling is fragmented, polyphonic (many voiced) and collectively produced" (p. 1). Like Boje, our answer is to include in this narrative both traditional stories, or incidents or events that are chronologically narrated from the beginning to the middle to the end, and narrative fragments, which display fragmentation, discontinuities, partial and temporary understandings, and sometimes lack the closure typical of formal narratives.

3. During every game of the 1996–97 ABL and 1997 WNBA inaugural seasons analyzed in this study, sports commentators referenced the involuntary exile experienced by U.S.-born professional women basketball players. The only game commentary about U.S. men basketball players playing on foreign professional

teams found in this study occurred during the October 27, 1996, New England Blizzard versus Atlanta Glory game, when sportscaster Tracy Warren noted that "Clarissa Davis-Wrightsil's husband [is] also a professional player [camera showed him in the stands] playing over in Tokyo." However, the diaspora narratives made quite clear that the difference was that male basketball professionals had not been playing in exile because there were no U.S. teams for which to play.

4. The term "symbolic annihilation" was first used by sociologist Gaye Tuchman (1978) to describe the absence of women from mass media news and entertainment (print, television, and film).

5. As we noted at the beginning of this chapter, language—including sports commentary—is never neutral. Fornoff (1993) has reminded us that, in sport the "F" word has eight letters, not four. "Feminism," as Creedon explains, "is the 'F' word because the four-letter word means business as usual; the eight-letter word threatens to change things" (1994, p. 7).

REFERENCE LIST

Altheide, D. L., & Snow, R. P. (1979). *Media logic*. Beverly Hills, CA: Sage.

Barker, C. (2000). *Cultural studies: Theory and practice*. London: Sage.

Berg, B. J. (1986). *The crisis of the working mother: Resolving the conflict between family and work*. New York: Summit.

Boje, D. M. (2001). *Narrative methods for organizational & communication research*. London: Sage.

Brummett, B., & Duncan, M. C. (1990). Theorizing without totalizing: Specularity and televised sports. *Quarterly Journal of Speech, 76*, 227–246.

Clarke, A., & Clarke, J. (1982). Highlights and action replays—Ideology, sport and the media. In J. Hargreaves (Ed.), *Sport, culture and ideology* (pp. 62–87). London: Routledge & Kegan Paul.

Clifford, J. (1994). Diasporas. *Cultural Anthropology, 9*, 302–338.

Creedon, P. J. (1994). Women, media and sport: Creating and reflecting gender values. In P. J. Creedon (Ed.), *Women, media and sport: Challenging gender values* (pp. 3–27). Thousand Oaks: Sage.

Csikszentmihalyi, M., & Lyons, B. (1982). *The selection of behavioral traits: Reasons for admiring people*. Unpublished manuscript, University of Chicago.

Daddario, G. (1994). Chilly scenes of the 1992 Winter Games: The mass media and the marginalization of female athletes. *Sociology of Sport Journal, 11*, 275–288.

Daddario, G. (1998). *Women's sport and spectacle: Gendered television coverage and the Olympic games*. Westport, CT: Praeger.

Duncan, M. C. (1986). A hermeneutic of spectator sport: The 1976 and 1984 Olympic games. *Quest, 38*, 50–77.

Duncan, M. C., & Brummett, B. (1987). The mediation of spectator sport. *Research Quarterly for Exercise and Sport, 58*, 168–177.

Duncan, M. C., & Hasbrook, C. A. (1988). Denial of power in televised women's sports. *Sociology of Sport Journal, 5*, 1–21.

Duncan, M. C., & Messner, M A. (1998). The media image of sport and gender. In L. A. Wenner (Ed.), *MediaSport* (pp. 170–185). London: Routledge.

Duncan, M. C., Messner, M. A., Jensen, K., & Wachs, F. L. (1994). *Gender stereotyping in televised sports: A follow-up to the 1989 study*. Los Angeles: Amateur Athletic Foundation of Los Angeles.

Duncan, M. C., Messner, M. A., Williams, L., & Jensen, K. (1990). *Gender stereotyping in televised sports*. Los Angeles: Amateur Athletic Foundation of Los Angeles.

Eitzen, D. S., & Baca-Zinn, M. (1989). The de-athleticization of women: The naming and gender marking of collegiate sports teams. *Sociology of Sport Journal, 6*, 362–370.

Fejes, F. (2000). Making a gay masculinity. *Critical Studies in Mass Communication, 17*, 113–116.

Fornoff, S. (1993). Lady in the locker room. Champaign, IL: Sagamore.

Giddens, A. (1991). *Modernity and self-identity*. Cambridge: Polity Press.

Gilroy, P. (1997). Diaspora and the detours of identity. In K. Woodwood (Ed.), *Identity difference*. London: Sage.

Graydon, J. (1983). But it's more than a game. It's an institution. *Feminist Review, 13*, 5–16.

Griffin, P. (1992). Changing the game: Homophobia, sexism, and lesbians in sport. *Quest, 44*, 251–265.

Griffin, P. (1993). Homophobia in women's sports: The fear that divides us. In G. L. Cohen (Ed.), *Women in sport: Issues and controversies* (pp. 193–203). Newbury Park: Sage.

Grossberg, L. (1996). Identity and cultural studies—Is that all there is. In S. Hall & P. duGay (Eds.), *Questions of cultural identity* (pp. 87–107). London: Sage.

Halbert, C., & Lattimer, M. (1994). "Battling" gendered language: An analysis of the language used by sports commentators in a televised coed tennis competition. *Sociology of Journal, 11*, 298–308.

Hall, S. (1992). The question of cultural identity. In S. Hall, D. Held, & T. McGrew (Eds.), *Modernity and its futures*. Cambridge: Polity Press.

Hall, S. (1996). Introduction: Who needs identity? In S. Hall & P. duGay (Eds.), *Questions of cultural identity* (pp. 1–17). London: Sage.

Harris, J. C. (1994). *Athletes and the American hero dilemma*. Champaign, IL: Human Kinetics.

Harris, J. C., & Hills, L.A. (1993). Telling the story: Narrative in newspaper accounts of a men's collegiate basketball tournament. *Research Quarterly for Exercise and Sport, 64*, 108–121.

Heroes of young America: The twelfth annual poll. (1991). In M. S. Hoffman (Ed.), *The world almanac and book of facts 1991* (p. 32). New York: Pharos.

Hochschild, A. (with Machung, A.). (1989). *The second shift: Working parents and the revolution at home*. New York: Viking/Penguin.

Kahn, J. J. (1979). The hero world of the adolescent male: A descriptive/Jungian perspective (Doctoral dissertation, California School of Professional Psychology, 1978). *Dissertation Abstracts International, 39*, 3520B–3521B.

Kane, M. J. (1989). The post Title IX female athlete in the media: Things are changing, but how much? *J.O.P.E.R.D., 60*(3), 58–62.

Kane, M. J. (1995). Resistance/transformation of the oppositional binary: Exposing sport as a continuum. *Journal of Sport and Social Issues, 19*, 191–218.

Kane, M. J., & Lenskj, H. J. (1998). Media treatment of female athletes: Issues of gender and sexualities. In L. A. Wenner (Ed.), *MediaSport* (pp. 186–201). London: Routledge.

Kane, M. J., & Parks, J. B. (1992). The social construction of gender differences and hierarchy in sport journalism—Few new twists on very old themes. *Women's Sport and Physical Activity Journal, 1*, 49–83.

Kane, M. J., & Greendorfer, S. L. (1994). The media's role in accommodating and resisting stereotyped images of women in sport. In P. Creedon (Ed.), *Women, media, and sport: Challenging gender values* (pp. 28–44). Thousand Oaks, CA: Sage.

Langellier, K. M. (1989). Personal narratives: Perspectives on theory and research. *Text and Performance Quarterly, 9*, 243–276.

Leonard, W. M. II. (1980). *A sociological perspective of sport.* Minneapolis, MN: Burgess.

Mercer, K. (1990). Diasporic culture and the dialogic imagination: The aesthetic of black independent film in Britain. In M. Alvarado & J. O. Thompson (Eds.), *The media reader* (pp. 24–35). London: British Film Institute.

Messner, M. A., Duncan, M. C., & Jensen, K. (1993). Separating the men from the girls: The gendered language of televised sports. *Gender and Society, 7*, 121–137.

Murray, K. (1989). The construction of identity in the narratives of romance and comedy. In J. Shotter & K. Gergen (Eds.), *Texts of identity* (pp. 176–205). London: Sage.

Okin, S. M. (1989). *Justice, gender, and the family.* New York: Basic Books.

Sabo, D. (1994, June 6). *The body politics of sports injury: Culture, power, and the pain principle.* Paper presented at the annual meeting of the National Athletic Trainers Association, Dallas, TX.

Sabo, D., & Jansen, S. C. (1998*). Prometheus unbound: Constructions of masculinity in sports media.* In L. A. Wenner (Ed.), *MediaSport* (pp. 202–217). London: Routledge.

Sabo, D., & Jansen, S. C. (1992). Images of men in sport media: The social reproduction of the gender order. In S. Craig (Ed.), *Men, masculinity, and the media* (pp. 169–184). Newbury Park, CA: Sage.

Smith, G. J. (1976). An examination of the phenomenon of sports hero worship. *Canadian Journal of Applied Sports Sciences, 1*, 259–270.

Sommers, T., & Shields, L. (1987). *Women take care: The consequences of caregiving in today's society.* Gainsville, FL: Triad.

Tuchman, G. (1978). The symbolic annihilation of women. In G. Tuchman, A. K. Daniels, & J. Benet (Eds.), *Hearth and home: Images of women in the mass media* (pp. 3–38). New York: Oxford University Press.

Tudor, A. (1998). Sports reporting: Race, difference, and identity. In K. Brants, J. Hermes, & L. van Zoonen (Eds.), *The media in question: Popular cultures and public interests* (pp. 147–156). London: Sage.

Trujillo, N. (1991). Hegemonic masculinity on the mound: Media representations of Nolan Ryan and American sports culture. *Critical Studies in Mass Communication, 8*, 290–308.

Trujillo, N., & Ekdom [Vande Berg], L. R. (1985). Sports writing and American cultural values: The 1984 Chicago Cubs. *Critical Studies in Mass Communication, 2*, 262–281.

Trujillo, N., & Vande Berg, L. R. (1994). From wild western prodigy to the ageless wonder: The mediated evolution of Nolan Ryan. In S. Drucker & R. Cathcart (Eds.), *American heroes in a media age* (pp. 221–240). New York: Hampton Press.

Vande Berg, L. R. (1998). The sports hero meets mediated celebrityhood. In L. A. Wenner (Ed.), *MediaSport* (pp. 134–153). London: Routledge.

Vander Velden, L. (1986). Heroes and bad winners: Cultural differences. In L. Vander Velden & J. H. Humphrey (Eds.), *Psychology and sociology of sport: Current selected research: Vol. 1* (pp. 205–220). New York: AMS Press.

Wahl, G., & Wertheim, J. (1998, May 4). Paternity ward: Fathering out-of-wedlock kids has become commonplace among athletes, many of whom seem oblivious to the legal, financial and emotional consequences. *Sports Illustrated, 88,* 62–71.

Wang C. (1997). Pouring the foundation: The inaugural season. *WNBA Official Souvenir Yearbook* (pp. 6–7). New York: Professional Sports Publications.

Williams, L. D. (1994). Sportswomen in black and white: Sports history from an Afro-American perspective. In P. J. Creedon (Ed.), *Women, media and sport* (pp. 45–66). Thousand Oaks: Sage.

"Women sports stars: A new set of role models." (1996, March). Editorial. *Glamour,* p. 108.

Women's Sports + Fitness. Sheryl, Dawn, Lisa, Dot. Reebok, Nike, AT&T. (1997, March). *Women's Sports + Fitness,* pp. 6–39.

Wood, J. T. (1994). *Who cares? Women, care, and culture.* Carbondale: Southern Illinois Press.

CHAPTER 3

Dueling Genders: Announcer Bias in the 1999 U.S. Open Tennis Tournament

Andrew C. Billings

In 1973, more than 50 million people watched tennis icons Billie Jean King and Bobby Riggs in the tennis equivalent of the ultimate "Battle of the Sexes." Although King won the match that day, the battle for recognition of female athletes was just beginning. For decades, women have sought equal respect, equal television time, and equal pay for their sporting achievements. Rarely have they found the respect they were seeking (Chaudhary, 1999; Mateo, 1986). The 1987 Wimbledon men's singles champion Pat Cash even observed that women's tennis is to the men's game what horse manure was to thoroughbred racing (*London Times*, 1999). However, in the last years of the century, the opinions started to change. Former men's top seed and NBC sportscaster John McEnroe (1999) wrote that "the fact is that fans buy tickets to watch great tennis played by great personalities competing for titles in great events. And the women are selling the tickets" (p. 13A). Bandrapalli (1999) argued that, within today's sports market, "women's tennis is hip. It's hot" (p. 12). In fact, Walker (1999) reports that ratings for the 1998 U.S. Open Women's Final were 15 percent greater than those for the Men's Final, and Bandrapalli (1999) writes that HBO devoted 60 percent of its 1998 Wimbledon coverage to the women's game. The increased focus on female players appeared to result in a ratings increase of 19 percent. In the majority of recent Grand Slam events, ratings were higher for women's tennis than for men's (Bonham, 1998).

The reason for the increased appeal of women's tennis can be traced to several factors. First, controversies, such as the revelation that basketball player Julius Erving was the father of women's player Alexandra Stevenson and the "outing" as gay of several female tennis players, have brought attention to the sport (Acee, 1999; Pattullo, 1999). In addition, the World Tennis Association (WTA) rankings have placed American women higher than in previous years, with four American women's tennis players ranked in the world's top five in 1999 (Cronin, 1999). Still, the overwhelming reason for the increased popularity of women's tennis has been a combination of attitude, talent, and sex appeal (Bonham, 1998). Tennis stars such as Anna Kournikova and Martina Hingis are seen not only as tennis phenoms, but as covergirls who have posed for *Vogue* and *Vanity Fair*. As reported in *The London Times* (1999), "80 percent of spectators who positively prefer women's tennis are men. There is inevitably a sexual element to this" (p. 1). The result, argues Chaudhary (1999), is that "many of the women players have a higher profile than the men" (p. 9).

One might think that having a higher profile would result in equal pay and equal respect. Unfortunately, this has not happened. Prize money for women's tournaments still lags behind that for men's (Bandrapalli, 1999; Chaudhary, 1999). As for respect, consider that 1996 Wimbledon Champion Richard Krajicek recently called female players "lazy, fat pigs" (Foster, 1999, p. 5). Clearly, the Battle of the Sexes in 1973 has not led women to equal status a quarter of a century later.

Although several variables could explain the prejudices against women's tennis, the bias of sports commentators should not be overlooked. Many researchers (Daddario, 1994; Eastman & Billings, 1999, 2000; Halbert & Latimer, 1994; Tuggle, 1997) have studied and pinpointed gender bias in sports broadcasts. From the Olympics to tennis to women's basketball, female athletes remain the underdogs: They aren't strong enough, they aren't quick enough, they can't leap high enough. At least, the television media frame it that way.

Because men's and women's Grand Slam tennis tournaments are the only mixed-gender tournaments in mainstream sports, and because the U.S. Open represents the most prestigious tennis tournament that the United States hosts, this study evaluates potential sportscaster bias during the 1999 U.S. Open. During U.S. Open tennis telecasts, coverage moves back and forth between men's and women's matches, which makes comparisons between the genders particularly salient. Two studies that serve as starting points to analyze gender bias—Halbert and Latimer's (1994) study of the Battle of the Sexes and Eastman and Billings's (1999) study of gender bias in the Olympics—lead to important findings that have implications for the future of women's sports and for the construction of gender identity in modern society.

RELATED LITERATURE

The impact of televised sport cannot be understated. Prisuto (1979) argues that "televised sports play an active and significant role" in shaping

overall values and beliefs (p. 101). Brummett and Duncan (1990) l
that televised sports provide three categories of viewing pleasure:
ism, voyeurism, and narcissism. They write that "to understand how each
kind of pleasure works, one must consider the discourse, social context
and practices, and technological capabilities associated with televised
sport" (Brummett & Duncan, 1990, p. 244). Decades ago, Lippmann (1922)
postulated that media shape theory, a view that suggests that the pictures
of the world that the media give its receivers eventually become social
reality. Myth becomes fact. Therefore, when notable differences are found
in the manners in which male and female athletes are characterized, those
differences, or biases, shape current social views.

Such biases have been pinpointed by many researchers in the past several decades. Morris and Lydahl (1983) divide sports commentary into
two dimensions: basic (giving accounts of the game) and elaborative (commenting on the dramatic impact of the game). In both types of comments,
scholars such as Daddario (1994, 1997), Tuggle (1997), and Tuggle and
Owen (1999) have found marked differences in the ways sports commentators characterize and summarize male and female athletes. Taking the
lead of Reid and Soley (1979), Kane (1989) analyzed *Sports Illustrated* articles and found that the magazine tended only to cover "socially acceptable" women's sports, such as tennis, figure skating, or gymnastics. Tuggle
and Owen (1999), in their analysis of the 1996 Atlanta Olympics, found
similar results: Although NBC showed women's sports almost half the
time, the network almost exclusively televised those events that were
physically attractive to televise, including gymnastics, diving, and sprint-
ing. The more visually unattractive sports, such as field hockey, shot put,
discus, softball, and soccer, were relegated to short segments between
main events, if they were covered at all.

Mateo (1986) even classifies sports on the basis of gender biases. So-
called men's sports are those viewed as high contact sports (e.g., basketball, football, hockey), whereas so-called women's sports involve finesse
and elegance (e.g., figure skating, gymnastics). Golf and tennis are categorized under Mateo's (1986) final heading, neutral sports. Harrison, Lee,
and Belcher (1999) find results similar to Mateo's (1986) in their logistic
regression analysis of gender biases toward sport participation. Football,
a high contact sport, is considered the most masculine of all the sports
studied, whereas gymnastics is the most feminine. Tennis, though found
to be a slightly more feminine sport, is fairly androgynous. Yet, as both
studies note, undeniably, sports have been classified according to gender
for decades.

Using a battle of the sexes in the spirit of Riggs versus King, Halbert
and Latimer (1994) studied sportscaster gender bias in a match between
Martina Navratilova and Jimmy Connors. In several salient areas of study,
they found that the depiction of Navratilova was much less favorable than

that of Connors. Granted, Connors won the match. Yet, Halbert and Latimer (1994) found differences throughout the match, even before the outcome was determined. These findings, combined with the work of Eastman and Billings (1999, 2000), yield seven areas of study integral for the purposes of this research.

First, the amount of clock time given to male and female athletes is important with regard to the overall salience of mixed-gender sporting events. Eastman and Billings (2000) studied coverage of female athletes in televised sports programs and newspapers. Using a 76-night database, they found that CNN's *Sports Tonight* devoted just seven percent of its coverage to female athletes and ESPN's *SportsCenter* only devoted five percent. Newspaper coverage was a bit more balanced, with women receiving 11 percent of all coverage in the *New York Times* and 19 percent in *USA Today*. Although there were more men's sports contested on a given night, the television and newspaper analyses underscore the dominance of men's sports coverage.

The greatest strides toward equal coverage has been in the Olympics. Higgs and Weiler (1994) analyzed the clock time in the 1992 Barcelona Summer Olympics and found that 56 percent of all clock time was devoted to men's athletics, with the remaining 44 percent devoted to female athletes. Eastman and Billings (1999) counted the clock time for the 1994 Lillehammer Games, and the split was identical to that in 1992 (56 percent to men, 44 percent to women). Tuggle and Owen (1999), who studied the 1996 Atlanta Summer Olympics, found that the gap between coverage of male and female athletes had closed to 53 percent/47 percent. However, in the recent 1998 Nagano Olympics, the gap widened to a larger difference than any of the previous studies: 60 percent to men and 40 percent to women. Any analysis of Olympic coverage, however, must be reconciled with the fact that nearly two-thirds of all Olympic participants are men (Mayo, 1996; Suk, 1998). Because of this difference in the number of participants, male athletes might be expected to receive more coverage than female athletes. Thus, clock time alone cannot definitively answer whether mixed-gender sports telecasts tend to favor male athletes.

Second, Halbert and Latimer (1994) noted that naming practices appear to be a large problem in gendered sports coverage. Messner, Duncan, and Jensen (1993) pointed out that women frequently are referred to by their first names, whereas male athletes commonly are called by their last names. The use of differential naming practices can reinforce negative stereotypes of female athletes. Whereas first names may personalize an athlete more, last names may distance the viewer from the athlete and thereby create a distinction that is more likely to make the athlete seem superior and heroic in comparison to the viewer.

Third, gender marking, which was evident in the study of the Navratilova/Connors match, makes certain assumptions about male and female athletes. Halbert and Latimer (1994) found that comments about Connors rarely included the word "men's" to qualify a statement, whereas Navratilova's skills often were limited to the "women's" category. For example, Connors's serve was considered the "best in the game," whereas Navratilova's skills were listed as the reason she was "set apart in *women's* tennis for so many years" (Halbert & Latimer, 1994, p. 302, emphasis added). Gender marking thus reinforces a bias against women by serving as a qualifier of their abilities. In comments such as the one pertaining to Navratilova, the underlying assumption is that Navratilova's skills were not good enough to set her apart in tennis as a whole; instead, they set her apart in women's tennis only. These comments cause the casual listener to assume that women's tennis is substandard to men's, in that women's tennis apparently needs a qualifier.

Fourth, the amount of praise and criticism that male and female competitors received was identified in both Halbert and Latimer's (1994) and Eastman and Billings's (1999) studies as crucial to the perception of female athletes. Halbert and Latimer (1994) detected an immense difference in the ratios of praise to criticism for Navratilova and Connors. Navratilova was criticized more often than she was praised (29 praises versus 41 criticisms), whereas Connors was praised more than four times as often as he was criticized (70 praises versus 16 criticisms). Eastman and Billings (1999) analyzed 3,256 adjectival descriptors in the coverage of the 1994, 1996, and 1998 Olympics, though instead of praise and criticism, they call their categories explanations for success and explanations for failure. They found more explanations for the success of men than the success of women in both 1996 and 1998. More specifically, male athletes were depicted as succeeding because of exceptional courage, experience, composure, and athletic skills, whereas women had no common explanatory theme for why they succeeded.

Fifth, Eastman and Billings (1999) also analyzed several other key factors associated with gender bias. For all three Olympics (1994, 1996, and 1998), they categorized the number of comments about the physical attractiveness of the male and female athletes. All three Olympic telecasts contained significantly more comments about the attractiveness of female athletes. In combination with Bonham's (1998) observation about the sex-symbol status of several current professional women's tennis players, this finding suggests that the sex-symbol variable is a key element in the analysis of tennis telecasts.

Sixth, Eastman and Billings (1999) categorized comments about the physical strength of athletes. As might be expected, comments about the strength of male athletes significantly outnumbered similar comments about the strength of female athletes, often by greater than a 2:1 ratio.

A final facet of Eastman and Billings's (1999) analysis pertained to comments about the emotions of athletes. Surprisingly, no significant differences between men and women were determined by their study. However, because the Olympics often is depicted as the kind of athletic event in which everyone would be emotional, a second look at this variable is warranted in a study of professional tennis, a venue in which men may been viewed as better able to control their emotions, whereas women may not.

HYPOTHESES

On the basis of analyses by Halbert and Latimer (1994), Bandrapalli (1999), and Eastman and Billings (1999) in reference to both professional tennis and the depiction of male and female athletes across the sporting spectrum, seven hypotheses were constructed to test announcer bias during the 1999 U.S. Open Tennis Tournament:

H1: Female players will receive significantly more television clock time than will male players.

H2: There will be significantly more naming practices toward female players than toward male athletes.

H3: There will be significantly more gender marking of female players than of male players.

H4: The ratio of praise to criticism will be higher for male players than it will be for female players.

H5: Comments about the physical attractiveness of female players will be significantly more frequent than will comments about the physical attractiveness of male players.

H6: Comments about the strength of female athletes will be significantly less frequent than will comments about the strength of male athletes.

H7: Comments about the emotions of female athletes will be significantly more frequent than will comments about the emotions of male athletes.

METHOD

For this study, U.S. Open tennis coverage by CBS and the USA network was videotaped from 6:30–11:00 P.M. on weeknights and from 11:00 A.M.–6:00 P.M. on weekends. However, several factors decreased the number of hours available for analysis. First, technical difficulties occurred on two nights of programming, eliminating the possibility of analysis on these nights. Second, several major rain delays, including one that lasted more than six hours during weekend coverage, resulted in fewer hours of actual tennis coverage. Third, the U.S. Open tennis coverage had large segments of time devoted to commercials, promotions, and in-studio commentary. Despite these factors, 36 hours of U.S. Open tennis coverage, an amount that warrants analysis, were used as a database.

When the hours were recorded, all adjectival descriptors used to describe male and female athletes were recorded and separated according to gender. Only athletes participating in the tournament were counted, and only descriptors uttered by CBS employees were deemed important for analysis. Descriptors from players before and after the matches were not entered into the database, because any potential bias they exhibited would not be a function of network bias.

Overall clock time was determined using a VCR real-time counter, and the percentage of minutes devoted to men's and women's coverage was compared with the number of comments about male and female athletes in each of the seven categories.

The announcer comments were organized into seven categories pertaining to (1) naming practices, (2) gender marking, (3) praise, (4) criticism, (5) attractiveness, (6) strength, and (7) emotions. These divisions then were separated into individual content analysis categories. To verify the reliability of the categorizations, an independent coder analyzed one three-hour tape. According to Holsti's (1969) formula, intercoder reliability was 96 percent.

RESULTS

Of the approximately 36 hours of network coverage, more than 35 were devoted to singles competition. No mixed-doubles matches were aired, so all descriptors occurred in same-sex matches. A total of 3,612 descriptors was categorized into the seven descriptive categories. Of all the descriptors, 1,559 (43%) referred to men, and 2,053 (57%) pertained to women.

Regarding the hypothesis 1, the results concur with Bandrapalli's (1999) findings. Women's tennis constituted 59 percent of all tennis coverage (20 hours, 42 minutes), leaving just 41 percent of the coverage devoted to the men's game (14 hours, 25 minutes). Hypothesis 1 therefore is confirmed, because women's tennis constituted the majority of U.S. Open coverage.

In addition, women were much more frequently referred to by their first name than were men, in support of hypothesis 2. Table 3.1 indicates the descriptor breakdown by category and gender.

Female players were referred to by their first names 50 percent of the time; men were referred to by their first names only 22 percent of the time. The leading women's tennis players were most often called Martina, Lindsay, Venus, or Serena. Men's players, rarely called by their first names, were referred to by their last names. For example, men's champion Andre Agassi was referred to as "Andre" only 28 percent of the time, whereas women's champion Serena Williams was referred to as "Serena" a whopping 64 percent of the time. Thus, hypothesis 2 is confirmed, in that naming practices are very evident in the data.

In contrast, gender marking was found to be a less prevalent concern.

Table 3.1.
U.S. Open Announcer Descriptors by Gender

	Male Athletes	Female Athletes
Naming Practices	717	859
Gender Marking	157	195
Praise	253	347
Criticism	212	378
Physical Attractiveness	48	113
Strength	134	108
Emotion	38	53
TOTAL	1,559	2,053

Total number of descriptors = 3,612

Men's tennis matches were referred to as "men's tennis" instead of "tennis" a total of 157 times. Women's tennis received similar gender markings 195 times. Although women were the subject of more instances of gender marking than were men, the proportion of gender marking comments was equal in terms of the greater number of women's matches shown in comparison with the men's matches. Gender marking occurred at rates of 9 per hour for women and 10 per hour for men. Consequently, hypothesis 3 is rejected; there were no discernable gender marking differences.

The ratio of praise to criticism also was calculated for both male and female athletes. Women were praised a total of 347 times and criticized a total of 378 times. In contrast, men were praised 253 times and criticized 212 times. Thus, the ratio of praise to criticism for women was .9 to 1, whereas the ratio for men was 1.2 to 1. This difference is significant ($\chi^2 =$ 5.34; degrees of freedom [df] = 1; $p = .04$), and hypothesis 4 is confirmed.

The fifth hypothesis pertained to differences by gender in the number of comments about an athlete's physical attractiveness. Although the most publicized sex symbol in women's tennis, Anna Kournikova, was not entered in the tournament, comments about the women's beauty were much more prevalent. Of all the comments pertaining to physical attractiveness, 113 (70%) were about women's physical attractiveness, whereas only 48 (30%) comments were made about men. Even with the difference in clock time between women's and men's coverage, this discrepancy is significantly different from the null ($\chi^2 = 10.4$; df = 1; $p = .02$). Therefore, hypothesis 5 is confirmed; women's physical appearances were much more of a conversational focus than were men's appearances.

Hypothesis 6 postulated that comments depicting an athlete's strength would center more often on men. Men's strength was referred to 134 times, whereas women's strength was referred to a total of 108 times. This bias toward men is even more notable considering that they received more strength comments than women despite constituting only 41 percent of the database. A very evident significant difference was calculated ($\chi^2 = 34.4$; df = 1; $p = .01$) that confirms hypothesis 6.

Finally, hypothesis 7 argued that female athletes would be characterized as more emotional than would male athletes. However, comments describing emotions yielded a 59/41 percent split between female and male athletes, respectively, which represents a near-perfect match to the percentage of coverage time. Women athletes were judged as emotional in 53 cases, whereas men were similarly described as emotional 38 times. Such an even balance rejects hypothesis 7, because all athletes were portrayed as equally emotional in competition.

DISCUSSION

Extracted from the results are several trends that are noteworthy in the discussion of gender bias in televised sport. First, this study supports findings that women's tennis is the only known professional sport in which female athletes receive more television coverage than do their male counterparts. The women received 59 percent of all coverage, which is apparently typical, as Bandrapalli (1999) indicated that a 60 percent share of Wimbledon coverage was devoted to women players. Although figure skating and gymnastics are two other sports in which both the genders compete and women receive the lion's share of airtime, both these sports are largely amateur and relegated to major coverage only once every two years when an Olympics occur. Women's tennis is the only regular example of a gender split that favors women at least four times per year when the Grand Slam tennis tournaments are telecast for two-week periods. In the U.S. Open used for analysis, it should be noted that the top men's player, Pete Sampras, was forced to withdraw before the tournament started because of an injury and the world's second-ranked player, Patrick Rafter, dropped out in the first week. These absences could explain the lack of men's coverage. However, men's matches are inherently longer (best of five sets) and two American men advanced to the final (Andre Agassi and Todd Martin), so any clock time discrepancies that occurred because of the lack of participation of Pete Sampras and Patrick Rafter should have been counteracted. Thus, women's dominance of clock time is highly relevant to the discussion of gendered sports as a whole.

Second, several gender biases were still showcased by sportscasters responsible for the U.S. Open commentary. Male athletes were referred to by their last names much more frequently than were women. Previous research has indicated that this practice contributes to the notion that women are personal and accessible (Messner et al., 1993), whereas men are impersonal and inaccessible because they are sports superstars. However, at least part of the large discrepancy between the genders in naming practices likely occurred because of the presence of the Williams sisters: Serena, the eventual women's champion, and Venus, a semifinalist. Because two prominent female athletes had the same last name, sportscasters relied on the first name of each sister to avoid confusion about which was playing. Because both of the Williams sisters did so well, and because they are both Americans with high-profile personalities, these two athletes constituted a significant segment (23%) of the database and thereby likely skewed the results for naming practices.

A second difference detected in the telecasts was that women were criticized more frequently than they were praised, whereas men were praised more than they were criticized. This was consistent with the findings of Halbert and Latimer (1994) regarding the match between Jimmy Connors and Martina Navratilova. However, Halbert and Latimer found the rate of praise to criticism to be .7:1 for Navratilova and 4.3:1 for Connors, an overwhelming difference. In contrast, this study yielded results of .9:1 for women and 1.2:1 for men, which may indicate a shift toward equality, even if bias against female athletes still exists.

More typical stereotypes found not only in tennis but in sports coverage as a whole were also identified. Men were characterized as strong; women were characterized as attractive. The significant differences detected in these two categories cannot be explained easily and appear rather to be the result of deeply rooted stereotypes about male and female athletes. The results of this study suggest that these two stereotypes may be the hardest to debunk.

Still, two findings suggest that gender equity is starting to occur. In addition to the obvious finding that women received more on-air coverage, no significant differences were detected in the areas of gender marking and player emotion. The lack of gender marking for women's tennis is particularly important because it suggests that women's tennis may be losing the stigma of being considered subservient to the men's game. The fact that female athletes were not portrayed as more emotional than male athletes indicates that women are portrayed as hard-nosed athletes who will not falter under pressure.

CONCLUSION

Gender bias in televised sports persists throughout an increasingly saturated sports-television market. The signs of progress indicated in this study of professional tennis are not likely to influence gender attitudes about all sports. However, women's tennis appears to be leading the way in the battle for equal treatment in television coverage. Several of these findings indicate a shift in the overall impressions about women's tennis. Men's tennis is still seen as providing the superior athletes, but women's tennis is regarded as something of a breed unto itself. That it is now televised more than is the men's game indicates that people may appreciate the skills associated with the women's game more than the raw power exemplified in men's tennis. Ultimate gender equity can be reached in this way, as an increasing portion of television audiences finds that though men's and women's tennis is played differently, both can be entertaining, and both can be respected.

REFERENCE LIST

Acee, K. (1999, August 15). The world according to Alexandra; New-found status providing Stephenson with forum, options. *The San Diego Union-Tribune*, p. C1.

Bandrapalli, S. (1999, June 25). Wimbledon's unequal pay scale. *The Christian Science Monitor*, p. 12.

Bonham, D. (1998, September 6). Hollywood, "Hot looking players" teaming up to save tennis. *The Denver Rocky Mountain News*, p. 12G.

Brummett, B., & Duncan, M. C. (1990). Theorizing without totalizing: Specularity and televised sports. *The Quarterly Journal of Speech, 76*, 227–246.

Chaudhary, V. (1999, June 21). Women players' volley over equal pay; Protest campaign during Wimbledon fortnight aims to highlight injustice of lower prize money in three of the grand slams. *The London-Guardian*, p. 9.

Cronin, D. (1999, October 27). World tennis rankings, *USA Today*, p. 17.

Daddario, G. (1994). Chilly scenes of the 1992 Winter Games: The mass media and the marginalization of female athletes. *Sociology of Sport Journal, 11*, 275–288.

Daddario, G. (1997). Gendered sports programming: 1992 Summer Olympic coverage and the feminine narrative form. *Sociology of Sport Journal, 14*, 103–120.

Eastman, S. T., & Billings, A. C. (1999). Gender parity in the Olympics: Hyping women athletes, favoring men athletes. *Journal of Sport and Social Issues, 23* (2), 140–170.

Eastman, S. T., & Billings, A. C. (2000). Sportscasting and sports reporting: The power of gender bias. *Journal of Sports and Social Issues, 24* (1), 192–212.

Foster, P. (1999, June 17). Men are no match for the Centre Court Spice Girls: The new breed of tennis women mix power with grace. *The London Daily Telegraph*, p. 5.

Halbert, C., & Latimer, M. (1994). "Battling" gendered language: An analysis of the language used by sports commentators in a televised coed tennis competition. *Sociology of Sport Journal, 11*, 298–308.

Harrison, L., Lee, A. M., & Belcher, D. (1999). Race and gender differences in sport participation as a function of self-schema. *Journal of Sport and Social Issues, 23* (3), 287–307.

Higgs, D. T., & Weiler, K. H. (1994). Gender bias and the 1992 Summer Olympic Games: An analysis of television coverage. *Journal of Sport and Social Issues, 18*, 234–246.

Holsti, O. R. (1969). *Content analysis for the social sciences and the humanities.* Menlo Park, CA: Addison-Wesley.

Kane, M. (1989). The post-Title IX female athlete in the media: Things are changing, but how much? *Journal of Physical Education, Recreation, and Dance, 60 (1),* 58–62.

Lippman, W. (1922). *Public opinion.* New York: Harcourt, Brace.

The London Times. (1999, June 20). The spice girls of centre court, p. 1.

Mateo, S. (1986). The effect of sex and gender-schematic processing on sport participation. *Sex Roles, 15 (7/8),* 417–432.

Mayo, M. (1996, July 19). 100 years of gold and glory: Let the celebration begin. *Fort Lauderdale Sun-Sentinel,* p. 1G.

McEnroe, J. (1999, June 8). Gender inequity at center court; Women tennis pros draw crowds; men draw bigger checks. *The Minneapolis Star-Tribune,* p. 13A.

Messner, M. A., Duncan, M. C., & Jensen, K. (1993). Separating the men from the girls: The gendered language of televised sports. In D.S. Eitzen (Ed.), *Sport in contemporary society* (pp. 219–233). New York: St. Martin's Press.

Morris, B. S., & Nydahl, J. (1983). Toward analyses of live television broadcasts. *Central States Speech Journal, 34,* 195–202.

Pattullo, A. (1999, June 25). Buster flustered by girls in shorts. *The Scotsman,* p. 46.

Prisuto, R.H. (1979). Televised sports and political values. *Journal of Communication, 29,* 94–102.

Reid, L. N., & Soley, L. C. (1979). *Sports Illustrated*'s coverage of women in sports. *Journalism Quarterly, 56,* 861–863.

Suk, S. (1998, February 22). Nagano Olympics full of winter games firsts. *Japan Economic Newswire,* p. 1.

Tuggle, C. A. (1997). Differences in television sports reporting of men's and women's athletics: ESPN *SportsCenter* and CNN *Sports Tonight. Journal of Broadcasting & Electronic Media, 41 (1),* 14–24.

Tuggle, C. A., & Owen, A. (1999). A descriptive analysis of NBC's coverage of the Centennial Olympics. *Journal of Sport and Social Issues, 23 (2),* 171–182.

Walker, S. (1999, July 2). Sponsors snub women's tennis: Companies leaving over smaller audiences and dwindling interest. *The Ottawa Citizen,* p. B3.

CHAPTER 4

The Talk of the Town: A Rhetorical Analysis of the Browns' Departure from and Return to Cleveland

Daniel J. O'Rourke III

November 6, 1995, was a newsworthy day in northeast Ohio. The Cleveland *Plain Dealer* covered international stories, such as the assassination of Israeli Prime Minister Yitzhak Rabin, as well as local topics including upcoming elections and the financial crisis of the city schools. However, on Tuesday, November 7, these stories were subsumed beneath the banner headline, "Browns bolt" (1995). For Cleveland sports fans, the unthinkable had happened. Art Modell, the principal owner of the Cleveland Browns, announced in a Monday afternoon press conference that he was moving the team to Baltimore, Maryland. Cleveland's largest newspaper thought this story so significant that it dedicated four-and-a-half pages of its 10-page news section to coverage of the event. In the eyes of Browns' followers, and many Ohioans, the terms "Cleveland" and "Browns" were synonymous. In its championship years and losing seasons, the Browns came to symbolize the city that knew both manufacturing boons and the deflation of rust-belt economics. Politicians and industries could fail, but the heroes of Sunday afternoons in Municipal Stadium were tested and true. Some fans heard the fateful announcement and described feeling a personal sense of loss, as though experiencing a divorce or the death of a loved one ("Modell Trashed," 1995; Rushin, 1995). One of the icons of Browns' history, a giant of a man forever to be known as Lou "The Toe" Groza, said that when he heard the news, all he could do was cry (Morgan, 1997).

To non-sports fans, such descriptions of the departure of a football team would seem overly dramatic. The significance of the relocation of a sports franchise clearly pales in comparison with the assassination of a world leader. The impact of a failed school system would have irreparable consequences on a community and generations of its citizens. Even local elections should have more long-term consequences on a city and county than the departure of a sports franchise. In support of such sentiments, some economists have argued that the financial losses due to the migration of a professional sports team are negligible. They assert that the entertainment dollars spent on sports merely shift from one venue to another (Morgan, 1997). Still, the outpouring of heartfelt emotion and anger after the press conference of November 6 cannot be denied. Editorials from newspapers across the country blasted the ownership of the Browns for its lack of loyalty and unbridled greed ("Columnists around," 1995). Protests followed in Cleveland, Pittsburgh, Baltimore, and numerous cities around the nation. Thousands of letters, telephone calls, and e-mail messages flooded the headquarters of the National Football League (NFL) and the offices of its team owners. A member of Congress proposed legislation to prevent this and future moves by sports franchises as a violation of interstate commerce laws (Williamson, 1995). The message was clear: In this country, professional sports represent something more than political or economic games between wealthy and powerful team owners. Professional and amateur sports are a part of our collective culture and represent one of the symbolic threads that can either bring communities together or tear them asunder.

The purpose of this chapter is to explore the symbolic relationship that can form between a community and a professional sports team. In 50 years of competing in Cleveland, the Browns became more than the local franchise. The Cleveland Browns were the storied home team. Newspaper articles began as simple accounts of wins and losses, but over the years, they were woven into a community mythology. Quarterbacks became representative heroes, and opponents were enemies to be vanquished. Victories and defeats brought tribal celebrations and battle scars. Local radio and television stations trumpeted the arrival of the competitive season and chronicled the history of past campaigns. Slowly but surely, these stories became part of the collective consciousness of people in Ohio, and the Cleveland Browns became mythic representatives of their community. I will not argue that sports are the sole creators of a community's mythology. For some citizens, the Cleveland Symphony composes international narratives that extend far beyond the scope of any sports myth. Instead, this chapter examines the story of professional football in Cleveland, Ohio, as the source of a modern mythology. For five decades, this mythology flourished in the rich narrative soil of this midwestern community. The depth of its roots only became apparent when the owner of the franchise tried to transplant the team. Fortunately for fans, the team was removed, but the mythic roots remained.

Like it or not, America is a nation obsessed with sports. Small towns across the nation introduce themselves on roadside signs as the home of a state championship team. Our major colleges and universities are known more for their basketball, football, and baseball teams than for their music, chemistry, or communication programs. And then there are professional sports. Billions of dollars are spent each year on tickets for games, sporting equipment, athletic apparel, and products promoted by sports figures ("Why Sports?," 1998). It is difficult to walk down a street in this country without encountering someone wearing a team jacket, baseball cap, or other article of clothing with a corporate sports logo on it. The media facilitates the promulgation of sports by producing multiple all-sports television channels, myriad magazines dedicated to one or more sports, and newspapers that tout more local and national sports coverage. In 1998, more people watched the Super Bowl than voted in the 1996 presidential election ("Why Sports?," 1998). America is not alone in this obsession. One need only think of World Cup riots or the fact that Michael Jordan was the most recognized person on the planet during his professional career. Still, the availability of leisure time, media saturation, and the diversity of sports in this country make the United States the preeminent promoter and consumer of sports in the world.

The amount of attention paid to sports in this country, however, begs the question: Why has the subject been studied so little by academics? Two researchers have argued in an essay in *The Chronicle of Higher Education* that, despite the importance of sports in American culture, too few scholars select this area as a field of specialization and that critical work about sports has been marginalized (Gorn & Oriard, 1995). Indeed, I would argue that virtually every significant social issue of the twentieth century has been played out on the courts, as well as adjudicated in them. To discuss racism and ignore the story of Jackie Robinson would be an oversight. Drug abuse has been seen through the eyes of professional athletes struggling with steroid use and addiction. Sexism has been reflected in the issue of Title IX, and economic inequity is evidenced in the astronomical salaries of those few who become professional athletes. Even complex global, political, and military struggles have been personified by sports figures. Be it Joe Louis versus Max Schmelling, the United States' defeat of the Soviet hockey team, or Muhammed Ali versus the U.S. Selective Service, sports have simplified and characterized the struggles of nations, movements, and governments.

In the aforementioned article in *The Chronicle of Higher Education*, Gorn and Oriard (1995) assert that one reason sports might not be studied is that they are "unscripted." The authors theorize that professors are essentially linguistic creatures who struggle to understand the "nonverbal" phenomenon of sports. One of the arguments of this chapter is that just the opposite is true. I assert that, in the Burkean sense, all sports begin in the realm of physical motion. Athletes are bodies in motion who pit their physical skills against an opponent or object. However, once this motion occurs, announcers and analysts immediately convert the experience into symbolic action for the consumption of those in attendance or fans watching, listening, or reading about the contest through the media (Burke, 1966). In their study of sports broadcasting, Brummett and Duncan (1990) observe that the discourse of announcers is fundamentally narrative, in that it often seeks to overlay a story on the actions taking place on the field. To extend this narrative pattern, journalists seek to explain the reasons for the success or failure of a team in the next editions of their newspapers. Sportscasters offer scores and synoptic highlights to those who missed the game, and fans carry favorite stories or complaints back with them into discussions with friends, family, or coworkers in the week to come. For a true fan, such stories become part of a larger narrative field that links him or her with other similarly engaged individuals. For this reason, I assert that the narrative of sports may best be understood as a myth of identity and community.

SPORT AS MYTH

In a previous study of mythic criticism, I proposed the following definition of myth: A myth is "a sacred story of identity, not reliant on logical proofs that defines an aspect of an individual or a community's world and their place in it" (O'Rourke, 1992, p. 51). The purpose of this definition was to provide a link between classical perceptions of myths as "sacred stories" and the contemporary perception of myth as "A purely fictitious narrative usually involving supernatural persons, actions or events and embodying some popular idea concerning natural or historical phenomena" ("Myth," 1971/1994). The impetus for this association was Kenneth Burke's (1941/1973, pp. 110–111) perception of history as "an unending conversation." In Burke's view, all of human history can be understood as an ongoing story passed from one generation to the next. The metaphor used to explain this conversation is a cocktail party. Simply put, each person, and indeed each generation, arrives at a party that has been going on for some time. Before anyone can enter the conversation, he or she must learn the language and topics of discussion. Slowly, the person becomes comfortable with the group and ventures into the verbal fray. The evening wears on, and eventually, he or she must leave. Still, the party continues with new guests and new topics of conversation (Burke, 1941/ 1973).

Burke's metaphoric vision of history as an intergenerational conversation is fairly simple and straightforward. Since the dawn of human symbol use, each generation has learned its language and culture from its symbolic forebearers. New situations and challenges arise in every era that force symbol users to adapt and expand the inherited terms to explain new phenomena. Eventually, each generation passes, leaving the voices of tomorrow to craft new symbols for the future. One of the interesting applications of this conversational view of history is the study of the evolution of myths. Sociologists and anthropologists tell us that in the prescientific world, primitive people "acted out" dramas of significant tribal events (Bellah, 1964; Cassirer, 1944). Tales of origin, feats of bravery, and important moments in tribal history were recorded in the performance of these dramas. Over time, humans became more adept at the use of symbols, and stories were translated into words to explain the ancient rites. In this way, myths were linked with rituals as a unique form of narrative.

In the prescientific world, humans defined their world through the telling of myths. A storyteller would offer a tale about the origin of the tribe, and that tale would resonate among the people until a more popular narrative arose to take its place. There were no proofs or tests of the tale other than the credibility of the speaker and the ability of the story to answer a fundamental question. In this way, myths became sacred as they answered the essential questions of life: "Who are we?" "Where do we come from?" and "What is our purpose?" The truths offered by these narratives gave people a symbolic sense of identity. Physically, humans needed one another to survive in a hostile world and procreate. Symbolically, humans joined together in communities when they shared stories, defined truths, or identified common goals. The first myths were these stories of identity and community.

The advent of the scientific method challenged myths to prove themselves. No longer was the credibility of an elder or the poetry of an ancient fable enough to explain the workings of nature. Thus, myths were relegated to the realm of folktales and fables by those seeking quantifiable answers to questions about the physical world. It is important to note, however, that questions of identity and purpose are rarely answered in measurable terms. Thus, some sacred myths of identity and community persisted as they were passed from generation to generation. In particular, religious communities founded on faith in ineffable truths maintained sacred myths and rituals as a means of distinguishing their sacred communities from the rest of secular society.

The persistence of sacred myths in the unending conversation of history suggests that some aspects of the definition of humanity were beyond the scope of the scientific method. Fundamental questions of identity and purpose are rooted in the human experience. To discover "who I am" or "what my purpose is," many have turned to sacred scriptures. In the predominantly secular society of the world today, it is also possible that people might turn to other significant communities, such as the family, the nation, or the corporate world, in search of stories of identification and direction. The quests for identity and purpose can be hard to define, however, and may lead some to seek affirmation or distinction in the established stories of others. We may strive to be like the best among us or know that "we" are not like "them." Humans never tire of heroic tales of an individual or team overcoming adversity. Such stories are the basis of numerous newspaper columns, movie scripts, and inspirational parables told to children. We use these stories to identify with the best qualities of humanity and remind ourselves of our potential. Unfortunately, our darker sides also use narrative themes to scapegoat those different from ourselves or parody actions that challenge our perceptions and traditions. In this way, many of our baser human fears, hopes, and emotions are relegated to the realm of myth, which provides a narrative justification of their existence. The best scientific evidence available tells us the causes of AIDS, yet stories appear in the news about schoolchildren ostracized because of a faulty blood transfusion. Racial stereotypes persist, in part because of the retelling of insensitive jokes and anecdotal evidence about the intelligence of one group or the work ethic of another. It seems that twenty-first-century women and men are not so far removed from their primitive narrative ancestors. Heroic tales and scapegoating myths persist in the unending conversation of our collective lives. Today, these stories are facilitated greatly by media that enable the myths to reach much larger audiences in much less time. It is in this rich mythic ground that sports narratives can flourish.

In *A Hard Road to Glory*, Arthur Ashe (1988) observes that sports traditionally have prospered in democratic societies. From the time of the Olympic Games, free societies have recognized that one did not have to be born to privilege to possess extraordinary skills. This is not to suggest that competitive athletics have always been open to all people. Ashe's history of the African American athlete chronicles many struggles for acceptance. For the purpose of this study, two points can be drawn from Ashe's statement. First, athletics reflect the competitiveness found in other cultural venues of a free society. Political elections and the rivalry of the free market are examples of competition in a democratic culture. As noted previously, the complexities of such issues have led writers and analysts to characterize these struggles in simple sports terms. In American culture, sports metaphors and symbols have become a coin of the realm for leaders, writers, and citizens to describe the conflicts of everyday life. We are "underdogs" in "the fourth quarter." Elections are cast as "horse races." Successes are "home runs" or "knockouts." The list of appropriated terms is quite extensive. Second, though sports have not been completely open to all people, no other institution has provided as much access for minorities and women to achieve success or cultural acceptance. Some critics have charged that athletes are manipulated as pawns in the corporate culture of contemporary professional sports (Early, 1998). Historically, however, women and minorities have found the doors more open at the highest levels of competition in sports than in any other realm. Athletes such as Joe Louis, Jackie Robinson, Babe Didrickson, Muhammed Ali,

Greg Louganis, and Casey Martin have used their tremendous talents to challenge stereotypical perceptions of race, gender, sexual orientation, and disability. The very public nature of sports provides fans much information about these figures and their strengths and weaknesses. Whereas once athletes were perceived as gods, the proliferation of sports media has subjected athletes to the same scrutiny as politicians, royalty, and celebrities. In the mythology of traditional American culture, Horatio Alger may stand as archetypal story of success. In the complex and ethnically diverse world of contemporary American culture, it is sports that provide us with many of our most poignant narratives of success and failure.

The highly public nature of sports activities and reporting accents its mythic potential. Basketball great Bill Russell (1992) once observed that the four most public activities throughout history have been politics, religion, art, and sports. Trujillo (1991) noted that the media are drawn to sports because they preserve the masculine hegemony in American culture. In this way, the male-dominated media reflect their own "sports hero-worship" and preserve stereotypical narratives of male dominance. In recent years, the media have expanded their coverage to include stories of top female athletes such as Mia Hamm or Marion Jones. Still, the professional sports of football, baseball, and basketball are "men-only" games that create heroes, not heroines, and can reify the male-dominated mythologies of the past. This critical assessment of myth should remind us that Kenneth Burke (1941/1973) once wrote that literature was "equipment for living" (pp. 293–304). Burke's point was that a sufficient number of conditions recur in the human experience that readers should learn from the well-articulated stories of our ancestors. In the increasingly aliterate society of today, readers are being replaced by viewers who see the world through the lens of the media. The broadcasting of sports has become one of the primary "texts" of modern society. Games are simple with clear winners and losers. They are presented in a dramatic fashion with clashes of hometown heroes and marauding villains. The form of the contest is ephemeral, in that it lasts but a few hours, yet enduring, in that the game will be played by the same rules tomorrow. In the public consciousness of America, citizens have integrated the narratives of the "big three" sports—baseball, football, and basketball—into their unending story. The myth of professional football, however, stands alone as the most powerful and potent sports story in contemporary American culture.

Michael Novak (1985) writes that "Baseball, football, and basketball are more than highly organized, institutionalized rituals; they are public liturgies" (p. 35). Every weekend, millions of Americans travel to ballparks and arenas or sit in front of their televisions to observe these athletic contests. Brummett and Duncan (1990) add that broadcasts of games create a kind of "communal voyeurism" that engages the mediated fan with the crowd in attendance and the athletes in competition. The question then becomes: How do athletic contests and spectators watching these games become rituals and myths? Novak (1985) observes that in today's pluralistic society, the community formed through teamwork in sports, tested under stress and provocation, might be one of the most profound experiences in life. The narrative extension of this drama to the fans is a vicarious association that can be as powerful to those who observe it as to those who play the game. Christopher Lasch (1985) suggests that for some fans, sport becomes more than mere entertainment. Athletic contests in the modern era may no longer decide life and death issues, but, he contends, they have the capacity to dramatize and clarify the most significant issues in the lives of their fans. In other words, we may find it difficult to define winners and losers in our daily lives. How do you define a success in life? How much must a person earn? Whom must he or she defeat? The vagaries of life are less clear than the victories and losses on the playing field. Thus, those who identify with a team become part of a winning (or losing) community. Heroes on the sports fields teach us how to deal with victory and defeat. We might adapt Burke to suggest that "sports narratives" are modern equipment for living. I would contend that this is particularly true for football fans in America.

It has been suggested that baseball is the sport of America's past and basketball the sport of the world's future, but there can be little doubt that professional football holds a preeminent position in American contemporary sports culture. Each January, more than 100 million viewers watch the championship game of the NFL (McDonough et al., 1994). It could be argued reasonably that the Super Bowl has become an American holiday. To its credit, the NFL has successfully blended the themes of teamwork, controlled violence, individual achievement, and community rivalry into the most successful professional sports product in the history of the world. To understand how this "game" became part of American culture, I offer the story of one franchise: The Cleveland Browns.

THE CLEVELAND BROWNS' STORY

The stories of the NFL and the Cleveland Browns are born in and of the state of Ohio. In 1920, representatives of four teams met in Canton, Ohio, to form the All-American Football Conference, which became the NFL in 1922. The four teams represented were from Ohio cities: Akron, Canton, Dayton, and Cleveland (McDonough et al., 1994). To commemorate this event, the NFL chose Canton, Ohio, as the site for its Hall of Fame. It is fitting that the repository for the game's greatest stories and records would be in this small Ohio town.

In 1946, a Cleveland franchise joined a rival league, the second incarnation of the All-American Football Conference. However, the first mythic character of the Browns' story actually began his coaching career only a few miles from Canton in the town of Massillon, Ohio. Paul Brown became the coach of the Massillon High School Tigers in 1932. During the next nine years, he compiled a record of 81–7–2 and won 6 high school state championships (Pluto, 1997; www.massillonproud.com/football). This success warranted an opportunity to lead the Buckeyes of Ohio State University where, in only his second year, Brown directed his team to the national championship (Smith, 1999). So revered was Brown among Ohio sports fans that there was little doubt who should coach the expansion league professional team to be based in Cleveland in 1946. The Cleveland Rams had won the NFL championship in 1945, but fearing competition from the rival team led by Brown, they moved to Los Angeles the next year (Manoloff, 1995; Smith, 1999). The Rams' fears were completely founded. On September 6, 1946, a crowd of 60,135 saw the Cleveland Browns defeat the Miami Seahawks 44–0. This was the largest crowd ever to witness a professional football game at that time (Smith, 1999). The Cleveland Browns proved to be both a financial and competitive success, due in large part to the vision of their coach. In the seven home games of the 1946 season, the Browns averaged more than 57,000 fans per game (Smith, 1999). In the first four years of the All-American Football Conference, the Cleveland Browns won four consecutive league championships (Smith, 1999). It was evident to fans of professional football that Paul Brown and his Cleveland teams were winners.

By the time the Cleveland team was invited to join the NFL in December 1949 (along with the Baltimore Colts and the San Francisco 49ers), Paul Brown had become a mythic figure in Ohio sports lore. A contest was held by a local newspaper to name the new Cleveland NFL franchise. The fans selected the name "Browns" in honor of the famous coach (Pluto, 1997). Sports fans in Cleveland had suffered years of frustration with its American League baseball franchise, the Indians, primarily at the hands of the legendary New York Yankees. For the first time, the city of Cleveland was associated with winning. The final test for the new Cleveland Browns of the NFL was to challenge the great franchises of New York, Los Angeles, Chicago, and Philadelphia. In their first eight years in the NFL, the Cleveland Browns played in seven league championships and won three titles (Smith, 1999). Once again, the city of Cleveland identified itself as a city of champions.

The success of Paul Brown and his Cleveland football team is the first ingredient in the creation of a popular sports myth. In the pretelevision era, fans ritualistically traveled to cold, lakefront Municipal Stadium to be a part of the collective drama. Nearly 400,000 fans participated in the inaugural season of the Browns in the All-American Football League (Smith, 1999). A community of followers was cultivated by attending home games and reading the extensive coverage the successful team received in the local press. The NFL seized on this success and manufactured rivalries between franchises in nearby cities. Over time, Pittsburgh and Cincinnati became mortal enemies of the Cleveland team. Midwestern cities that were largely indistinguishable to casual viewers poured their identities into their respective sports franchises and claimed bragging rights over vanquished opponents. Comparisons to tribal conflicts between ancient enemies on the field of battle is a bit dramatic but metaphorically appropriate for these annual or semiannual rituals. To anyone who has observed thousands of fans dressed in team colors confronting their similarly clad brethren, comparisons to tribal battle might not seem so far fetched.

Other factors also became threads in the mythic tapestry of the Cleveland Browns' sports narrative. Cleveland is a diverse, multicultural urban community that accepted waves of immigrants as labor for heavy industry. In 1946, Paul Brown recruited two African American athletes to join his football team. Marion Motley and Bill Willis broke the color line in professional football by becoming the first African Americans to start a game since the 1930s. Eight months before Jackie Robinson played for the Brooklyn Dodgers, men of color starred as athletic heroes at Municipal Stadium in Cleveland, Ohio (Smith, 1999). Over the years, the Browns became a model for the kind of ethnic integration that blue-collar communities sought. Players such as Otto Graham, Dante Lavelli, Jim Brown, Lou Groza, Dick Modzelewski, and Paul Warfield taught a community that a player (or a coworker) should be judged by his or her abilities rather than the color of his skin, her religion, or his ethnic heritage.

Still, there was something to the Browns' story that ran deeper than identifying with a winner or challenging a sports rival. The Browns won their last NFL championship in 1964 by defeating the Baltimore Colts. From 1965 to 1996, the Browns seemed to reflect the city's economic and political struggles. Changes in the economy moved America away from a manufacturing base toward new technologies and a revolution in the information industry. The Midwest became known as "the Rustbelt," reflecting the number of closed steel mills, vacant metal processing plants, and heavy industries that abandoned Ohio, Michigan, and Pennsylvania in search of cheaper foreign labor. Cleveland, in particular, became the national symbol for cities in decline. During this period, industrial chemicals were dumped in the nearby Cuyahoga River, causing the river to catch fire. This paradoxical image of a "burning river" was satirized in a song by Randy Newman, and the city of Cleveland quickly became the butt of the nation's jokes (www.randynewman.com/sail_away.html). Similarly, the Cleveland Browns were struggling for respectability but becoming a symbol of frustration. In the 1980s, the Browns lost two championship games to the Denver Broncos. In the first, Denver quarterback John Elway drove his team 98 yards in the final few minutes to win the game. In the second, Browns' running back Ernest Byner fumbled on the two-yard line and failed to score the winning touchdown. "The Drive" and "The Fumble" are now part of a Browns' narrative that not only represents a team's shortcomings, but also reflects the larger frustrations of a city struggling to recover (Smith, 1999). In their 50-year history, the Cleveland Browns came to symbolize the successes and failures of their patron city and their fans. The hopes for urban renewal that escaped the city council and mayor were born again every fall in the hearts of Browns' fans in the promise of *their* team. The promise died on November 6, 1995, when owner Art Modell announced that he was moving *his* team to the city of Baltimore.

A RHETORICAL REBELLION

The issue of moving a sports franchise can be examined from several perspectives. It is an economic concern because entertainment revenues and thousands of jobs are lost. There also are the legal constraints of contracts with stadiums, vendors, licensing agents, and media outlets. We might also consider the intangible elements of corporate citizenship and community responsibility. All of these issues are viable points of inquiry. Of course, Cleveland was not the first sports franchise to move in search of financial gains. From the Brooklyn (Los Angeles) Dodgers to the Houston Oilers/Tennessee Titans, team owners have sought greater fan support, better market demographics, and more luxurious stadium accommodations. The bottom line in professional sports is dollars, and all of these considerations mean added profits.

In the case of Art Modell, the Cleveland Browns, and the city of Cleveland, one thing is clear: The financial history of the organization and its negotiations with civic leaders was very complicated. Art Modell purchased the Cleveland Browns in 1961 for the then-unheard of price of $4 million (Pluto, 1997). Thirty-five years later, the franchise was valued at nearly $200 million, yet the owner was deeply in debt and at the end of his credit. In *Fumble!* (Poplar and Toman, 1997), the Browns' financial advisor Michael G. Poplar documents Modell's attempts to run a successful and profitable sports franchise. The costs of an aging stadium, revenues lost to other Cleveland sports franchises, poor investments, and players' salaries in the era of free agency cost Art Modell millions (Poplar and Toman, 1997). The threat of inheritance taxes and the promise of a tremendous financial package from the state of Maryland left the Browns' owner with what he declared to be "no choice"(Poplar and Toman, 1997). The city of Cleveland had committed millions of dollars to revitalization projects that included the construction of the Rock and Roll Hall of Fame and new stadiums for the Cleveland Indians and Cleveland Cavaliers. A referendum was on the November 7 ballot to raise taxes to renovate the Browns' Municipal Stadium, but it was declared "too little, too late" by the frustrated owner (Poplar and Toman, 1997). The $200 million package put forth by the state of Maryland was worth the gamble for the financially strapped Modell. It is unlikely, however, that even in his worst-case scenarios could he have imagined the response that would follow.

Art Modell sat on the stage for the November 6 press conference and added a rhetorical dimension to the mix. Stories had appeared in the Cleveland sports press for days about the possibility of losing its NFL franchise to another city. The irony in this sports drama was that the city of Baltimore had lost its NFL franchise 12 years earlier to another civic raider, the city of Indianapolis. Baltimore Colts owner, Robert Irsay, loaded his team equipment into Mayflower moving vans in middle of the night and absconded with the legends of Johnny Unitas, Lenny Moore, and John Mackey. On this day, the Governor of Maryland, Parris N. Glendening, Baltimore Mayor Kurt L. Schmoke, and Modell intermingled the narratives of these once-proud NFL rivals, the Browns and Colts, and created a goulash of sports history. Modell was introduced as the owner of the "Baltimore Browns," and the traditions of Graham and Brown were mixed with Unitas and Moore to the disdain of true Browns' and Colts' fans everywhere (Poplar and Toman, 1997). *Baltimore Sun* writer Ken Rosenthal observed that "Modell is going to stand up at today's news conference and talk of reviving the Colts' tradition. He's destroying an even grander tradition but never mind" ("Columnists around," 1995, p. D-15). John Eisenberg, also of the *Baltimore Sun,* echoed those sentiments, writing, "Congratulations if you made it through yesterday's announcement ceremony without becoming nauseated. . . . And it was official: There is no decency left in the world" ("Columnists around," 1995, p. D-15).

Sportswriters around the country quickly weighed in on the move. Bob Ryan of the *Boston Globe* wrote that "[t]he Cleveland Browns have as much moral right to leave Cleveland and head to Baltimore as the British Parliament does to relocate in Berlin. . . . Morality, responsibility, fairness, decency and most of all, loyalty now mean nothing—Nothing!—in professional sports" ("Columnists around," 1995, p. D-15). Charlie Vincent of the *Detroit Free Press* added, "In Baltimore they learned twelve years ago when the Irsay family—owners of the Colts—backed up a fleet of trucks in the middle of the night, loaded up the franchise and moved it to Indianapolis. . . . Now, it seems the people of Baltimore have forgotten that hurt and outrage and sense of abandonment, because on Monday they welcomed the Browns" ("Columnists around," 1995, p. D-15). Ann Killion of the *San Jose Mercury News* added, "What lasts is tradition. The only redeeming value sports has in our culture is that it brings communities together, it gives us shared experience, a community passion, a family tree" ("Columnists around," 1995, p. D-15). To extend the family metaphor, Michael Ventre of the *Los Angeles Daily News* declared, "After bringing sorrow and misery to Ohio, he [Modell] will now go down in the annals of professional football as the worst kind of money-grubbing opportunist. . . . He is a father who deserted his family for money" ("Columnists around," 1995, p. D-15).

Normally, the story would end there. Fans would lament the loss of the team, and a few editorials would blast the team owners and promise a brighter future for the scorned city. However, it seems that the audience for messages about the Cleveland Browns was somewhat unique. First, there was the base of 10,000 fans that occupied the "Dawg Pound" in Municipal Stadium. These rabid supporters have been known to drink heavily, disdain clothing in frigid weather, paint their skin in team colors, wear rubber dog masks, and carry dog biscuits to games. Second, these fans were usually accompanied at the game by 60,000 other Browns' fans. Even in the worst seasons, attendance at Browns' games was consistently among the highest in the NFL (Munson, 1995). Third, the Browns developed a unique mythic community in their 50-year history in Cleveland. The advent of global media enabled sports fans around the world to follow favorite teams. Rushin (1995) noted that the official team fan club, the Browns Backers, claims the largest fan base of any professional sports team with over 200 chapters and 63,000 members worldwide. Sportswriter Martin Fennelly of the *Tampa Tribune* noted, "My brother is a Browns fan and he has never been to Ohio. It starts with the helmets, he once told me. The helmets are plain, the way football should be" ("Columnists around," 1995, p. D-15). The Browns rejected a team logo on their helmets because former coach Paul Brown thought it unseemly. For 50 years, the Browns played simple football near the birthplace of the professional game. Fans around the world rewarded this team with their loyalty, a loyalty that Art Modell did not return. Fourth, city leaders, particularly Mayor Michael White, felt betrayed by the actions of Modell. Negotiations had been ongoing between the team owner and the mayor up until the announcement of the team's planned departure. Thus the mayor, the Dawg Pound, tens of thousands of loyal fans, and a global community of backers rejected Modell's message and planned to fight for *their* team.

The first reaction from fans was raw and emotional. Radio call-in shows and local media provided an outlet for Browns' followers to vent their anger and frustration. One fan declared, "Art Modell has murdered my memories. He's murdered a friend" (Rushin, 1995). Others expressed their frustration at the loss of a community, a link to past and future generations. Thirteen-year-old Jenny Sheeler said that she watched games with her parents and sister and felt a sense of loss that she would not share that experience with her children (Rushin, 1995). The Cleveland *Plain Dealer* contacted the president of the Browns Backers in Southern California to hear his reaction. Jeff Wagner said that the response of the 2,000-member organization was virtually unanimous: "This is like your wife having an affair behind your back," he said (Alexander, 1995, p. D-6). Unfortunately, there was also a destructive impulse that accompanied these emotions. An evening security guard at the Browns' stadium reported receiving calls that spoke of depression and suicide, as well as acts of violence (Poplar and Toman, 1997). Threats against Modell's life were taken seriously, and the team owner chose not to attend the Browns' final home game against the Cincinnati Bengals (Morgan, 1997). Current and former players joined in the verbal fray. Former wide receiver Reggie Rucker said, "It's like my whole history is gone. . . . The last time I felt this bad was when I got divorced" (Robbins, 1995, p. D-6). Hall of Fame quarterback Otto Graham could only add, "It is like a death in the family" (Robbins, 1995, p. D-6).

Cleveland Mayor White sought to direct this emotion and immediately began a two-pronged campaign against Modell. First, city attorneys were directed to pursue litigation against the Browns' owner for breaking his lease at Municipal Stadium. The Browns had three years remaining on their contract with the city of Cleveland, and the mayor intended to collect on that debt (Poplar and Toman, 1997). Second, NFL bylaws required that a majority of team owners approve any franchise movement. In previous cases, such as the controversial movements of the Oakland Raiders, some minor dissent had been voiced. Still, NFL owners are first and foremost businesspeople in search of maximum profit for themselves and the collective league. No such previous action had ever been vetoed, and it was doubtful that this trend would change. Nonetheless, White adopted a "No Team, No Peace" public relations campaign directed at league officials and team owners (Green, 1997). Addresses, telephone numbers, e-mail addresses, and fax machine numbers for team and league offices were published and posted on Web sites. A full-page ad was published in the Cleveland *Plain Dealer* on January 14, imploring readers to "Make the Most Important Call in Browns' History" and tell "Mr. Tagliabue: The Browns belong in Cleveland. Fifty years of loyal support can't be ignored" ("Tomorrow," 1996, p. A-15). The NFL offices were inundated with pleas to vote against the move to Baltimore. This fan-based campaign, coupled with the dearth of negative media, led NFL Commissioner Paul Tagliabue to seek some sort of compromise with city officials.

On February 8, an agreement was stuck. Art Modell would be allowed to move his NFL franchise to Baltimore, but the name and colors of the Cleveland Browns would remain for a future NFL franchise to be located in the city of Cleveland (Koff, Heider, & Grossi, 1996). The league agreed that a franchise would be returned to the city by either relocation of an existing team or a new franchise to be granted in 1999. In exchange for this three-year hiatus from professional football, the NFL offered to contribute $48 million toward the construction of a new football stadium in Cleveland. The city agreed and also settled the lawsuit against Modell for the remainder of the payments due according to the lease (Koff, et al., 1996). Modell demonstrated that it was *his* NFL franchise at great cost to his personal and professional reputation. The city of Cleveland and Browns' fans around the world proved that it was *their* team by reminding the NFL what 50 years of loyalty sounded like.

EPILOGUE

Art Modell's Baltimore Ravens won the Super Bowl in January 2001. Some might say that the owner finally achieved his dream by winning another championship. Others have argued that half a life was lost by turning against a community that supported him for 35 years (Rushin, 1995). It is interesting to note that while Modell and his associates were moving their equipment and personnel to Baltimore, the Hall of Fame agreed to act as a temporary repository for the Browns' records and memorabilia. It was almost as if a ritual of rebirth was being performed for the Cleveland Browns by the sanctuary of professional football.

The rhetorical campaign by the city of Cleveland and the fans of the Cleveland Browns represents a unique moment in the history of modern professional sports. Beloved teams such as the Brooklyn Dodgers and the Baltimore Colts relocated and left fans equally distraught and forlorn in the past. Furthermore, there should be no disillusion that demographics and corporate influences will not lead franchise owners to move their teams in the future. The purpose of this study is to demonstrate that a sports team, be it professional or amateur, can become something more than a corporate commodity. In this era of downsizing, rightsizing, and supersizing, a sports team can become a repository for a community's hopes, dreams, and frustrations. The stories of winning and losing, of challenge, and of upsets can weave a mythic web through a people and create a community of believers known as fans. Legendary teams such as the Boston Celtics, the Notre Dame Fighting Irish, the Green Bay Packers, and the Cleveland Browns have provided generations of followers with stories that unite them in a common bond. Fathers and daughters, mothers and sons have shared moments and memories that link them with other Browns' fans all over the world. Sports narratives create a mythic community that can defy space and time and teach us the lessons of competition. Americans cheered as one when their little-known hockey team defeated the mighty Soviet Union team in 1980. We also become a little misty eyed when we see athletes compete so valiantly at the Special Olympics.

The story of the Cleveland Browns fans' confrontation with Art Modell and the NFL demonstrates that sports can be about more than dollars and cents. Ultimately, the NFL capitulated because it would be bad for business to suffer such a public relations disaster and alienate loyal fans around the world. But the *campaign* to save the Browns reminds us of the stories that bring us together—fathers taking their sons to their first games, the anguish fans felt when Elway scored, or the power of a run by Jim Brown. Professional sports will grow more lucrative and aloof in the future as broadcasting contracts soar and players' salaries increase accordingly. Let us remember, however, the heroic stories of our youth and the modern sports dramas that bring us together as a community of fans. In the future, the rhetorical battle for the Browns may be a shining moment for anyone who has ever identified with an athlete or an amateur or professional sports team. The corporate control of sports will continue to increase as fans endure the threats of private seat licenses, tennis shoe sponsorship of athletes, and sports management in the era of free agency. The battle for the Cleveland Browns was a narrative battle for possession of our collective mythology, for *our* team and *our* stories. The rhetorical battle for the Browns also was a victory for any child who has ever hung a poster of a sports hero over her bed. The NFL can franchise teams and license sports merchandise, but it can neither create a storied home team nor destroy the memories indelibly etched in the minds of its true fans.

REFERENCE LIST

Alexander, E. (1995, November 7). Backers feeling betrayed. *The Plain Dealer*, p. D-6.

Ashe, A. R., Jr. (1988). *A hard road to glory: A history of the African-American athlete.* New York: Warner Brothers.

Bellah, R. N. (1964). Religious evolution. *American Sociological Review, 29,* 358–374.

Browns bolt. (1995, November 7). *The Plain Dealer*, p. A-1.

Brummett, B., & Duncan, M. C. (1990). Theorizing without totalizing: Specularity and televised sports. *Quarterly Journal of Speech, 76,* 227–246.

Burke, K. (1941/1973). *The philosophy of literary form: Studies in symbolic action.* Berkley: University of California Press.

Burke, K. (1966). *Language as symbolic action.* Berkeley: University of California Press.

Cassirer, E. (1944). *An essay on man.* New Haven, CT: Yale University Press.

Columnists around nation react to Browns move. (1995, November 12). *The Plain Dealer*, p. D-15.

Early, G. (1998, August 10/17). Performance and reality: Race, sports and the modern world. *The Nation, 267,* 11–20.

Gorn, E. J., & Oriard, M. (1995, March 24). Taking sports seriously. *The Chronicle of Higher Education*, p. A-52.

Koff, S., Heider, T., & Grossi, T. (1996, February 9). City, NFL strike a deal. *The Plain Dealer*, pp. A-1, A-18.

Lasch, L. (1985). The corruption of sports. In W. L. Umphlette (Ed.), *American sports culture: The humanistic dimensions* (pp. 50–67). Cransbury, NJ: Associated University Presses, Inc.

Manoloff, D. (1995, November 7). Rams left town in fear of Browns. *The Plain Dealer*, p. D-6.

McDonough, W., King, P., Zimmerman, P., Carucci, V., Garber, G., Lamb, K., et al. (1994). *75 seasons: The complete story of the National Football League.* Atlanta: Turner Publishing, Inc.

Modell trashed a loyal history. (1995, November 12). *The (Wooster) Daily Record,* p. E-2.

Morgan, J. (1997). *Glory for sale.* Baltimore, MD: Bancroft Press.

Munson, L. (1995, December 4). A busted play. *Sports Illustrated, 83,* 62–63.

Myth. (1971/1991). *The Compact Oxford English Dictionary.* (2d ed.). New York: Oxford University Press.

Novak, M. (1985). American sports, American values. In W. L. Umphlette (Ed.), *American sports culture: The humanistic dimensions* (pp. 34–39). Cransbury, NJ: Associated University Presses, Inc.

O'Rourke, Daniel J. III (1992). In his image: A rhetorical analysis of the mythic androcentricism of the Roman Catholic Church. Unpublished doctoral dissertation, Purdue University, West Lafayette, IN.

Pluto, T. (1997). *When all the world was Browns' town.* New York: Simon & Shuster.

Poplar, M G., & Toman, J. A. (1997). *Fumble! The Browns, Modell and the move: An insider's story.* Cleveland: Cleveland Landmark's Press.

Robbins, L. (1995, November 7). Former Browns stunned by move. *The Plain Dealer,* p. D-6.

Rushin, S. (1995, December 4). The heart of a city. *Sports Illustrated, 83,* 58–70.

Russell, B. (1992). Sports. In G. Plimpton (Ed.), *The Norton book of sports* (pp. 409–415). New York: W. W. Norton & Company, Inc.

Smith, R. (1999). *Cleveland Browns: The official illustrated history.* St. Louis, MO: The Sporting News.

Tomorrow, make the most important call in Browns' history. (1996, January 14). *The Plain Dealer,* p. A-15.

Trujillo, N. (1991). Hegemonic masculinity on the mound: Media representations of Nolan Ryan and the American sports culture. *Critical Studies in Mass Communication, 8,* 290–308.

Why Sports? (1998, August 10/17). *The Nation, 267,* 3.

Williamson, G. (1995, November 7). Dewine, Hoke to seek congressional action. *The Plain Dealer,* p. A-5.

www.massillonproud.com/football.

www.randynewman.com/sail_away.html.

CHAPTER 5

Sport, (Dis)Ability, and Public Controversy: Ableist Rhetoric and *Casey Martin v. PGA Tour, Inc.*

James L. Cherney

Communication about sport occasionally involves controversy about its meaning, significance, and cultural value. At such moments, sport's rhetorical and communicative dimensions become particularly salient. Like any major institution, sport speaks to us (Douglas, 1986). Its rules, traditions, and arguments tell us much about its perspective, orientation, and beliefs. At such moments, we should not lose the opportunity to listen.

Sport and disability historically have shared a complicated relationship. On one level the relationship is causal, as professional contact sports often disable players. American football, in particular, appears particularly productive. A recent cover story in *Sports Illustrated* notes that two out of every three former players' football injuries limited their recreational ability in retirement, and more than half also had a "curtailed ability to do physical labor" (Nack, 2001). Robert McRuer (2000) observes that this causal relationship should mark sporting events as intimately related to disability, but the relationship is typically repressed and sublimated:

[b]ecause of the ever-present threat of catastrophic injury, [sport is] a site where the absolute contingency of able-bodied identity is made manifest. Disability always circulates threateningly around the performance at sporting events, even thought it is ultimately *always* subordinated to able-bodiedness: games stop momentarily when there is an injury, but the narrative perspective doesn't shift to one identified with disability.

On another level, sport appears to encourage ableist thinking. Ableism, or discrimination against people with disabilities, includes any systematic preference for able-bodied persons as superior beings. In this context, sports can be read as "showcase[s] for able-bodied performances" where athletes compete and win based on their physical skills, stamina, and strength (McRuer, 2000). Throughout the history of Western civilization, sport has promoted ableist thinking by its focus on the body and physical performance in artificial challenges. The wealth and status commanded by professional athletes, and the extremely small minority of people with disabilities that belong to this group, stand as strong evidence of the ableist nature of professional sport. Sport's historical treatment of people with disabilities provides further evidence for this claim. Strands of ableist thinking appear in the controversies surrounding disabled players, as in the debate over Casey Martin's use of a golf cart on the Professional Golf Association (PGA) Tour.[1] On its face, professional sport appears to be a prime example of institutional machinery actively perpetuating ableism.

In particular, sport institutionalizes the ableist practice of locating ability in the body. It assumes an ideal of the stable and controllable body as the foundation of ability and as the essential characteristic from which ability derives. Like the notion of biology as destiny, this norm masks the way "ability" is a function of social institutions that create cultural expectations and rules of behavior that define a particular physical skill as an ability. Simply put, the social structures that make one person's bodily capacity "abled" and another's "disabled" construct ability far more than any body. Yet locating ability in the body disguises the action of this cultural machinery, especially when the institution in question is the well-established and historically popular world of sport.

However, sport defies such simple condemnation. The popularity of modified sports among people with disabilities, who sponsor activities ranging from Deaf basketball leagues to the Special Olympics, suggests sport's redeeming qualities can be rediscovered in a less ableist context.[2] Disability and sport also connect through those arenas in which people with disabilities are integrated to compete with able-bodied athletes. Although segregated sports continue to be a source of controversy (Allen, 1999; Goggin & Newell, 2000; Reilly, 2000; Shapiro, 1993), many read examples of successful integration as important evidence of the American spirit of equality and values of persistence and courage (Chimelis, 2000; Golen, 1999).

Furthermore, sport creates a unique calculus for interpreting the body. Whereas ableist institutions such as the medical establishment tend to regard any deviation from the norm with suspicion, sport rewards deviation, at least when that deviance favors performance according to its rules.[3] Sport does not rely on the simple condemnation of deviance, but rather privileges those whose bodies are different enough to give them an advantage in a specified activity. All of this suggests the need to further examine sport as an important cultural institution intimately involved with ableist thinking in our culture.

Sport as a concept generally speaks with an ableist bias, and the material values and monetary stakes of professional sport has made its ableism particularly significant and controversial. Indeed, disputes over excluding people with disabilities from sport would be much less emphatic were there few or no material consequences involved. In a professional context, sport's crafting of ability takes on additional significance. Sport defines particular physical skills as ability by defining arenas in which those skills give players access to substantial rewards. A person whose body exhibits particular skills—whether general skills, such as strength, exceptional reaction time, or hand-eye coordination, or particular skills, such as throwing a curveball or serving a tennis ball at 120 miles per hour—is made "able" by the rules of the games that reward those skills. Furthermore, sport constantly directs attention to these "abilities" as arising from the body. Throughout professional sport, in its traditions, rules, and modes of display, attention is placed on the body of the athlete as the source of ability rather than on the rules and traditions without which the relevant "abilities" would be largely irrelevant. Were professional sport recognized as a purely artificial institution that elevates skills of questionable value for no other reason than to provide certain skill-exhibiting bodies with incredible wealth, its appeal and significance would likely diminish substantially.

To investigate these implications, this chapter performs a case study of the controversy surrounding golfer Casey Martin. Martin's federal case to apply the Americans with Disabilities Act (ADA) to the PGA Tour, to allow him to ride a golf cart during professional tournaments, ranks among the most significant controversies over the ADA to date. The popular public debate over Martin's suit generated more published lay commentary in the space of two weeks than appeared in three years of debate over the ADA itself.[4] But Martin's case became much more than the latest battle over the rights of people with disabilities, in that developing arguments over whether he should ride and whether walking is essential to the sport of golf posed a series of questions that have been resolved only tenuously by the Supreme Court's decision in the case (*PGA Tour, Inc. v. Martin*, 2001). To what extent should society protect ableist institutions as a means of crafting social pressure to develop physical performance? What role can, or should, technology play in sports, and do extensions of that role undermine the value of sport as a contest of the limits of the human condition? If we permit Martin the use of a cart on a golf course, on what grounds do we deny recognition to the wheelchair runners of the Boston Marathon as the "true" winners of the race (in that they consistently complete the course at times faster than the runners in the men's and women's divisions)?

To contextualize the relationship between such questions and the Casey Martin controversy, the next subsections briefly detail two related issues from a broader perspective. First, I examine the ways sport provides some measure of social control by creating a space for some deviant persons, and second, I discuss some of the ways that sport and technology intersect.

SPORTS AND "SPORTS": DISABILITY AS A GIFT

Sport rewards certain freakish bodies. It turns a person who has a skill with a relatively low social utility—say, hitting a small white ball a long distance with a piece of wood—into a hero. A batter's differences from "normal people" who cannot hit the ball as well make him or her superior according to the rules of the game. Put another way, sport rewards both "freaks" and those who pursue training regimens that develop their bodies in specialized ways. From the perspective of its socializing impact on bodies, a primary social function of the institution of sport is to assimilate, reward, and promote what might be otherwise threatening freakish bodies.

Sport long has been associated with social control and with the controlled outlet for aggression. Among sport's well-known social effects is the provision of dramas for spectators to consume and vicariously participate in; it thus controls crowds and provides an outlet for pressures that might otherwise be brought to bear against the state. But sport also controls the large and powerful offspring of future generations, especially those "sports" who differ substantially from the general population.[5] As strong and potentially threatening offspring, these freaks are often co-opted as children into an institution that teaches them rules, to respect officials and authority, and "sportsmanship" and gives them a controlled outlet for their aggressive tendencies.

From this perspective of sport's cultural function as a freak assimilator, the rejection of certain freaks becomes quite disturbing. In this context, the popular myth that sport promotes excellence in bodies operates as a façade that protects and hides, among other things, sport's more important function of segregating and controlling freakish "sports." To maintain this myth, the group more conventionally labeled freak—people with disabilities—must be driven from the field of play. Were sports recognized as a type of strictly regulated freak show, the negative associations of that activity would likely reduce its appeal to those "sports" currently pacified through it. Given the negative associations of disability in our ableist culture, sport would likely collapse if athletes were widely viewed as disabled. Yet sport clearly rewards bodies that deviate from the norm by elevating some of them to wealth, fame, and fortune.

Furthermore, sport encourages a focus on particular body parts as gifts, particularly those talented arms and legs that provide an individual with

noteworthy skills. Although athletes probably recognize this myth as fallacious on some level, for they condition their whole bodies and engage
in cross-training activities, the celebration of a particular piece of the body
pervades the narrative of sport. As catcher "Crash" Davis comments to
pitcher "Nuke" LaLoosh in *Bull Durham* (Burg, Mount, & Shelton, 2000),

You've got a gift. . . . You've got a gift. When you were a baby the gods reached
down and turned your right arm into a thunderbolt. You've got a Hall-of-Fame
arm, but you're pissing it away.

Sportscasters often describe sports figures by a similar metonymy: football
kickers "have enough leg" when they make a field goal, and baseball
outfielders "have the arm" when they throw to the infield to make an out.
Communicating through this metonymy reinforces the idea that it is the
body that makes ability rather than the structure and rules of the game
that allow a particular "skill" to be recognized as "ability." This same
metonymic move becomes crucial in the Casey Martin debate, for he has
all the elements of a professional golfer except for a "failing" in one leg.

Sport and Technology

As expected at the intersection of any two major institutions, sport and
technology exhibit a complicated relationship. Sport often relies on and
utilizes various technologies while forbidding the use of others. Professional baseball players use the basic tool known as the bat, but the technology incorporated into the bat is closely regulated. Metal bats and bats
spiked with illegal substances (such as cork or rubber balls) are illegal.
Bats also must fit within allowed parameters of size, weight, and balance
(Major League Baseball, 2000). Even this specific example identifies a basic
pattern in the relationship of sport and technology: The game requires
using the tool, but rules dictate strict standards for the tool to ensure that
that the tool does not interfere with the game. Generally speaking, sport
traditions dictate that no player should be given any advantage over any
other because of the technology incorporated into their particular tools.

In sport, the game is a contest of human bodies struggling on the proverbial "level playing field" to achieve victory because of some characteristic of those bodies themselves. In the myths that surround it, sport
rewards the bodies that exhibit talent, skill, training, mental toughness,
will power, and dedication. Players are supposed to have equal access to
any technology that enhances performance, and technologies that "artificially" enhance performance by acting directly on the body, such as steroids and other drugs, are closely scrutinized and generally prohibited.
In short, sport locates technology, gives it its place, and tries to make it
stay there.

Thus, the sport/technology relationship combines elements of dependency and antagonism. Without any technological developments, sport would be reduced to the most basic competitions of physical bodily exertions, such as wrestling or running. All modern professional sports, from football to golf, depend heavily on technological aids and prostheses that shape the nature of the game itself. In general, these aids are simple tools: basic extensions of the arm (bats, racquets, golf clubs, hockey sticks) and basic missiles (balls, shuttlecocks, pucks). Technology also shapes the arenas in which these sports are played, for which rules strictly limit the type of playing surfaces (grass, artificial turf, ice) and the boundaries of the game (end zones, goals, baskets, golf holes) while creating conditions without which the sport cannot be played. Ostensibly for safety reasons, sport also allows a variety of protective equipment, including helmets, gloves, specialized shoes (including skates), padding, and other clothing. In specific sports, this protection has evolved into essential tools for the game. The baseball glove, as an extension of the arm, enhances a player's ability to catch a ball, and the football helmet, as reinforced protection for the skull, enhances a player's ability to tackle.[6] Yet, even when technology plays a central role in a sport, it is closely regulated so that it does not give any player or team an "unfair advantage" over others.[7] This basic assumption about the proper role of technology in sport underlies one of the major arguments in the Casey Martin controversy: whether allowing him to use a cart would create an unfair advantage.

CASEY MARTIN V. PGA TOUR, INC.

From 1998 to 2001, we witnessed the most public controversy over the ADA since it was signed into law in 1990. In a very short period, the controversy generated more newspaper articles, letters to the editor, and talk show airtime than during the congressional debates over the ADA itself.[8] Yet this public debate centered on nothing more earth-shattering than the question of whether a professional golfer should be allowed to use a golf cart. When Casey Martin sued the PGA Tour for the right to use a cart during competitions as a reasonable accommodation for his disability, he never expected to become a celebrity who, as sportswriter Tim Rosaforte (1998) put it, "had more media attention than Bill Clinton and Paula Jones" (p. 10). Whereas the size of the controversy alone makes it worthy of analysis, the passions it enflamed make it even more important that we understand this public debate. Supporters of both the PGA Tour and Casey Martin were so completely divided on the question of his suit that they often resorted to wisecracks, slurs, and ad hominem attacks instead of substantial arguments. Such behavior is not surprising in any controversy involving radically opposed ideological factions, such as in the debates over abortion, the constitutionality of flag burning, or teaching creationism in schools. But why was *this* such a controversy? Why was this case so important, so emotionally charged, for so many people?

My examination of *Casey Martin v. PGA Tour, Inc.* and the public debate surrounding the case focuses on understanding the ideological structures, orientations, and worldviews represented by the two sides. I contend that the dispute achieved its scope and intensity because the two primary sides simply could not communicate with each other in a constructive manner. Both understandings of the stakes involved operated from such diametrically opposed premises about sport and its social functions that very little ground was shared in this debate. As such, the controversy teaches us about both the dynamics of contemporary controversies and the meaning of sport in our culture. Central to this debate is the relationship of sport and disability, the social status of ability generally, and the growing notion that we live in an ableist culture. In my reading of the controversy, the unstated, yet central, question in the debate is whether and to what extent professional sport is an ableist institution.

The Debate over Martin

Casey Martin is a golfer with a rare circulatory condition known as Klippel-Trenaunay-Weber Syndrome that has limited the physical development of his right leg. When placed under stress, blood pools in and below his knee (*Casey Martin v. PGA Tour, Inc.*, January 30, 1998). His leg is highly susceptible to fracture, a risk compounded because his leg will be amputated when it breaks ("Casey Martin–PGA Tour," 1998; Kelley, 1998; Midgen, 1998; D. Robertson, 1998). After being allowed to use a cart in the first two rounds of qualifying for the Nike Tour, a lower echelon and stepping stone to the PGA Tour, Martin was informed by Tour officials that he would not be able to use a cart during later qualifying rounds or competition on the Nike Tour (*Casey Martin v. PGA Tour, Inc.*, January 30, 1998). The PGA rules prohibit players from using carts during competition in all but the most limited of circumstances.[9]

Martin filed for an injunction with the Federal District Court in Eugene, Oregon, and won a temporary order allowing him to use a cart in the later two qualifying rounds and in two tournaments on the Nike Tour. He won the first of these competitions, the Lakeland Classic in Florida. Martin then sued for a permanent injunction under the ADA in late January 1998 ("Casey Martin timeline," 2001). The case made national headlines and sparked a heated debate. On February 19, 1998, United States Magistrate Judge Thomas M. Coffin ruled in Martin's favor (*Casey Martin v. PGA Tour, Inc.*, February 19, 1998). The PGA Tour subsequently appealed to the 9th Federal Circuit Court, which on March 6, 2000, upheld the lower court's decision (*Casey Martin v. PGA Tour, Inc.*, 2000). On September 26, 2000, the United States Supreme Court granted certiorari and then heard arguments on the case on January 17, 2001. In a rather surprising decision announced on May 31, 2001, the Supreme Court upheld Coffin's verdict by a vote of 7–2 (*PGA Tour v. Casey Martin*, 2001).

Because public argument arose out of the PGA Tour's defense against Martin's initial suit, their basic positions shaped most of the issues. The Tour defended its autonomy, arguing that the sport (and its organization) was not subject to the ADA (Joe Gordon, 1998; Kelley, 1998; Slezak, 1998), as well as its traditions, which it associated with the historical importance of golf as a beneficial social institution ("Casey Martin–PGA Tour," 1998; Sandomir, 1998), and its sense of fairness, claiming that to allow Martin to use a cart would violate the ethics of the sport by giving him an unfair advantage (Blauvelt, 1998a; Faculak, 1998; Hirsley, 1998a; B. Robertson, 1998). Supporters of the Tour additionally argued that attempting to accommodate Martin would create a "slippery slope" and "open a Pandora's box" by which golf and other sports would be constantly subjected to scrutiny in courts by people who felt their abilities would not allow them to compete without accommodation ("Another Golfer," 2001; Campos, 2001; Faculak, 1998; Fraley, 1998; Joe Gordon, 1998; Hart, 2001; "Killing Standards," 2001; "Martin's win," 2001; Seigle, 2001; Sirak, 1998).

Martin's supporters responded to each of these claims in turn. They described the Tour's claim to autonomy as the elitist actions of a power-hungry group unwilling to give up its discriminatory practices (Blauvelt, 1998b; Coulson, 1998; Kelley, 1998; Keown, 1998; Posnanski, 1998). Repeatedly decrying the previous history of the PGA Tour, which had resisted efforts to allow nonwhite golfers to compete and held tournaments at golf clubs where players of color were not allowed on the course, these supporters portrayed the claim of autonomy as a bald-faced attempt to insulate bigoted views from public scrutiny (Agnos, 1998; Ormsby, 1998; D. Robertson, 1998; Slezak, 1998).

The Tour's defense of its traditions also was met with a challenge from Martin supporters. Golf's most enduring tradition, they claimed, was to discriminate against those who were not white. Describing Martin as a Rosa Parks (like Parks, Casey just wants to ride) and a symbol of equality generally, Martin supporters loudly hailed his suit as a necessary blow against a recalcitrant establishment and an important symbol of access for people with disabilities (Agnos, 1998; Harber, 1998; Midgen, 1998; D. Robertson, 1998; Slezak, 1998; Wolfe, 1998). Except when the issue of tradition became implicated in the question of whether a cart would give Martin an unfair advantage ("Casey Martin–PGA Tour," 1998; Chambers, 1998a; Joe Gordon, 1998; Kelley, 1998; Sandomir, 1998; Slezak, 1998), this issue disappeared shortly after it arose.

The most dramatic aspect of the controversy was whether giving Martin use of a cart would give him an unfair advantage over other golfers (Blauvelt, 1998a, 1998b; Chambers, 1998b; Hirsley, 1998a, 1998b). The Tour enjoyed a significant amount of support in this case from an unlikely (and somewhat paradoxical) source: Martin's win in only his second Nike Tour tournament ("Casey Martin timeline," 2001). Because Martin's supporters had to admit that Martin would not have been likely to win if he had not used a cart (indeed, that position supported his entire case for accommodation), the Tour was able to exploit his very success to suggest that he had been not only accommodated, but "given a leg up" over the other players.

The foundation of this "unfair advantage" argument was the contention that walking was fundamentally a part of golf competitions because it created fatigue that affected play (Blauvelt, 1998a; B. Robertson, 1998). The Tour argued that walking was the "X factor" that could never be eliminated without removing an essential part of the game (Faculuk, 1998). Martin's supporters launched a number of responses to this position, ridiculing the Tour's claim that golf was a strenuous activity and even going so far as to question the idea of golf as a sport (Erickson, 1998; Posnanski, 1998; B. Robertson, 1998; Sandomir, 1998). Golf, they argued, was about hitting a ball, as evidenced by the number of amateur players who used carts and the use of carts on the PGA Senior Tour (Causey, 1998; Coulson, 1998; Jariabek, 1998; Kelley, 1998; Midgen, 1998; D. Robertson, 1998; Slezak, 1998). The Tour responded with what might be called its most significant mistake in the controversy: it declared that the Senior Tour was a "nostalgia event" and not serious athletic competition (Babineau, 1998; Elliot, 1998; Jeff Gordon, 1998; Kelley, 1998).

The "nostalgia event" argument initiated several responses from within the Tour's ranks of professional golfers. Both regular Tour players and Senior Tour players loudly criticized the characterization and cited numerous examples of intense athletic competition at Senior Tour events (Babineau, 1998; Elliot, 1998; Jeff Gordon, 1998; Kelley, 1998; Mizell, 1998; Slezak, 1998). Even many of those who agreed that to allow Martin to ride would create an unfair advantage disagreed that the Senior Tour was merely nostalgic instead of athletic (Elliot, 1998). This division within the ranks may have led some of the Tour supporters to join the Martin side of the controversy, but even without such a shift, for some, it marked the beginning of the end of the Tour's case (Broder, 1998; Kelley, 1998).

The Decision

Judge Coffin's decision resolved the central legal questions of the controversy, but many public observers were not satisfied with the conclusion, and the PGA Tour's subsequent appeals continued its search for a legal remedy to its central complaint. In a judgment rendered over competing claims for summary judgment, Coffin denied the PGA position that it was not bound by the ADA. Finding that the PGA Tour was a public accommodation under Title III of the Act, Coffin reserved the question of whether Martin was an employee of the Tour and other substantive questions for the trial of the case (*Casey Martin v. PGA Tour, Inc.*, January 30, 1998). The central questions of the summary judgment issued on January 30, 1998, were whether the PGA Tour met the ADA's definition of public accommodation or whether it met the "private club" exemption recognized under the ADA (*Casey Martin v. PGA Tour, Inc.*, January 30, 1998). In each case, Coffin sided with Martin.

Coffin found that the Tour did not qualify as a private club because it operated primarily as "an organization formed to promote and operate tournaments for the economic benefit of its members" and "is part of the entertainment industry" (*Casey Martin v. PGA Tour, Inc.*, January 30, 1998, at *9). Unlike a private club, organized "for social and recreational purposes"(*Casey Martin v. PGA Tour, Inc.*, January 30, 1998, at *12), the PGA Tour "is a commercial enterprise" (*Casey Martin v. PGA Tour, Inc.*, January 30, 1998, at *9). Coffin argued that "[t]he success of the Tour in generating revenue for its members is in direct proportion to public participation as spectators and viewers of the Tour's tournaments. Without this public participation, the primary object of the Tour could not be achieved" (*Casey Martin v. PGA Tour, Inc.*, January 30, 1998, at *9–10). As a commercial enterprise, the Tour not only fails to meet the standard for the private club status, but also clearly falls under the definition of a public accommodation, generally defined as a private entity whose operation affects public commerce.[10] In addition to this finding, Coffin considered the seven criteria used to identify a "bona fide private club" in *United States v. Lansdowne Swim Club*. He found that the Tour did not exhibit the characteristics of private clubs associated with genuine selectivity, membership control, history of organization, use of facilities by nonmembers, club's purpose, whether the club advertises for members, and whether the club is nonprofit (*Casey Martin v. PGA Tour, Inc.*, January 30, 1998, at *13–16). Finally, Coffin noted that the Tour's use of golf courses as the locations of its tournaments aided his conclusion, because golf courses are specifically identified as places of public accommodation covered by the ADA (*Casey Martin v. PGA Tour, Inc.*, January 30, 1998).

After the summary judgment, the case was limited to a few basic points. The Tour did not contest that Martin was disabled under the definition of the ADA, so the only remaining defense issues were whether the ADA applied to professional golf tournaments and whether "walking is a substantive rule of its competition and that a waiver of the rule would, accordingly, result in a fundamental alteration of its competitions, which the ADA does not require" (*Casey Martin v. PGA Tour, Inc.*, February 19, 1998, at *4). Coffin declared that the first of these was satisfactorily resolved in his summary judgment, so the only claims resolved in the final decision pertained to whether Martin's proposed accommodation was a "reasonable modification" that would neither require the PGA Tour to perform a "fundamental alteration of the nature of its business or programs in order to accommodate the disabled, nor ... result in undue hardship to the [PGA Tour]" (*Casey Martin v. PGA Tour, Inc.*, February 19, 1998, at *6).

After reviewing the case law that discussed the "fundamental alteration" issue in ADA cases involving sporting activities, Coffin found that allowing Martin the use of a cart during competition would meet both the applicable criteria and was a "reasonable accommodation" of the type envisioned by the ADA (*Casey Martin v. PGA Tour, Inc.*, February 19, 1998). Finding that "the use of a cart is certainly not unreasonable in the game of golf" and that "the Rules of Golf do not require walking," Coffin noted that "even the PGA Tour permits carts at two of the events it stages [the Senior Tour and the first two preliminary rounds of the Qualifying School Tournament]" (*Casey Martin v. PGA Tour, Inc.*, February 19, 1998, at *21).[11] Because the Tour does not penalize participants who use carts in those events, Coffin reasoned, "This is certainly compelling evidence that even the PGA Tour does not consider walking to be a significant contributor to the skill of shot making" (*Casey Martin v. PGA Tour, Inc.*, February 19, 1998, at *21).

Coffin finally examined whether using a cart would give Martin an unfair advantage over other competitors, and thereby "fundamentally alter the nature of [the Tour's] accommodation" (*Casey Martin v. PGA Tour, Inc.*, February 19, 1998, at *22). He identified this issue as the "ultimate question in this case" and devoted the remainder of the decision to its discussion (*Casey Martin v. PGA Tour, Inc.*, February 19, 1998, at *22–23). After reviewing the role of walking in the United States Golf Association (USGA) (2000) Rules of Golf and similar documents and accepting the PGA Tour's contention that walking fatigued participants to some extent, Coffin concluded that Martin's unique circumstances—his disability— meant that Martin would not enjoy an unfair advantage from riding in a cart during competitions. Coffin concluded,

The fatigue [Martin] endures just from coping with his disability is undeniably greater than the fatigue injected into tournament play on the able-bodied by the requirement that they walk from shot to shot. Walking at a slow pace—to the able-bodied—is a natural act, of little more difficulty than breathing. It is how we were designed to move from place to place. ... As [Martin] easily endures greater fatigue even with a cart than his able-bodied competitors do by walking, it does not fundamentally alter the nature of the PGA Tour's game to accommodate him with a cart. (*Casey Martin v. PGA Tour, Inc.*, February 19, 1998, at *31–32)

In May 2001, the United States Supreme Court ultimately affirmed Coffin's decision and found in favor of Martin by a 7–2 decision, with Justices Anton Scalia and Clarence Thomas dissenting. The majority decision, delivered by Justice John Paul Stevens, essentially agreed with Coffin on all points, finding that though a general elimination of the rule on carts might fundamentally change the game of golf, allowing Martin to use a cart was a reasonable accommodation in his case (*PGA Tour, Inc. v. Casey Martin,* 2001).

In addition, the majority court denied the Tour's new claim that public accommodation law did not pertain in this case because it only applies to customers or clients of the accommodation. The Tour based this argument on a subsection of Title III of the ADA, which specifies that "For the purposes . . . of this subparagraph, the term 'individuals or class of individuals' refers to the clients or customers of the covered public accommodation that enters into the contractual, licensing or other arrangement" (42 U.S.C. 12182 (b)). Interpreting this definition narrowly, the Tour argued that Martin was in effect a provider of the exhibition or entertainment made available to the public by the golf tournament and not a proper customer or client of the PGA Tour. The majority denied the application of this definition to Title III as a whole and argued for a broader interpretation of the term, finding that it is "entirely appropriate to classify the golfers who pay [the PGA Tour] $3,000 for the chance to compete in the Q-School and, if successful, in the subsequent tour events, as petitioner's clients or customers" (*PGA Tour, Inc. v. Casey Martin,* 2001, at *34–35). The dissent, in contrast, heartily endorsed the Tour's claim, and this contention formed the basis of its rationale for breaking with the majority (*PGA Tour, Inc. v. Casey Martin,* 2001, at *53–63).

The Supreme Court decision operates legally as the final resolution of this case. But it did little to stem the public controversy over Martin's suit against the PGA. In the week following the decision, public clamor over the case again became major news.[12]Although many expressed support for Martin, a majority articulated confusion, angst, or dissatisfaction with the verdict. In general, the negative reaction to the verdict revealed a continued belief in the sanctity of sport as an institution above reproach and safe from government interference. Rather than resolving the Martin matter, the Supreme Court decision simply provided the public with an opportunity to reiterate the same arguments it had made when the controversy began. Reaction to this final decision revealed again that the opposing sides of the Martin controversy were locked in an ideological struggle that must be understood as a conflict over the meaning and value of sport in our culture rather than a simple dispute over reasonable accommodation.

ANALYSIS OF THE CASEY MARTIN CONTROVERSY

In terms of argument theory, the two sides in the Casey Martin dispute failed to reach common ground because they operated in different argument fields. As Toulmin, Rieke, and Janik (1984) explain, arguments have different goals, reasonings, and procedures in different fields, and what stands as acceptable support, reasoning, and warrants can vary widely from field to field. Occupying different ideological grounds, the combatants in this dispute operated as if from distinct fields and identified different goals and critical issues. To the pro–Martin advocates, the issue at hand was the exclusiveness and historically discriminating structure of the PGA, which some suggested ought to stand for "Please Go Away" ("Dole supports," 1998; Goldman, 1998). To this group, golf and other sports traditionally have exhibited unfairly discriminating attitudes, particularly regarding race, and excluding Casey Martin simply proved that such elitist thinking continued to shape professional sports. Although few expressed it outside of circles such as disability studies discussion groups, this view generally attacked professional sport as an ableist institution, dedicated to promoting the norms of ableist culture.

On the other side, pro–PGA Tour advocates argued that upholding the rules of the game required that Casey Martin only be allowed the advantages available to the other golfers. According to this group, golf and other sports traditionally have upheld the cultural values of fair competition, athleticism, and sportsmanship, values associated with such revered cultures as that of ancient Greece. Although few made this point directly, it lurked beneath virtually every argument made in the PGA Tour's defense.

From an argument theory standpoint, the controversy gained its notoriety and intensity largely because these two positions did *not* clash. There is no reason that both of these positions cannot simultaneously be accepted: Sport can be an ableist institution and uphold ancient cultural values at the same time. What we understand as the values of fair competition, athleticism, and sportsmanship may all be structured by ableism, most particularly the idea that ability arises in the body. In other words, professional sport is an ableist institution because it stands for and teaches these cultural values. Until such a premise is accepted, however, the two sides appear to compete because accusations of "discrimination" carry a recognizably negative valence, whereas claims of proudly upholding Greco-Roman ideals carry a positive valence.

In short, the two sides saw themselves as debating the point while providing evidence that, from the perspective taken here, identified sport as an ableist institution. In argument theory's terms, the Tour's defense was nonresponsive, based largely on a non sequitur, and completely consistent with the notion that it practiced ableism. As in many debates in which the clash becomes impossible because the two sides are so diametrically opposed that they cannot even agree about what is being debated, this controversy quickly boiled down to a collection of assertions, ad hominem attacks, and examples of blatantly fallacious reasoning. The pro–Martin side, having made its case that the Tour had a history of discrimination,

felt assured of victory; the pro–Tour side, having made its case for upholding the rules of a value-laden activity, felt the same confidence.

What I find most interesting and important is the way that these decisions operate with and inscribe ableist ideals even in their support of
Martin's case. Finding the use of a cart a reasonable accommodation for
Martin alone, the courts relied on expressly ableist rhetoric. The limited
application of the decision is important for a few reasons. First, it located
the legal ground for defining "reasonable accommodation" on a case-by-
case basis, which the PGA Tour had argued set an inappropriate (and
difficult-to-meet) standard (*Casey Martin v. PGA Tour, Inc.*, February 19,
1998). Second, it resolved the issues of the case by attending to the different qualities of Martin's body, rejecting the PGA Tour argument that the
rules had to be drawn without regard for whether a body was normal.
On one hand, this seems to reject the ableist tendency to naturalize the
social construct of the "normal" body, or at least remove the privilege a
body enjoys because it is "normal." On the other hand, the decision states
unequivocally that walking is a "natural" activity for which people are
"designed." Because this statement requires reading "natural" as "normal," it suggests that this idea has simply been set aside rather than discarded. Third, and most important for my purposes, the argument
qualifies the impact the decision has on institutional ableism. By looking
to the body as the location of ability and finding that Martin's particularly
limited ability allowed him a particular accommodation in this case, the
decision inscribes the norm that bodies construct ability. The two ableist
ideas connect at a fundamental level: the orientation that regards walking
as a "natural act" and the way "we were designed to move from place to
place," which locates the ability to walk in the design of the body. In these
decisions, the ideals operate as sustaining reflections of each other. Martin
deserves accommodation not because his case challenges structures that
locate ability in the body, but precisely because his body lacks certain
abilities.

This emphasis became symbolized by the mute testimony offered by a
video showing Martin's leg without its protective stocking. Both Coffin
and observers argued that the video was the most powerful argument for
Martin's case (*Casey Martin v. PGA Tour, Inc.*, February 19, 1998; "Martin
reveals," 1998). According to Coffin, the video clearly showed Martin's
leg as "weakened," a source of "severe pain and discomfort," and, in a
word, disabled. Richard Sandomir (1998) observed:

Nothing in the PGA Tour's rigid defense—that golfers must walk because the
resulting fatigue tests their competitive mettle—can compare with the powerful
videotaped depiction of Martin's Klippel-Trenaunay-Weber Syndrome. Standing
before a camera, Martin showed how blood settles in hardened black-and-blue
patches below a damaged knee that swells instantly. Only when he laid down did
blood return via constricted veins. (p. 8.12)

The metonymy of the body implicit in the visual evidence of Martin's leg reinforces a reading of the ableist dimensions of the decision, for it clearly reduces Martin and his case to a single disabled leg while reinforcing the view that ability is determined by the body.

CONCLUSION

Jackson Miller (1999) argued that

few people would dispute the notion that sports mirror the values and beliefs of the dominant culture. The role which sporting events play in shaping cultural values, however, is typically downplayed or ignored. Viewing sports as cultural performances, as I am suggesting here, means acknowledging the power of sporting events to *create* culturally shared beliefs and values. (p. 189)

Limiting sport to cultural performance, however, nearly glosses over the role of sports players as performers. Miller (1999) is relatively uninterested in the performance of the players as rhetorical artifact and focuses instead on how the entire ritual of the game becomes a cultural performance shared and created by the players, the managers and coaches, the owners, the media, and the fans. Although I am not uninterested in the interactions of these same parties, I am mostly interested in the way these groups' notions of the acceptable "player" have shaped, and create or extend, ableist norms of the body.

I read sport as the typically masculinist, elitist, and ableist celebration of bodies trained "to perfection" (and paid exceedingly well) in a voyeuristic arena designed to highlight feats of physical bravado for the praise of typically less skilled, but generally masculine and ableist, audiences. In such a context, it is interesting to watch people with disabilities try to "make it big" in a forum where they are inherently unwanted. For many years, professional sports have segregated themselves from those with less powerful, less skilled bodies. Such bodies cannot be denied the right to participate in such an important cultural institution as sport, but they can be denied the limelight of its upper echelons. Women, children, and the disabled are all given their own place to play, safely kept out of the "big leagues" where the fans and the money tend to congregate.

Many sport fans can easily describe people who have challenged this institutionalized idea. Citing figures like Casey Martin, such fans would argue that sport does not necessarily discriminate against people with disabilities. But such examples merely prove the ground in which I formed my position. Sport is not about these few who have made it despite their disabled bodies. Sport is about perfection of the body and the eternal search for the names that will embody that perfection for the next generations of athletes. Golf fans that admire Casey Martin implicitly recognize this, for they appreciate what they read as his "inspirational effort." This approval appears to validate uncritically the institutional ableist bias and creates the impression that sport is indeed an egalitarian enterprise offering a level playing field that is open to everyone.

Yet statistically, disabled people who participate in sports do so in segregated groups, such as Deaf basketball leagues, the Special Olympics, the Paralympics, or the wheelchair races that accompany many major marathons. Very rarely (and only under the strictest rules for passing) do people with disabilities find a place in the world of professional sports. Even women, whose "normal" physical strength and stamina mark them in ableist culture as relatively less abled than men, have found a niche only by crafting their own courts, teams, and competition. As strong and as durable as the female athlete's body has grown, it is still confined to its own space.

Sport rests on ableist norms that are literally written into the rules. The games often dictate that players (for their own safety and that of others) are not allowed to participate when they are "injured" or "unfit to play." Players who reach this status temporarily are placed on the "disabled list" until their bodies return to form; players that acquire this status for good—thereby becoming disabled—retire.[13] Until Martin rode, we had never seen a professional game played in which the rules were structured to even the playing field for disabled participants. We have yet to see a marathon runner face off against a wheelchair rider with equal credit given to the winner. We have yet to see a person who cannot see, run, or throw be allowed to take to the professional baseball field or basketball court. Accessibility, of course, is the key term, for though all the examples of the past might show that certain "supercrips" can make it in the world of professional sports without accommodation, no one can sensibly argue that all professional sports are accessible to people with disabilities. As long as sport constructs its rules as mere reflections of acceptable notions of fairness and sportsmanship, its propagation of the idea that ability is located in the body (and not in the skills privileged by its rules) will continue to generate ableism.

In the Casey Martin controversy, the ableism inherent in professional sport became clear: Access was to be earned by performance within the rules rather than by altering them to make the game more accessible. Martin's case was only taken seriously—by both his supporters and the PGA Tour—because of his history of success on the golf course. We could simply dismiss this as a conservative attraction to the way its always been done, but then we would miss the critical point. Professional sport is inherently an ableist institution whose rules are built on, teach, and (re)create ableist thinking.

At the beginning of this chapter, I recounted various reasons to regard professional sport as an ableist institution: its closeting of the intimate causal relationship of sport and disability, the relatively few people with disabilities that participate, its segregation of most who do in special leagues, its metonymic reduction of players to their parts, and its consistent location of ability in the participants' bodies rather than in its rules. Using this operating premise as a lens, this analysis of the Casey Martin controversy strongly reinforces the notion of sports as an ableist institution and brings some of its dimensions into focus. The controversy is best understood when viewed as an ideological battle over sport and its ableist implications. Understood this way, the PGA Tour's strenuous objections and the loud outcries by its supporters are so easy to understand that they seem almost justified. Whether recognized by the courts or not, the implicit message of the Martin decision is that sport does not provide a level playing field open to all, that certain bodies enjoy unwarranted privileges created by its rules, and that the resulting disparity discriminates. Giving Casey Martin a cart means that the rules are, at least in some cases, unfair and rebuts the position of sports as an unquestionably wholesome and moral activity above reproach or scrutiny.

In contrast to such thinking, the Casey Martin case may be read as a dramatic blow against a recalcitrant ableist culture. And, for Martin at least, it is an impressive victory. But I find it nearly impossible to over-caution against any optimism resulting from the case. The lingering resentment of the decision reveals that, though the message may have been understood on some level, a large number of the Tour's supporters find it unpersuasive, if not downright dangerous. Furthermore, as the Court itself carefully pointed out, the decision did not craft a clear legal precedent to force sports to become more accessible, but rather required that each petitioner bring requests for accommodation on a case-by-case basis (*PGA Tour, Inc. v. Casey Martin*, 2001). Anyone interested in receiving reasonable accommodation may need to go all the way to the Supreme Court to get it. Finally, the decision must be read in the context of the Court's recent and extremely limiting decisions that have undermined the ADA (see *Board of Trustees of the University of Alabama v. Patricia Garrett*, 2001). Especially in this context, the ableist rhetoric pervading Casey Martin's case—even that offered on his behalf, such as the "mute testimony" of his leg—reminds us that the decision should not be read as a rejection of ableist ideology per se. A cynical reading might point out that whatever impact the courts had on ableism in sports, they more than made up for it by inscribing ableism in the law. Nevertheless, the Martin case and the controversies surrounding it reveal at least a growing recognition of sport as a potentially discriminatory enterprise, and the ableist rhetoric involved speaks to both our and future generations about the need to alter the orientation of our ableist culture.

NOTES

1. Consider the story of Eddie Gaedel, who was prohibited from playing professional baseball because he was only three feet, seven inches tall. In what is widely recognized as a "publicity stunt" on August 19, 1951, Gaedel took a turn at bat for the St. Louis Browns against the Detroit Tigers. Because the strike zone is defined by the size of the batter, Gaedel's strike zone has been estimated at one and one-half inches. He was walked on four pitches by Bob Cain and then replaced at first base by a pinch runner. It was Gaedel's only time at bat. The American League president prohibited Gaedel from playing baseball again. See Geoffrey C. Ward (1994), William Marshall (1999), Burt Solomon (1997), and Mike Shannon (1999).

2. I use the convention of capitalizing the term "Deaf" when referring to the culture and those that belong to it, reserving "deaf" to refer to the audiological condition of not being able to hear. See Carol Padden and Tom Humphries (1988).

3. Mordecai Peter Centennial "Three-Finger" Brown, for example, excelled as a baseball pitcher because he threw a natural curve ball with his disabled hand. Injuries from a childhood accident with a corn grinder required the amputation of his forefinger, rendered his middle finger "mangled and left crooked," and made his little finger into a stub. He learned to pitch with the lower two fingers and use the stub to place extra spin on the ball. See Harold Seymour (1971) and Mike Shatzkin (1990).

4. At the peak of the controversy, the first two weeks of February 1998, I collected more than 400 relevant editorials, articles, and letters to the editor from Lexis/Nexis. When researching my thesis on the ADA a few years before, I found less than half that amount in the same database for the three years preceding its passage. I focused on this two-week period because it appeared that the amount of published material related to the controversy dropped off significantly after that time.

5. These two senses of "sport" occasionally operate as a terrific pun, as in the following conversation between Charles Wallace Murray and Calvin O'Keefe, characters from Madeline L'Engle's (1962/1976) *A Wrinkle in Time*. In this dialog, Charles Wallace, a savant-like freak, and Calvin, a basketball star, find a point of identity in their status as deviants:

"Most peculiar moron I've ever met," Calvin said. "I just came to get away from my family."

Charles Wallace nodded. "What kind of family?"

"They all have runny noses. I'm third from the top of eleven kids. I'm a sport."

At that Charles grinned widely. "So'm I."

"I don't mean like in baseball," Calvin said.

"Neither do I."

"I mean like in biology," Calvin said suspiciously.

"A change in gene," Charles Wallace quoted, "resulting in the appearance of offspring of a character which is not present in the parents but which *is potentially transmissible to its offspring.*"

"What gives around here?" Calvin asked. "I was told you couldn't talk." (p. 36)

The etymology of these two meanings reveals only an indirect connection between the freak and the athlete. According to the *Oxford English Dictionary* (*OED*) (Murray, 1971), the primary definition of sport is as follows: "I.1. Pleasant pastime; entertainment or amusement; recreation, diversion." Athleticism appears a secondary concern; "sport" refers to "participation in games or exercises . . . or amusements collectively," because of their entertainment and recreation value. This sense of "sport" seems closely connected with the image of the jester, "II. 4. A matter affording entertainment, diversion, or mirth; a jest or joke," which has been linked extensively to the freak. See Leslie Fiedler (1978).

When a freak appears, it is as if Nature amuses or plays. Secondary definitions of the verb "sport" read: "4. A. Of Nature: to produce or develop abnormal or irregular forms or growths *as if in sport.* b. Of plants, animals, etc.: To deviate or vary abnormally from the parent stock or specific type; to exhibit or undergo spontaneous mutation" (emphasis added). This play has dark overtones, as in the *OED* example attributed to Edward Bancroft: "surrounding forests, where Natural sports in primaeval rudeness." The term connotes a sense of a mischievous prank, the trickster's play that can cause harm, and the cruel games required to entertain an elemental force.

Note that this definition of sport is virtually identical to that used by Aristotle (1942/1994, p. 175) to identify the monster: "[A]nyone who does not take after his parents is really in a way a monstrosity, since in these cases Nature has in a way strayed from the generic type" (qtd. in Thompson, 1997, p. 19). Further research should inquire what significance the shift in terminology from monster to sport to freak has had for evolving views of disability.

6. The football helmet provides another example of closely regulated technology, in that its use as an aid in tackling is accepted, but a player is penalized for using it too forcefully or in cases in which using the helmet while tackling is deemed fairly likely to injure the tackled player (NFL Rules, 2001).

7. The result is the proverbial "level playing field" that is said to create the appropriate conditions for play but not unduly influence the performance of any given player. This mythic construct ignores a variety of influences that favor particular players. Slight but unavoidable differences in equipment or arenas may favor one player's skill over another. Professional baseball fields are not all the same size, and the conditions of a particular locale can influence individual players' performances. Domed stadiums, differences in playing surfaces, and environmental factors such as climate and altitude are suspected to affect players' performance, and playing in familiar surroundings ("at home") is deemed advantageous. Furthermore, the presence and interaction of spectators and fans can influence the performance of players, creating the phenomenon of the twelfth man in football and a sixth man in basketball when a game is played at home. These invisible players can influence a game by encouraging emotional play, affecting officials' impressions and penalty calls, and physically interfering with the ability of teams to perform, as when a crowd makes a great deal of noise to hinder play calling by the opposing team in football.

8. See endnote 3.

9. Players are allowed to use a cart to reduce delays arising when they must return to the tee to restart a hole after a lost ball and when a final round playoff requires that they move quickly to a different hole on another part of the course.

No player is allowed to ride a cart for any reason during the course of "normal" play.

10. For example, Title III of the ADA defines "public accommodation" with these terms and provides an extensive list of examples. 42 U.S.C. 12181 (7) reads in part, "The following private entities are considered public accommodations for the purposes of this title, if the operations of such entities affect commerce. . . ."

11. The Rules of Golf referred to here are jointly written by the United States Golf Association and the Royal and Ancient Golf Club of Scotland and are generally accepted as the rules governing play by all amateur and professional golfers. Those rules do not require walking or prohibit carts but suggest in Appendix I that if "it is desired to require players to walk in a competition, the following condition is recommended: 'Players shall walk at all times during a stipulated round'" (USGA, 2000).

12. In the week following the decision, I collected more than 270 different documents from Lexis/Nexis related to the Casey Martin case.

13. Major League Baseball's rule 3.17, of the *Official Rules 2000 Edition*, specifies that players on the disabled list "may not take part in any activity during the game such as warming up a pitcher, bench jockeying, etc. Disabled players are not allowed to enter the playing surface at any time or for any purpose during the game."

REFERENCE LIST

Agnos, A. (1998, February 10). PGA has it all wrong [Letter to the editor]. *San Francisco Chronicle*, p. A20. Retrieved February 13, 1998, from http://web.lexis-nexis.com/universe/.

Allen, K. (1999, December 6). Olympic sized fight over disabled rights. *USA Today*. Retrieved December 6, 1999, from http://www.usatoday.com/sports/ccovmon.htm.

Americans with Disabilities Act of 1990, 42 U.S.C. § 12101 *et seq.* (West 1993).

Another golfer might get a ride: Martin ruling could aid Indiana man. (2001, June 5). *Star Tribune*, p. 2C. Retrieved June 8, 2001, from http://web.lexis-nexis.com/universe/.

Aristotle. (1942/1994). *Generation of animals* (A. L. Peck, Trans.). Cambridge: Harvard University Press.

Babineau, J. (1998, February 8). Comment offends senior players. *Orlando Sentinel*, p. D12. Retrieved February 12, 1998, from http://web.lexis-nexis.com/universe/.

Blauvelt, H. (1998a, February 9). Martin "anxious" for decision: He could learn this week whether he may use a cart. *USA Today*, p. C10. Retrieved February 13, 1998, from http://web.lexis-nexis.com/universe/.

Blauvelt, H. (1998b, February 11). PGA Tour: Benefits of cart magnified in course of season. *USA Today*, p. C3. Retrieved February 13, 1998, from http://web.lexis-nexis.com/universe/.

Board of Trustees of the University of Alabama v. Patricia Garrett, No. 99–1240, 2001 U.S. LEXIS 1700 (U.S. February 21, 2001).

Broder, D. S. (1998, February 11). Showdown over a golf cart. *The Washington Post*,

p. A21. Retrieved February 13, 1998, from http://web.lexis-nexis.com/universe/.

Burg, M., Mount, T. (Producers), & Shelton, R. (Director). (1988). *Bull Durham* [Motion picture]. United States: MGM Contemporary Classics.

Campos, P. (2001, June 2). Martin case only further handicaps us. *Rocky Mountain News*, p. A22. Retrieved June 9, 2001, from http://web.lexis-nexis.com/universe/.

Casey Martin–PGA Tour trial set to resume today. (1998, February 10). *The Washington Post*, p. D2. Retrieved February 13, 1998, from http://web.lexis-nexis.com/universe/.

Casey Martin timeline. (2001, January 16). *Scripps Howard Hews Service*. Retrieved January 17, 2001, from http://espn.go.com/golfonline/tours/2001/0114/1015735.html.

Casey Martin v. PGA Tour, Inc., No. 97-6309-TC, 1998 U.S. Dist. LEXIS 1503 (D. Or. January 30, 1998).

Casey Martin v. PGA Tour, Inc., No. 97-6309-TC, 1998 U.S. Dist. LEXIS 1980 (D. Or. February 19, 1998).

Casey Martin v. PGA Tour, Inc., Nos. 98-35309, 98-35509, 2000 U.S. App. LEXIS 3376 (9th Cir. March 6, 2000).

Causey, P. R. (1998, February 7). Readers would give Martin a ticket to ride on the tour [Letters to the editor]. *The Los Angeles Times*, p. C3. Retrieved February 12, 1998, from http://web.lexis-nexis.com/universe/.

Chambers, M. (1998a, February 10). Casey Martin case: Groups close ranks. *New York Times*, p. C7. Retrieved February 13, 1998, from http://web.lexis-nexis.com/universe/.

Chambers, M. (1998b, February 11). Head of PGA testifies of cart's unfair edge. *New York Times*, p. C8. Retrieved February 13, 1998, from http://web.lexis-nexis.com/universe/.

Chimelis, R. (2000, June 26). Situation drops in on the fly. *Springfield Union-News*, p. D1.

Coulson, D. (1998, February 7). Readers would give Martin a ticket to ride on the tour [Letters to the editor]. *The Los Angeles Times*, p. C3. Retrieved February 12, 1998, from http://web.lexis-nexis.com/universe/.

Dole supports Casey Martin's fight. (1998, January 29). *Dayton Daily News*, p. 7C. Retrieved June 5, 2001, from http://web.lexis-nexis.com/universe/.

Douglas, M. (1986). *How institutions think*. Syracuse, NY: Syracuse University Press.

Elliott, M. (1998, February 8). Tour of duty. *Tampa Tribune*, Sports, p. 9. Retrieved February 12, 1998, from http://web.lexis-nexis.com/universe/.

Erickson, S. (1998, February 7). Skills make a golf pro [Letter to the editor]. *Omaha World-Herald*, p. 45. Retrieved February 12, 1998, from http://web.lexis-nexis.com/universe/.

Faculak, S. III. (1998, February 7). Letters to the green. *San Francisco Chronicle*, p. B2. Retrieved February 12, 1998, from http://web.lexis-nexis.com/universe/.

Fiedler, L. (1978). *Freaks: Myths and images of the secret self*. New York: Simon & Schuster.

Fraley, G. (1998, February 7). Rangers' rookie owner following veteran's example.

Dallas Morning News, p. 2B. Retrieved February 12, 1998, from http://web.lexis-nexis.com/universe/.

Goggin, G., & Newell, C. (2000). Crippling paralympics? Media, disability, and Olympism. *Media International Australia incorporating Culture and Policy, 97*, 71–83.

Goldman, C. D. (1998). Legal access: PGA: please go away! *Braille Forum*, p. 36.9. Retrieved June 13, 2001, from http://www.acb.org/Magazine/1998/mar/bf039811.html.

Golen, J. (1999, December 25). Hockey's a fit for amputees. *Springfield Union-News*, pp. C1–C2.

Gordon, Jeff. (1998, February 9). Tipsheet. *St. Louis Post-Dispatch*, p. C2. Retrieved February 13, 1998, from http://web.lexis-nexis.com/universe/.

Gordon, Joe. (1998, February 8). Golf notes: Authority an issue—Martin case weakens PGA. *Boston Herald*, p. B29. Retrieved February 12, 1998, from http://web.lexis-nexis.com/universe/.

Harber, P. (1998, February 8). PGA needs a ride into the millennium. *Boston Globe*, p. 17. Retrieved February 12, 1998, from http://web.lexis-nexis.com/universe/.

Hart, B. (2001, June 3). Court puts its own spin on golf: Now rules for every other sport are ripe for rewriting. *Chicago Sun-Times*, p. 35. Retrieved June 9, 2001, from http://web.lexis nexis.com/universe/.

Hirsley, M. (1998a, February 8). No gimmes in disabled golfer's suit. *Chicago Tribune*, p. 14. Retrieved February 12, 1998, from http://web.lexis-nexis.com/universe/.

Hirsley, M. (1998b, February 11). PGA: Cart use could mean money edge. *Chicago Tribune*, Sports, p. 3. Retrieved February 13, 1998, from http://web.lexis-nexis.com/universe.

Jariabek, R. (1998, February 7). Readers would give Martin a ticket to ride on the tour [Letters to the editor]. *The Los Angeles Times*, p. C3. Retrieved February 12, 1998, from http://web.lexis-nexis.com/universe/.

Kelley, S. (1998, February 9). Hypocritical comments by golf's greats reveal emptiness of PGA Tour's case. *Seattle Times*, p. D1. Retrieved February 13, 1998, from http://web.lexis-nexis.com/universe/.

Keown, T. (1998, February 11). Figure skating is fine, CBS, but don't force-feed us. *San Francisco Chronicle*, p. C1. Retrieved February 13, 1998, from http://web.lexis-nexis.com/universe/.

Killing standards with kindness. (2001, June 4). *Pittsburgh Post-Gazette*, p. A11. Retrieved June 9, 2001, from http://web.lexis-nexis.com/universe/.

L'Engle, M. (1962/1976). *A wrinkle in time.* New York: Dell.

Major League Baseball. (2000). *Official rules 2000 edition.* Retrieved June 8, 2001, from http://www.mlb.com/.

Marshall, W. (1999). *Baseball's pivotal era, 1945–1951.* Lexington: University Press of Kentucky.

Martin reveals "nightmare" leg: Withered limb focus of lawsuit against PGA Tour. (1998, February 3). *Ottawa Citizen*, p. F2. Retrieved June 19, 2001, from http://web.lexis-nexis.com/universe/.

Martin's win in cart case is only right, but has perils: Ruling opens "rich source of litigation." (2001, June 1). *Arizona Republic*, p. B8. Retrieved June 9, 2001, from http://web.lexis-nexis.com/universe/.

McRuer, R. (2000, June). *Critical bodies: Conceptualizing AIDS and/as disability*. Paper presented at the annual conference of the Society for Disability Studies, Chicago, IL.

Migden, C. (1998, February 10). Let Casey Martin play [Letter to the editor]. *San Francisco Chronicle*, p. A20. Retrieved February 13, 1998, from http://web.lexis-nexis.com/universe/.

Miller, J. B. (1999). "Indians," "Braves," and "Redskins": A performative struggle for control of an image. *Quarterly Journal of Speech, 85*, 188–202.

Mizell, H. (1998, February 11). Presents from the past. *St. Petersburg Times*, p. C1. Retrieved February 13, 1998, from http://web.lexis-nexis.com/universe/.

Murray, J. A. H., et al. (Eds.). (1971). *The compact edition of the Oxford English Dictionary: Complete text reproduced micrographically* (Vol. 2). Glasgow: Oxford University Press.

Nack, W. (2001, May 7). The wrecking yard. *Sports Illustrated, 94*, 60–75.

NFL Rules (2001, June 19). *Behind the football stripes*. Retrieved June 19, 2001, from http://members.tripod.com/refereestats/index.htm.

Ormsby, M. (1998, February 10). PGA's pig-headed elitism lives in battle with Martin. *Toronto Star*, p. C12. Retrieved February 13, 1998, from http://web.lexis-nexis.com/universe/.

Padden, C., & Humphries, T. (1988). *Deaf in America: Voices from a culture*. Cambridge, MA: Harvard University Press.

PGA Tour, Inc. v. Casey Martin, No. 00–24, 2001 U.S. LEXIS 4115 (U.S. May 29, 2001).

Posnanski, J. (1998, February 9). PGA walks twisted path in Martin case. *Kansas City Star*, p. D1. Retrieved February 13, 1998, from http://web.lexis-nexis.com/universe/.

Reilly, R. (2000, December 11). Paralympic paradox. *Sports Illustrated, 93*, 98.

Robertson, B. (1998, February 7). Readers would give Martin a ticket to ride on the tour [Letters to the editor]. *The Los Angeles Times*, p. C3. Retrieved February 12, 1998, from http://web.lexisnexis.com/universe/.

Robertson, D. (1998, February 8). Have a heart, PGA, and let Martin ride. *Houston Chronicle*, Sports, p. 3. Retrieved February 13, 1998, from http://web.lexis-nexis.com/universe/.

Rosaforte, T. (1998, January 23). All over but the shouting. *Golf World, 51*, 10–14.

Sandomir, R. (1998, February 8). A by-the-book defense versus Martin's reality. *New York Times*, p. 8.12. Retrieved February 12, 1998, from http://web.lexis-nexis.com/universe/.

Seigle, G. (2001, June 7). The ADA has no place in sports. *Hartford Courant*, p. A19. Retrieved June 8, 2001, from http://web.lexis-nexis.com/universe/.

Seymour, H. (1971). *Baseball: The golden age* (Vol. 2). New York: Oxford University Press.

Shannon, M. (1999). Eddie Gaedel and Bill Veeck. In *Tales from the ballpark: More of the greatest true baseball stories ever told* (pp. 73–74). Chicago: Contemporary Books.

Shapiro, J. P. (1993). *No pity: People with disabilities forging a new Civil Rights Movement*. New York: Random House.

Shatzkin, M. (Ed.). (1990). *The ballplayers: Baseball's ultimate biographical reference*. New York: Arbor House/William Morrow.

Sirak, R. (1998, February 8). An exemption for Nicklaus is an open and shut case. *Buffalo News*, p. 2B. Retrieved February 12, 1998, from http://web.lexis-nexis.com/universe/.

Slezak, C. (1998, February 8). Elitism, hypocrisy alive and well on PGA Tour. *Chicago Sun-Times*, p. 15. Retrieved February 12, 1998, from http://web.lexis-nexis.com/universe.

Solomon, B. (1997). *The baseball timeline*. New York: Avon Books.

Thompson, R. G. (1997). *Extraordinary bodies: Figuring physical disability in American culture and literature*. New York: Columbia University Press.

Toulmin, S., Rieke, R., & Janik, A. (1984). *An introduction to reasoning* (2nd ed.). New York: Macmillan.

United States Golf Association. (2000). Rules of golf, App. I § C.7. Retrieved June 8, 2001, from http://www.usga.org/rules/rule_2000/index.html.

Ward, G. C. (1994). *Baseball: An illustrated history*. New York: A. A. Knopf.

Wolfe, K. (1998, February 8). Casey Martin wins whether or not he scores in court. *Milwaukee Journal Sentinel*, Crossroads, p. 3. Retrieved February 12, 1998, from http://web.lexis-nexis.com/universe/.

CHAPTER 6

Regulating Sport Rationality in America through the Moral Controversy of Extreme Fighting

Thomas Vaughn

Sport, similar to most institutions, engages in practices that mark the boundaries between legitimate interiors and renegade exteriors. As Kenneth Burke (1968) has noted, communities must continually refine the symbols that they use to create their sense of ethical cohesion and a spirit of common purpose. This process is propelled by defining certain practices as unwanted or profane, as forces that must be marginalized to maintain the pristine nature of a valorized interior where traditions are preserved. One of the primary ways that this process transpires is by defining the unwanted practices as irrational or as a challenge to the ethical cohesion that drives a given institution. Nowhere in the realm of sport has this process of moral exclusion been more pronounced than in regard to a new form of martial arts tournament. Within contemporary culture, promoters of these tournaments encounter both ambivalence and hostility emanating from the mainstream community. For at least three millennia, the martial arts have played an essential role in constituting the sporting ethic, as well as in defining the boundaries of civilization. As early as the Greek Olympiad, athletes would gather to perform acts of skill, stamina, and strength, thus embodying the ideals that defined the moral terrain of the *polis* (Golden, 1998).

Today, sporting events remain moments during which a community or nation generates narratives crucial to maintaining the moral order and set limits as to what is considered appropriate competition through the precepts of bravery, sportsmanship, and self-control. Complicating this issue, along with these sanctioned athletic performances, events outside the margins of the mainstream exist that simultaneously stabilize and challenge the boundaries of social acceptability. Pecking away at the fringes of the American sport ethic is a new type of martial arts tournament in which many of the rules that guide the conduct of other contact sports, such as boxing and football, are discarded. The essential goal is to use whatever means necessary to compel opponents to quit or ensure that they are unable to continue. Because it is still in the fledgling stages of development, this sport is known by various names: submission wrestling, no-holds-barred fighting, *pankration*, bare-knuckle fighting, tournament jujitsu (developed in Brazil), shoot wrestling (which disallows closed hand strikes), ultimate fighting, pitfighting, and freestyle martial arts. I have elected to use the term "extreme fighting" to designate this burgeoning sport because a significant portion of this essay focuses on the tournament culture of the midwestern United States, where many competitions use this descriptive title as a form of self-promotion. By examining this evolving culture and the public debate surrounding these tournaments, we are afforded an intriguing glimpse into the acquisition and denial of athletic legitimacy.

Debates over extreme fighting in America have been carried out at several different levels, ranging from local legislatures and judiciaries to the United States Senate. These debates have been followed sporadically by the popular press. Opponents to the events focus on the notion that, within a "civilized country," sports that demand little skill have no goal other than to brutalize another human being for the profit of those willing to appeal to the most base of human instincts, tantamount to human cockfighting. In short, extreme fighting is denied legitimacy by many state athletic commissions because it is deemed uncivil and therefore resides outside the accepted moral order that sports ideally are designed to preserve. Examining the discourse that emanates from the extreme fighting debate, particularly the resistance leveled against it by community leaders concerned with the sport-entertainment industry, provides insight into the current moral assumptions that underpin violence in the American mainstream by exploring visions of the ideal civilization propagated by athletic culture. In particular, this chapter argues that sport does not possess an inherent rationality, but rather that rationality must be ascribed from the outside, particularly in the case of morally controversial practices. This means both looking inside the extreme fighting culture and examining the public debate and perceptions surrounding it. Before embarking on a sustained analysis of this public debate, it is informative to take a brief look at the tournament culture itself, a culture that continues to grow and proliferate at the grassroots level despite sustained legal and political pressure.

NOTES ON AN INDIANA COCKFIGHT

As I stood in line outside the Armory of Muncie, Indiana, in August 1998, it occurred to me that I was probably doing research, even though

I had no specific project in mind or thesis percolating under the surface—
merely a spectator's interest in the martial arts. This uneasy feeling that I
should be taking notes may have stemmed from a recent reading of Clifford Geertz's (1972) classic essay on cockfighting in Bali, during which
the cunning anthropologist was afforded a rare glimpse into the culture
he was studying when he broke the delicate barrier between the legitimate
and the renegade. Although technically illegal in the eyes of a government
informed by European standards, the cockfight was an event that the populace enjoyed, partly because its illegal nature lent it a certain romanti-
cism. Men would gather with their cocks (the term has the same double
meaning in Balinese as in English), tie razors to the roosters' feet, then
risk enormous sums of money on the outcome of a fight to the death.
Risking a fortune on such a capricious event constitutes what Geertz
(1972) calls "deep play," a term borrowed from the Enlightenment social
theorist Jeremy Bentham, who viewed these irrational acts as subversive
because they satisfied no rational need and seemed both excessive and
disproportionate in terms of risk. .

Relating this idea to a distinctly American context, Gary Alan Fine
(1992) refers to these types of events as "morally controversial leisure"
and argues that examining the boundaries that delimit such performances
provides valuable insight into the discursive construction of sport ethics.
He writes that "deviant play is a rich arena for examining constructed
meanings because its deviant status demands a justification and a self-
consciousness from the participant" (Fine, 1992, p. 250). When exiting the
mainstream, the "deviant" proceeds with the awareness that a line has
been crossed into social deviance, an experience in which participants
revel. Such border crossings expose the assumptions and contradictions
that characterize the moral underpinnings of a society at a particular time.

As I stand there, I begin to think like an ethnographer and very quickly
find myself longing for a confederate, an informer with an insider's perspective who could allow me access to this underground ritual. Almost
at that precise moment, I am struck from behind by an inadvertent foot
belonging to a young woman who is being introduced to a Greco-Roman
hiplock by a female friend. The move is a simple one that involves throwing an opponent over his or her center of gravity using the hips. Both
women are very serious about their technique, and the one who made
contact with me apologizes while brushing dry grass off of her sweat-
pants. As it turns out, this was the break I needed, because it caused me
to bump into a machinist from Cincinnati who was there to watch a friend,
Kerry Schall, fight that evening. As luck would have it, Kerry had reserved
a front-row table that could seat about ten people and had an extra spot
that he wanted to sell. Much like Geertz among the Balinese, my foot was
in the door.

Extreme fighters compete in a cage elevated about five feet off the
ground. There are debates about the use of a chain-link fence to contain

the fighters, some arguing that it makes the fight seem more renegade than necessary and others that the fence is necessary to keep the fighters in the fight area when pushed. The only rules at this event are no biting, eye-gouging, or fish-hooking (placing a finger in the mouth to pull the lips taught). The extreme fights are interspersed among amateur, toughman-style boxing matches. The announcer exhorts the crowd to cheer because the "louder you yell, the harder they fight." This evening will be Schall's first extreme fight. With a background in wrestling and Judo, he weighs about 250 pounds and sports, like so many of the extreme fighters, a shaved head and a goatee. His body is not chiseled, but he carries little fat, and his size places him squarely in the heavyweight division.

Chris Dodson, Schall's eventual opponent, is ready to beat someone up after being cut from the Indianapolis Colts, and he takes out his frustration on an inexperienced and poorly trained opponent whom he dispatches with rapid hand strikes in a courtesy warm-up match. Schall stops by to visit with his friends before the fight and sits with a calm smile on his face, drinking a Bud Light. The machinist informs him that Dodson "is a pretty bad dude." Schall simply nods. This seems like a good time to begin my research, so I ask him if he is nervous. He thinks for a moment and then responds, in a tone that seems honest enough, that it will probably hit him when he gets in the cage. I then ask him what he does to help himself relax, and he replies, this time to the entire table, which is now focused on our conversation, that he "masturbates." Not only is Schall big, but he is clever, and I am not surprised when I later learn that he is a successful businessperson outside of the cage. Dodson enters the cage to a roar from the crowd, which appreciates his prior performance, and I notice that Schall looks small standing next to his opponent. Schall's wife, who is seated across from me, fiercely warns that anyone not cheering for Kerry had better leave.

The speed of the fight is shocking; it is over in less than a minute. Dodson drives Schall back against the cage. Dodson then stands next to the referee with blood flowing from both nostrils due to a well-timed forearm from Schall that struck the bridge of his nose. If the bleeding cannot be stopped, the fight will be called. Schall walks back and forth in the cage raising his hands and yelling in victory. The people at his table are beside themselves. He walks out the winner of his first fight, and his wife, clearly his biggest fan, embraces him—an act of affection that causes a portion of Dodson's blood to stain the front of her cream blouse. A somewhat calmer female friend takes her aside, dabs at the stain with a tissue, and says, "Oh, honey, AIDS."

The crowd moves between frenzy and boredom because the matches often become defensive stalemates. The best fight of the evening takes place between two students from rival high schools in the area. The high-point comes when the larger, stronger competitor uses a body slam to break a triangle choke applied by the better trained opponent. (This is one of the most complex moves in a sport that only a couple of years earlier was known only to Brazilians.) I look around and notice children at the event, one of whom is wearing the distinctive half-gloves worn by fighters to protect their hands while his father bounces him on his knee. Truly, it is a grassroots phenomenon.

At certain times, the fighting spirit moves into the crowd, and the announcer admonishes the audience, which now turns its attention away from the cage. I am reminded of David Nasaw's (1993) description of public amusements at the turn of the century, when people entered into public not only to be entertained, but to become part of the public spectacle. Just as young women then would allow their dresses to be blown up at the funhouse to amuse the crowds on the boardwalk, local characters now scuffle briefly in front of a fascinated crowd before being removed to the parking lot.

The promoters move quickly to the capstone of the evening: three professional fights, all of which turn out to be lopsided showcases for some of the better-known fighters in the area. In one fight, a large man with a bushy goatee stands ready for his opponent, and some young women in the front row begin to heckle him by calling him "Tank," referring to a pitfighting celebrity from the Ultimate Fighting Championship (UFC). Pseudo-Tank's opponent, Wade Hamilton, has spent a good bit of time on the midwestern circuit, and the fight is brief. Hamilton climbs to the top of the cage and, looking into the crowd, spots Schall, then points at him to indicate that he wants to fight him next. Schall simply smiles and motions with his finger for Hamilton to come hither. Later, the lights go down, and the show is over. It is 2:30 in the morning, and I have a three-hour drive home.

A year later, I find myself in Market Square Arena in Indianapolis (less than a month before it is scheduled to be torn down). The "Extreme Challenge" is in town, and the tournament, as usual, is surrounded by controversy, particularly over the idea that the sacred space where Reggie Miller once rained three-pointers on opponents and Elvis Presley did his last live show is to be defiled by this violent showcase. Wade Hamilton and Kerry Schall are also in town and will be meeting each other in the cage. As I find my way to my seat, I look up and find a student from one of my classes sitting next to me. We lock eyes, and there is a brief moment in which we both feel as though we have caught each other in an adult bookstore. I find out he is working on his technique in a local "fight club" composed of other students and that he hopes to get in the cage in about a year. I also find out that Wade Hamilton is an alumnus of our college as well—this is indeed an incestuous universe.

When Schall enters the stadium (now with several wins to his credit), his wife and entourage are all sporting new shirts that read "Meat Truck."

Schall's clever moniker is clearly the most popular item at the T-shirt stand, and he is in the process of turning the gym where he trains into a corporation entitled "Meat Truck Inc." He traps the powerful Hamilton against the fence in a tuck position and delivers knee strikes to the top of his opponent's head until Hamilton taps out. Schall has just earned a title shot. In a more legitimate setting than the local armory, the fight crowd remains in that zone between excitation and boredom, and the Indianapolis police stay busy removing rowdy spectators to the parking lot. Another night of extreme fights continues, and a few more dramas play themselves out in the cage. For many in the audience, it is not important who wins, but rather that the spectacle of violence has transpired.

This chapter maps the marginalization of extreme fighting from the broader culture, as well as the sport's attempts to become legitimate while maintaining a fan base that is attracted to the renegade nature of the tournaments. As the promoter of the show in Market Square Arena, Monte Cox, explained in a personal interview, the sport is often a victim of its own propaganda. A constellation of rhetorical *topoi* that mark the boundary between the extreme fighting culture and the mainstream provide insight into the relationship between sport and morality. To draw this map, I proceed through four main sections. The first examines attempts by certain promoters to develop new rules and craft a sense of control during the competitions to satisfy legislators' complaints about the irrationality of the events and make the competitions seem more "sportlike." The second section explores the way that the extreme fighting audience is often regarded as a mob possessing lower-class characteristics, a perception that promoters attempt to counteract by referencing the classical roots of the sport. Next, I examine the attacks on the moral character of the contestants and the fear that the violence in the cage will spread to infect society, particularly children. The final section considers the way in which fiction and reality are negotiated in modern sports, where the "real" is seen as a potential threat to the sporting illusion, and the line between competition and performance is blurred. Out of this discussion, a clearer vision of the regulatory influence of sport in modern culture is obtained. By marking the sport outside the bounds of competitive rationality, opponents of extreme fighting create a rhetorical universe in which the sport comes closer to a criminal behavior than a legitimate competition.

Molding Violence to Look Like Sport

At a recent show, the ring announcer and events promoter stimulated the expectant crowd before a series of extreme fights by shaking his head and, while tearing up his notes, shouted the following: "Rules! We don't need no stinking rules!" He went on to assure the audience that there would be blood on the mat by the end of the night. From these exhortations, it seemed unclear what the purpose of the exhibition was: to provide a template on which spectators could witness violence visited on the human body or skilled competitors pitting their athletic abilities against one another. This stimulation often leads to a certain level of disappointment among the crowd because a relatively small percentage of fights actually end in a knockout, and defensive contests can last 10 or 20 minutes while opponents work for position on the ground. Yet many promoters continue to focus on the violent spectacle that a no-holds-barred tournament can produce and use this as a means to market their product. One promoter, who asked not to be cited, informed me that after a particularly poor showing at the ticket counter for an event in Michigan, he paid a group of people to protest his own event. After informing the media, which produced stories decrying the tournament, his ticket sales substantially increased. Thus, the moral controversy surrounding the events remains one of the key reasons that many people attend them, not necessarily the promise of seeing a good competition.

One problem this raises for true fans of the tournaments is that particularly skilled fighters who win significant fights in a dramatic fashion are seldom reported on in the same way that an athlete in another venue might be discussed. All that is important is that a controversial event took place, not who performed well, scored a big upset, or perhaps emerged as a promising young rookie. The perception of thinly veiled brutality promoted both inside and outside the sport has played a significant role in its excoriation in the mainstream media.

Often when an event is organized and marketed in a particular area, the promoter must be prepared for legal action and the possibility of transferring venues. Monte Cox notes that one technique to deal with this is to schedule tournaments in a city that rests on a state border so that, if a last-minute shift is required, ticket holders can find the new location with relative ease. The first line of argument for those launching a legal challenge is that the lack of rules makes the events a form of legalized assault and battery on which the promoters profit. One legal activist in Wisconsin, Jeffrey Pawlinski, was able to halt one tournament by arguing that "it is really inappropriate, because I do not consider it a sport. I consider it a brutal spectacle" (Nichols, 1996). Because there seems to be no universal set of rules that define the sport and state athletic commissions view extreme fighting as either an unnecessary competitor to boxing or, at best, a practice completely outside their purview, the tournaments are vulnerable to these types of charges.

Perhaps the most widely covered controversy occurred in New York in 1997, when promoters of the UFC, extreme fighting's premier competition in America, sought entry into one of the most lucrative sporting markets in the world. The mayor of New York City, Rudolph Giuliani, was quick to respond, stating that "this is people brutalizing each other. I don't think something like this should be happening in New York State. I know it shouldn't happen in New York City" (Lewis & Liff, 1997, p. 3). After a brief legal struggle, the State Senate voted 33 to 0 to support any local bans on the competition. Community leaders took full advantage of the mandate, and the competition was moved to Dothan, Alabama (Van Gelder, 1997).

Certain stipulations, designed to address the lack of rules, have been proposed by opponents of the tournament. They have asked, for example, that all competitors wear headgear, a proposal that was rejected by tournament officials because this, ironically, would have posed a safety threat in a sport where headlocks and chokeholds can be used to end fights. Another stipulation was that the competitors be made to wear regulation boxing gloves. This was, of course, also rejected because it would completely eliminate all grappling and, for all intents and purposes, turn the event into a boxing contest. Thus, state officials, using the no-holds-barred rhetoric against event organizers, were able to define the event out of existence by enforcing rule parameters that imposed standards from other sports on the competition.

The intense controversy in New York did not end when the event transferred venues, because many journalists continued to report from Dothan. This reporting continued to follow preestablished patterns that dictated that the tournament be reported as a moral controversy rather than as a sporting event. One reporter summed up the contest by describing one of the early fights, during which a determined Walid Ismail failed to penetrate the defense of the first successful Japanese fighter in America, Nomi Takahashi. The writer reported, "Mr. Takahashi taunted him by running in place, then punching him in the face. Blood streamed down Mr. Ismail's cheeks like tears. An event employee wiped Mr. Ismail's blood off the mat with a white towel. It was time for the next bout" (*The New York Times Regional*, 1997, p. 43). No more cuts were opened during the competition, America got its first look at the phenomenal Vitor Belfort, and two legends of American wrestling, Dan Severn and Mark Coleman, fought in a title match; still none of these newsworthy events was mentioned, because any such description would have conceded the legitimacy of the sport. After the controversy, the practice of extreme fighting became increasingly problematic from a legal standpoint. In one case at Grand Canyon University in Arizona, a school known for its active martial arts program, a student sued the university after sustaining injuries in a class on self-defense (Steckner, 1998). The charge alleged that the instructor, a fighter known in extreme-fighting circles, had been holding sparring sessions during which the student's jaw had been broken. University officials were quick to distance themselves from the event by adopting the contradictory position that self-defense and the martial arts had a long tradition in Western culture, though the officials in no way condoned extreme fighting or encouraged its use.

One of the primary ways that many proponents of extreme fighting respond to these charges is by to pointing to high injury rates in other sports. Bob Meyrowitz, a UFC promoter involved in the New York controversy, pointed out that in Giants Stadium every Sunday, men are carried off the field with broken bones and torn ligaments, all so that team owners can profit from these injuries (Warner, 1997). The general disregard for this argument points to a telling aspect of sport culture: A spectacle such as football provides an illusion of control by requiring one of the most copious rulebooks of any sport in the world. It is not the regard for safety that is the issue, but rather the appearance that the violence is under control and the competitors are exercising a form of self-restraint dictated by a rule code. Many promoters have begun to recognize this situation and now strive to provide the appearance of regulation. Monte Cox has developed perhaps one of the most progressive sets of rules codes in the sport today, some of which protect the fighters and others simply provide the illusion of control. Fighters are now prohibited from headbutting, elbowing to the back of the neck, or delivering heel chops, and they all wear standardized protective gear. All of these rules protect fighters from potential injury. The heel chop, for example, is used by a fighter who has another in guard. The fighter then wraps his or her legs around the opponent's waist, and chops with a heel into the back of the opponent. This move is not immediately dangerous and causes little superficial damage, but it can cause kidney pain the next day. Other rules are explicitly created for cosmetic reasons, such as a prohibition against groin striking, which is impractical in a "real" fight and mitigated against by a protective device, and a rule against kicking a man while he is down, which more often than not results in the kicker's leg being grabbed and the fight turned in the other direction. Perhaps the most obvious cosmetic device is the use of rounds. This has little effect on fight safety and may disrupt the flow of the contest, but Cox notes that if viewers see something familiar, it gives the sport the appearance of control. Thus, extreme fighting has begun to employ a collection of rules that is designed to package the sport in a more rhetorically pleasing fashion, as well as enhance fighter safety.

The Curse of the Lowest Common Denominator

During the first UFC tournament, a telling event occurred. Carlton Gracie, the patriarch of a distinguished family of Brazilian Jujitsu fighters, was honored with a lifetime achievement award for his work in the martial arts. During the presentation, a solemn, 73-year-old Gracie stood by while the Denver, Colorado, crowd booed, whistled, and threw beverage containers around the arena to protest the brief lull in the violence. One preliminary conclusion this raises is that it is not the sport itself that is so objectionable, but the lower-class, blue-collar stereotypes with which it is associated. By adopting the language of the lowest common denominator, and then moving one step below it, extreme fighting advocates have participated in crafting a class boundary between themselves and legitimate sites of power. Take, for example, the controversy in Arizona, during which Senator John McCain emerged as an early enemy of the sport, a move that some argued (as it turns out, prophetically) was politically motivated and designed to improve his chances of obtaining the Presidency of the United States. Indeed, who would vote for a candidate whose home state allows thousands of screaming, drunk rednecks to cheer on a human cockfight? Election years can be lean for extreme fighting, because the manner in which its audience is constructed does not embody the ideal electorate.

In his analysis of the political commitments of boxing, John Hoberman (1984) argues that more community-based forms of government, such as socialism, resist brutal, illogical displays, whereas the totalitarian mind actively invites them, almost as if they were artistic expressions of coercion unfettered by persuasion. Interpreting the political commitments that mark a democratic sport is an interesting means to trace the ideology of the community. In America, one of the key factors that determine the viability of any form of recreation is that it is able to render a service to the existing political structure (Kraus, 1990). Athletes in mainstream sports are frequently called on to give testimonials about how their chosen sport taught them leadership, teamwork, self-worth, and so forth as a means to illustrate that the sport has value for the broader community. Public displays of violence, whether executions or extreme fighting tournaments, have been closely tied to the ethical degradation of sport and were critiqued by Enlightenment thinkers. In an analysis of the renegade nature of boxing, Don Atyeo (1979) notes that pugilistic exhibitions of brutality emerged when public executions were discouraged in Enlightenment Europe. As sensibilities became more refined, an interest in violence was perceived as a lower-class pursuit, though many members of the aristocracy remained fascinated. Thus, public violence was considered a crude and illogical act that only the mob could appreciate. As a way to help the lower classes help themselves, the aristocracy gradually drove these types of displays out of favor, and violence, which ironically turned out to be a key factor in Enlightenment policies (e.g., the use of technology in World War I), was temporarily driven underground.

During the Medieval period in Europe, the difficulties of survival and a repressive church spawned a festival culture in which people would gather in public to celebrate their existence with feasting and sometimes open displays of sexuality. Mikhail Bakhtin (1968/1984) notes that these rituals sometimes had a violent overtone, in which aggressive behavior such as burning a priest in effigy would play a key role in the development of the carnival atmosphere. There seems to be an element of catharsis present at the extreme fighting tournaments as well, primarily due to their interpenetration with the toughman contest. At these annual events, persons with little training put on a pair of boxing gloves and embark on punching frenzies that take place over the space of three one-minute rounds in which good defense is eclipsed by the willingness to behave aggressively. Events are performed in festive atmospheres with excesses of alcohol and ring girls wearing highly revealing apparel, which clearly locate them outside the bounds of family entertainment. The smaller extreme fighting tournaments still rely heavily on exotic dancers, who are sometimes used extensively when a fight card runs short due to quick bouts. Although this carnival atmosphere promotes some fan interest, it also reduces the importance of the competition. With professional or collegiate cheerleaders, though they clearly are present to elicit sexual arousal, there is at least a pretense of athletic or performative ability. Simply parading a woman with large breasts around a cage in a piece of lingerie reduces the expression of sexuality to its crudest and most raw form. The presentation of sexuality becomes a pure spectacle, not an attempt to generate team spirit.

Because the fans of extreme fighting are drawn heavily from the toughman culture, extreme fighting promoters have had to embark on an educational program for those who attend the tournaments. Take, for example, the first UFC held in Japan. Because the martial arts originated in Japan, audiences are familiar with various types of holds and joint locks. They will remain perfectly quiet until they see something to get excited about, such as one fighter almost cinching a knee lock, a hold that can take as long as five minutes to apply. When Kazushi Sakuraba defeated a much larger Brazilian, Marcus Conan Silvera, through the application of standing arm bar, his prowess was reported in many of the Japanese newspapers, and overnight, he became a national hero. Most Japanese fighters are now known for their flashy holds and creative locks, and the pure puncher, such as the UFC's Tank Abbott, is considered crude and inelegant. Thus, promoters have had to civilize the tastes of American fans so that they can understand the nuances of what is going on during the fight. This trend is apparent on the Internet, which is now the primary means by which tournament information is distributed. In an essay on gender relationships on the Internet, Laura Miller (1995) notes this terrain is often highly masculine and that its anonymity sometimes promotes hypermasculine aggression. Web sites devoted to extreme fighting often are no exception, and message boards abound with comments from teenage boys who threaten to beat, kill, and rape one another. After the New York controversy, many cable stations dumped the UFC events that had relied on pay-per-view for their viewership (now, less than 15 percent of households have access to the event). This blockage has led to an Internet campaign in which promoters urge fans to write and telephone cable companies to protest the blackout. Some initial failures in this campaign led Monte Cox to forward a message to all potential advocates asking them not to threaten cable company officials or use profanity when making their requests. Thus, the event promoters find themselves in a continual battle to civilize the appetites of the audience to which they are marketing their product so that they appear more like sports fans and less like a mob.

One promising avenue for legitimacy leads many proponents of the sport to the past, specifically to ancient Athens and the first Olympics, where the *pankration* formed the basis for all organized competition. Although these events also were controversial, this return to the classical roots of the sport has brought it some respect. Recent specials on both The Learning Channel and The History Channel have interspersed fighter interviews with discussions of the Greek Olympic culture. An interesting outcome of this discussion was one historian's observation that one of the greatest Greek champions would break his opponents' fingers until they quit. When this technique was suddenly remembered, several champions suddenly fell prey to "small joint manipulation," and the technique was quickly banned, much as it had been in ancient Greece. More important, this discussion has led to a serious debate among the Olympic committee about what it means to hold Olympic Games without the first and primary competitive spectacle. If *pankration* were to find its way back into the Games, it would move that sport much closer to cultural authenticity. With a connection to what is considered the pinnacle not only of skill, but also of moral legitimacy, promoters continue to battle against the stereotype of the drunk redneck in Alabama screaming obscenities when a fighter elects to use a more refined or defensive technique.

Moral Purgation and the Bad Man

In Western culture, sport and moral exhibition traditionally have been intertwined with an ethic that sometimes comes into conflict with the precepts of pure competition. Paul Plass (1995), drawing heavily on Rene Girard, notes that during the Roman games, sport and legal punishment were often blended. In these games, a villain might be forced to wear a sack over his head, be whipped, and fight wild dogs with nothing but a stick—not very sporting by current standards. Yet Plass writes that "the efficacy of public violence designed to deflect or absorb external danger comes in large measure from the shock its own abnormality administers" (p. 31). The public humiliation of a ready scapegoat maintained the moral order by integrating the villain's punishment with sport entertainment that, though both extreme and brutal, was perceived as just. It was when sport was divorced from criminal punishment as a result of European legal reforms that the exhibition of violence for the sake of itself became highly discouraged, if not outlawed.

Lacking the moral efficacy once accorded displays of violence, promoters and advocates of extreme fighting have crafted a discourse that attempts to maintain the dramatic intensity that the sport's deviant status generates while appealing to the moral narratives that mainstream sport ideally embodies. The question this raises is, why does a fighter win a competition? Is it superior athletic skill, or does the competitor work hard and illustrate good teamwork? Does a franchise win because the owner has spent excessive amounts on his or her payroll, or does it win because the team has come together around a winning strategy? For sport in America, with its connections to youth culture, this dilemma is a tightrope. It is often not enough to win; the winner also must appear morally deserving of that victory or the entire sport will be called into question (e.g., the 1998 World Series victory by the Florida Marlins; Ray Lewis as the most valuable player in the 2001 Super Bowl).

The most celebrated extreme fighter in America has been the UFC's David "Tank" Abbott, a fighter who clearly embodies this ethical dilemma for the burgeoning sport. If Tank could be said to embody an ethic, it is probably close to Thomas Hobbes's (1962) notion of the "will to power," according to which the naturally aggressive instincts of human beings must be regulated by a social contract designed to protect the vulnerable. With each beating he administers, Tank decries his opponents' lack of preparation and effeminate qualities, declaring, in effect, that they deserved to be hurt for even daring to enter the cage with such a man as himself. This taunting flies in the face of the traditional martial arts ethics, which emphasize fair play and congratulatory reconciliation after each match. Tank became a celebrity not for his fighting ability (his record is barely above .500), but for his psychological demeanor both in and outside the cage. Audiences hang on Tank's wit, such as the time he was asked his opinion about the Brazilian fighting that sometimes calls for the use of a short, oriental robe called a gee. Tank replied smugly that *he* would never wear a kimono. Although most of the athletes that enter the upper-level competitions are in phenomenally good shape, many writers focus on Tank's potbelly and alcoholism as the archetypal style and body type of the sport (Ferrell, 1997). Tank is not an athlete, but a criminal and rebel who smiled while beating a downed opponent. By winning enough fights against skilled opponents (though never winning a tournament), Tank has been able to maintain the idea that the competition is about brute force rather than skill and, more important, that it promotes aggressive and criminal behavior.

In the late 1990s, the sport was placed under heavy scrutiny in Canada, leading to another major controversy when the Mohawk nation decided to hold the banned events in Indian territory (Da Costa, 1998). The sport was becoming an illicit sideshow, much like the casinos sometimes associated with Native American reservations, a form of moral rebellion in the face of common sense and community judgment.

The degrading effect that extreme fighting might have on society quickly became a serious issue. In a report by George Lundberg of the American Medical Association calling for the complete ban of the sport, he elected to focus on the barbaric nature of the events rather than the actual threat to personal safety that they posed (Winkeljohn, 1997). It was not the threat of potential injury that was most concerning, but rather the possibility that this unethical behavior would spread to the youth culture. During the New York controversy, Governor George Pataki became one of the most outspoken critics of the UFC's proposed tournament, noting that "someone who wins by using choke holds and kicking people while they are down is not someone our children should be looking to emulate" (Dao, 1997, p. 5). Pataki was careful to point out that the issue was not athletic success, but the manner in which the victory is achieved.

This distinction can also be seen in an elementary school controversy in California, in which Paul Varelans, a fighter known for both his exceptional size and his exceptional sportsmanship in the cage, was scheduled to talk to a group of students about the martial arts and self-esteem. School officials came under fire once Varelans's background was discovered, though his appearance had nothing to do with his tournament background. One mother interviewed outside of the school simply stated, "[I]t seems like they could find a better role model" (Wilson, 1996, p. A21). A primary concern with the ethical nature of extreme fighting seems to revolve around the potentially low ethical standards held by particular fighters and the resultant potential for these standards to leak into the youth culture.

The crux of this argument pertains to the possibility that the individual psychology of certain competitors, such as the colorful Tank, will function as a roadmap for young men to give full vent to their aggressive tendencies. Unlike Charles Barkley and his famous "I am not a role model" comment, Tank seems to take a certain amount of pleasure in presenting himself as a object for emulation and reveling in the glory that his antisocial behavior theoretically promotes, such as rumors that circulated that he drank too much and beat his girlfriends. When asked about these rumors, Tank responded that sometimes a man just has to lay down the law. A particularly telling exchange occurred during an Internet chat that coincided with a UFC tournament featuring a question-and-answer session with this controversial icon. Someone asked Tank who was responsible for knocking his two front teeth out, and Tank responded that it had been his father, the only guy he truly respected. If Jungian, gender psychologists were to review this exchange, it might remind them of Robert Bly's

(1990) *Iron John* and the crisis of modern masculinity. According to Bly's thesis, to become a man, the wounded boy must come to grips with the pain inflicted on him by his father and recognize, as many overly effeminate men today do not, that in this wound there is strength. True manhood is only achieved when the man recognizes the pain of maturation, a key element in a sporting culture in which a young boy who drops a ball on the baseball field might be expected to be chastised by a disappointed father.

In this exchange, Tank also illustrates the confessional mind that Michel Foucault (1977) notes is so critical to the maintenance of community rationality. When the accused is brought into the public forum, they must recognize, in front of witnesses, the error of their behaviors and the moral irrationality of their acts. In Tank's case, the confession is not one of moral degradation, but rather one that points to natural male development. In a world in which the "girly man" (to quote a famous *Saturday Night Live* skit) has come to dominate, Tank still preserves the boundaries of something that many fans perceive as true manhood. In his universe, sport is nonexistent, and there is only one way to gauge rationality—through the competing poles of domination and submission.

REALITY OR EXCESS?

By calling a sport "extreme fighting," organizers communicate two things to a consuming public. The first is that what they are going to see is real, and the second is that what they are going to see is excessive. This expectation has established an interesting tension between the mixed martial arts and the world of professional wrestling, two realms that may appeal to the same audience and often are confused with each other by untrained observers. In professional wrestling, gymnastic, charismatic actors perform violent morality plays that pit good against evil for a largely adolescent male audience, and drama takes precedence over actual competition. The manhood of one fighter is challenged, and that fighter is called out to defend the honor of his country, girlfriend, principles, or whatever else. These events are usually given titles to indicate the nature of the fiction that is taking place. Extreme fighting tournaments, in an attempt to capitalize on the lucrative videotape distribution market found in professional wrestling, will sometimes bill events in a similar fashion with names like "Redemption," "Revenge of the Warriors," "Return of the Beast," "Judgment Day," "Young Guns," or "Superbrawl." Characterizing unscripted events in this fashion represents an attempt to apply moral coherence by mimicking the promotion of professional wrestling to appropriate an existing audience familiar with the hyperbolic performance of these scripted matches. This choice is important for those promoters who are attempting to bill their shows as "reality combat." In the case of professional wrestling, the notion that something is "raw" does not mean that it is more real, but instead that the performance is even more excessive than usual. By locating itself at this juncture between the real and the fictive, extreme fighting has set itself in a position that creates difficult expectations about the legitimacy of the sport.

Often, when critics attend tournaments and find that the violence level is not as high as they have been led to believe, the primary response is to say that "nothing" happened or that the event was a disappointment. One journalist described the violation of his anticipation of one event after the extensive controversy surrounding it created an expectation of profound violence as a disillusionment sparked by the realization that the fighting was actually not "extreme" in any way (Muller, 1997). He went on to note that his primary response was boredom (Muller, 1997). This experience represents one of the primary paradoxes of extreme fighting, because if "something" happens, then the sport is viewed as morally controversial, and if "nothing" happens, then it is a disappointment that does not live up to viewers' expectations. After events that do not feature a significant proportion of knockouts, some audience members will respond much as one spectator did after a tournament in Arizona (the same one from which Senator McCain sought to distance himself): "They got a bunch of little girls wearing tutus. . . . If I wanted to see wrestling, I'd watch my kids. They could definitely use more fist-to-fist action and blood" (Shaffer, 1998, p. 1). Thus, the reliance on the wrestling model, though it brings in a ready fan base, ultimately leads to substantial disappointment because the fighters are not equipped, nor would it be practical for them, to turn in "larger-than-life" performances. Rather than fulfilling the hyperbolic expectations of professional wrestling, extreme fighting is driven by the tactics of particular fighters for whom a patient strategy increases their chances of victory. When this happens, the popular press disregards these techniques as failures, despite the competitive success they bring to particular fighters, and thereby focus attention on the spectacle rather than on the sport.

The lack of excessive brutality also leads many writers to speculate that the true excess of the sport may revolve around sexuality rather than violence. John Marks (1997), for example, argues that "most of the time, the sport looks less like a genuine street brawl than an unappetizing X-rated film—beefy men committing banal acts under hot lights" (p. 46). Marks probably is referring to the appearance of the Brazilian guard, a strategically advantageous position from which a fighter baits a stronger opponent into a submission hold, which is quite similar to the missionary sexual position. Giles Whittell (1998) also notes that "the fighters spent long minutes grunting and slithering in and out of awkward clinches like actors in a homoerotic *Kama Sutra* for the big and tall" (p. 31). The move between the notions of extreme violence and X-rated content appears to have been quite natural for the popular press and even, on some occasions, for the fighters themselves. While being shown a tape of himself sitting on Paul Varelans and striking to the head, Tank Abbott suggested, "[Y]ou had better turn that off. I am getting sexually excited." In a subsequent fight, after losing in a quick knockout to the talented Brazilian Vitor Belfort (whom Tank called "cute" in a prefight interview), Tank summarized the fight by saying, "What can I think of him? I didn't even taste him. I got to s— his c— but he didn't even c—" (Whittell, 1998, p. 31). Turning to crude and unrestrained sexual commentary often functions to replace what was viewed as a poor performance. Even though the athletic skill was not there, the excess remains in place; obscenity simply replaces the violence. When excessive brutality is absent, other scandals must be sought to justify the marginalization of the spectacle.

This reasoning is not to say that those who are looking for brutality are always disappointed. In March 1998 in the Ukraine, "something" did happen. American fighter Douglas Dedge entered a no-holds-barred tournament, and while two referees, his corner attendants, and a crowd of hundreds looked on, he was beaten to death in public. In the action of the fight, the referee did not interfere quickly enough, and Dedge's trainers failed to report a medical condition that had led to blackouts prior to the event. He sustained a minute's worth of head blows with no protection until his opponent refused to fight any further. The video of this fight, which has already circulated on the Internet, led critics and promoters to condemn the event. Yet the death of Dedge indicates that the reality of extreme fighting has an excessive potential if tournament promoters are poorly prepared. In their book *Killing for Culture*, David Kerekes and David Slater (1995) argue that reality death videos, or "shockumentaries" as they are sometimes called, blur the gap between the performance and the reality of death. Viewers often feel that showing real violence in some way violates the ethics established by mainstream cinema, which dictate clean, aesthetic representations of these acts. When wrestler Owen Hart fell to his death in front of millions of fans during a pay-per-view event while attempting to rappel into the ring, it functioned as brief interruption in the fiction, though many fans assumed it was part of the performance. Both events likely soon will be fodder for shockumentary compilations. In Dedge's case, critics can say that his death was more than an unfortunate accident; it was the result of a sport, lacking in restraint and morals, achieving its ultimate *telos* in a way that the mythical snuff film never has: the murder of a human being for entertainment and profit. Despite the poor management of the tournament in the Ukraine, this incident will remain the single largest hurdle for event promoters to overcome. When an athlete such as a racecar driver is killed, the unfortunate event functions as an opportunity to revisit existing safety issues and regulations. In the case of extreme fighting, the blending of excess and reality lead the consuming public to view death or injury as a logical outcome rather than an aberration.

CONCLUSION

In his essay examining the role of *eros* in the maintenance of civilization, Sigmund Freud (1961) notes that society is composed of two competing forces: a death instinct that isolates persons through their violent drive to dominate and a sexual desire that forms the loose basis for all social institutions. This bleak view was revised by Herbert Marcuse (1955/1966), who noted that "the death instinct is not destructive for its own sake, but for the relief of tension. The descent towards death is an unconscious flight from pain and want. It is an expression of the eternal struggle against suffering and repression" (p. 29). Through the history of sport in America, this violent instinct has seemed to find one of its primary avenues for expression. By acknowledging this violent instinct, then channeling it in a rational manner, society is able to preserve its sense of moral consistency. The pounding hit on the football field is not an act of pure aggression but rather the act of a player who is working hard and who illustrates the competitive spirit by sacrificing his body to forward the goals of his team. What this chapter illustrates is that the process by which these logics develop in a sport context is gradual. Football is not rational because of any essential nature of the sport itself but because we actively ascribe that rationality to it. Extreme fighting has yet to gain any such legitimacy, and therefore, complaints that it is irrational or morally inconsistent continue to plague it.

It is, however, important to note that the nature of martial arts in America is changing permanently. The old karate model is now outdated, and schools that feature grappling training in the United States are increasing. If an instructor cannot teach a six-year-old child to do a triangle choke, the training is often considered outdated if not worthless. This trend suggests that extreme fighting will gradually shed its renegade status and move into the mainstream, where its excesses will decrease and its competitors can sell Gatorade uninhibited by detractors, just like athletes in other sports.

This conclusion does not mean that a systematic analysis of violence in sport culture is not worth discussing. Cultural critics such as Henry Giroux (1996) argue that young people now live in a fragmented culture in which anything that is considered outside the margins, an outlaw discourse, is a viable means to deal with the emptiness and economic deprivation that they experience. Although extreme fighting has not yet moved into inner cities to exploit the athletic talent of the urban poor as boxing has, this move may be one outcome of the eventual legitimacy of the sport. In the 1999 film *Fight Club*, audiences were exposed to a narrative that linked deep play to the alienation of contemporary masculinity. Indeed, many groups adopt the moniker "fight club" to describe their organizations, even though the violence experienced is more regulated than that portrayed in the film.

Another question this raises is why this sport, which is the oldest in the world, has suddenly reemerged now. Kirby Farrell (1998) offers some insight by describing the culture of the 1990s as one marked by trauma, a stressful event that causes a person to live out the violent episode in a symbolic fashion time and time again. Although the exact genesis of this trauma in modern culture is unclear, there seems to be a clear link between "reality programming" and violence, as well as with the desire to replay it among the mass media on a daily, if not hourly, basis. Whether the emergence of these tournaments stems from alienation or simple *mimesis*, the tournaments are beginning the challenge the moral boundaries of legitimate composition. Case studies such as this provide a unique opportunity to examine the process by which sport participates in the ritual reification of community values and the way that certain leaders seek to convince themselves and others that, despite a community's excess, our deep play is under control.

REFERENCE LIST

Atyeo, Don. (1979). *Blood and guts: Violence in sports*. New York: Paddington.

Bakhtin, Mikhail. (1968/1984). *Rabelais and his world* (Helen Iswolsky, Trans.). Bloomington: Indiana UP.

Bly, Robert. (1990). *Iron John: A book about men*. Reading, MA: Addison-Wesley.

Burke, Kenneth. (1968). *A rhetoric of motives*. Berkeley: University of California Press.

Da Costa, Norman. (1998, March 20). Mohawk chief defiant on ultimate fighting. *Toronto Star*, p. B9.

Dao, James. (1996, February 26). Pataki signs bill barring ultimate fighting. *New York Times*, p. 5.

Farrell, Kirby. (1998). *Post-traumatic culture: Injury and interpretation in the nineties*. Baltimore, MD: Johns-Hopkins University Press.

Ferrell, David. (1997, November 1). Out of bounds: A sport fights for its life. *Los Angeles Times*, p. 1.

Fine, Gary Alan. (1992). The depths of deep play: The rhetoric and resources of morally controversial leisure. *Play and Culture, 5,* 250.

Foucault, Michel. (1977). *Discipline and punish: The birth of the prison*. (Alan Sheridan, Trans.). New York: Random House.

Freud, Sigmund. (1961). *Civilization and its discontents*. (James Strachey, Trans.). New York: Norton.

Geertz, Clifford. (1972). Deep play: Notes on a Balinese cockfight. *Daedalus, 101,* 1–27.

Giroux, Henry. (1996). *Fugitive cultures: Race, violence, and youth*. New York: Routlege.

Golden, Mark. (1998). *Sport and society in ancient Greece*. Cambridge: Cambridge UP.

Hobbes, Thomas. (1962). *Leviathan*. London: Collier-Macmillan.

Hoberman, John. (1984). *Sport and political ideology*. Austin: University of Texas Press.

Kerekes, David, & Slater, David. (1995). *Killing for culture: An illustrated history of death film from mondo to snuff*. San Francisco: Creation Books.

Kraus, Richard. (1990). *Recreation and leisure in modern society*. Glenview, IL: Foresman.

Lewis, David, & Liff, Bob. (1997, January 19). Matches made in hell: Rudy vows to KO bloodsport. *New York Daily News*, p. 3.

Marcuse, Herbert. (1955/1966). *Eros and civilization: A philosophical inquiry into Freud*. Boston: Beacon.

Marks, John. (1997, February 24). Whatever it takes to win. *U.S. News and World Report*, p. 46.

Miller, Laura. (1995). Women and children first: Gender and the settling of the electronic frontier. In James Brook and Iain Boal (Eds.), *Resisting the virtual life: The culture and politics of information*, pp. 53–62. San Francisco: City Lights.

Muller, Bill. (1997, Oct. 9). The ultimate disappointment: No rules fighting falls flat. *The Arizona Republic*, p. 44.

Nasaw, David. (1993). *Going out: The rise and fall of public amusements*. New York: HarperCollins.

New York Times Regional. (1997, February 9). Meanwhile, in Alabama, the fight is family fare. *New York Times*, p. 43.

Nichols, Mike. (1996, June 13). Bouts could be blocked. *Milwaukee Journal Sentinel*, p. 1.

Plass, Paul. (1995). *The game of death in ancient Rome: Arena sport and political suicide*. Madison: University of Wisconsin Press.

Shaffer, Mark. (1995, December 11). Extreme disappointment: Fights not as fierce as rumored, fans at rage complain. *The Arizona Republic*, p. 1.

Steckner, Susie. (1998, January 30). Sparring injuries spur suit: Ultimate fighting alleged by student. *The Arizona Republic*, p. A20.

Van Gelder, Lawrence. (1997, February 6). Promoter postpones fight in Manhattan. *New York Times*, p. 7.

Warner, Gene. (1997, January 26). Crowd pleasing attraction triggers heated debate. *The Buffalo News*, p. 1B.

Whittell, Giles. (1998, April 4). Mortal combat. *The New York Times Magazine*, p. 31.

Wilson, Marshall. (1996, October 25). School's chief KO's speech by ultimate fighter. *The San Francisco Chronicle*, p. A21.

Winkeljohn, Matt. (1997, May 25). All sports risky. *The Atlanta Journal and Constitution*, p. 14E.

CHAPTER 7

The Resignification of Risk in Marketing Whitewater: Ritual Initiation and the Mythology of River Culture

Elliot Gaines

A SEMIOTIC CONSTRUCTION OF CULTURE AND THE SPORT PRODUCT

At the 1964 World's Fair in Flushing Meadows, New York, the automated amusement park–style rides sponsored by industrial giants like General Motors, Ford, and General Electric seemed to say that in the future, the successful evolution of industry and technology would provide so much affluence and free time that many people would actually work at jobs that involved doing things usually considered play. Leisure-time entertainment, recreation, and sports have indeed become big business and significant factors in American and world cultures. In considering the importance of the outdoor sport industry, this chapter examines sport communication through the semiotic construction of cultural identity among whitewater-rafting professionals. The purpose of this chapter is to demonstrate how the nature of risk in whitewater rafting is translated through the cultural strata of the business. I examine the historicity of the whitewater industry and trace the expression of the experience from adventure to commercial product.

BIRTH OF THE INDUSTRY

Around the same time as the 1964 World's Fair, whitewater rafting came into being as a commercial recreational sport. Sports are generally signified by physical activities, sometimes organized as games or competitions, that require certain skills, physical and mental, as well as such character-building qualities as teamwork, integrity, and determination. Sport is generally regarded as leisure, ". . . activities which are an end in themselves, a sort of physical art for art's sake, governed by specific rules, increasingly irreducible to any functional necessity, and inserted into a specific calendar" (Bourdieu, 1991, p. 359). Looking at the "whole range of sporting activities and entertainments . . . as a supply intended to meet a social demand," Bourdieu examines the social history of sport to "lay the real foundations of the legitimacy of a social science of sport as a distinct *scientific object* (which is not at all self-evident)" (pp. 357–359).

Beyond the limits of games and competition, this study considers "sport" in the context of the physical embodiment of participation in whitewater rafting and the social conditions that define a specific culture located in southern West Virginia. The cultural identity of these outdoor-recreation professionals (ORPs) is constituted by the embodied experience of specific activities performed simply for their own pleasure and challenge that are structured in relation to customers or guests that necessarily live outside the ethos of river life. Leisure studies and sports communication, building on this notion of production and consumption of sport, must explore "the constitution of the field and its esoteric culture" (Bourdieu, 1991, p. 359). In a remote location in the economically isolated state of West Virginia, the New River attracts in excess of 120,000 tourists each year—nearly half the visitors to all the rivers in the state (Leatherman, 1998). Much to the chagrin of many ORPs, the social conditions that enable the existence of their culture depend on the commercial success of the business.

Understanding a phenomenon such as an outdoor recreational business involves the study of many dimensions of culture and communication. A great body of scholarship addressing media and cultural studies has been produced "where semiotics provide the tools to demystify the ideological, verbal and visual signifying processes that are brought into modern consumer society through glossy magazine advertisements and aggressive TV commercials" (Schroder, 1991, p. 178). My strategy here is to apply these tools to the culture of ORPs engaged in whitewater rafting.

The people involved in providing the services for the operation of sports and recreational businesses need special skills and expertise specific to their particular activity to provide for the safety and enjoyment of participants. The lifestyle associated with many people dedicated to such activities constitutes its own culture. Not motivated by common American desires for material comforts and financial security, ORPs privilege their freedom to do what they love. In the words of one whitewater professional, "a bad day on the river is better than a good day at the office" (Krueger, 1998).

This chapter focuses on the semiotic structures of communication that distinguish the culture of whitewater-rafting professionals and their relationship with commercial customers that pay to share in the experience of the river. As methods for sport communication research, semiotics, phenomenology, and ethnography imbricate to examine the identity of whitewater rafters. Lanigan (1997) suggests that phenomenology is "a good description of the human world of perception, that locates a human world of expression" (p. 382). Identity is inscribed in the bodies of participants, the sport itself as a product, and the various levels of communication and ritual that are distinct to whitewater rafting.

THE COMMERCIAL CULTURE

As parts of a commercial business that has only existed for 30 years, West Virginia rivers attract almost 250,000 people annually, compared with 200 in 1968 (Leatherman, 1998). Considering how recently the business was invented, the semiotic structure of whitewater rafting as a sports product and the cultural identity of its participants raises interesting questions. Observing that sport functions as spectacle, entertainment, and activity, Bourdieu (1991) raises the following questions:

If such a model is adopted, . . . is there an area of production endowed with its own logic and its own history, in which "sports products" are generated . . . and what are the social conditions of possibility of appropriation of the various "sports products" that are thus produced? (p. 357)

Addressing these questions in the context of whitewater rafting, we must examine the history and nature of the activity that define it as a sport, the communication structure of marketing, and the cultural distinctions between production and consumption of the sports product.

As depicted in films like *The River Wild*, starring Meryl Streep (Hanson, 1994), the connotation of whitewater rafting is an adventurous sporting activity that is not for the faint of heart. Marketing strategies shift the context of meaning in promotional literature that states there is "a trip for everyone" (Cook, 1998, p. 24). During the 1990s, the fastest-growing whitewater market was families and children (Leatherman, 1998).

Jerry Cook (personal communication, 1998), president of ACE Whitewater and Adventure Center, asserts that rafting is the only commercial sport in which people who probably do not know each other must work together as a team. Rafting is a sport, not because of competition, but by virtue of cooperation and teamwork. The guide must communicate with people of various levels of experience, or more often, no experience, on the river to navigate the raft safely through the rapids. According to Hyde (1991), the New River is almost ideal

for commercial rafting in that the trip takes a day, with the first rapids being moderately difficult—ideal for learning paddling techniques early on. As the river enters the gorge with rugged mountains on either side, the river is restricted, and the gradient becomes steeper, creating numerous difficult rapids. By mid-trip, rafters are in the big stuff, and everyone is wet, yelling and paddling like mad. (p. 77).

Participants may represent variable ages, races, classes, genders, and physical abilities and conditioning. Great effort goes into giving commands for the crew to paddle the raft while the guide navigates, which is necessary because a boat must move faster than the current to be steered. At the same time, the guide must entertain the customers with local history, river stories, and conversation when floating through flat water. As a trainee at ACE Whitewater, I had to learn the names of the creeks that fed the river, the old towns, and landmarks; be certified in first aid and CPR; learn safety procedures; and master raft navigational skills.

Some people really do not understand the hazards of the river and assume it must be safe or it would not be marketed to the general public. According to senior guide Jack Lund (personal communication, 1998), who has more than 15 years of experience guiding, many guests simply do not belong on the river and risk great harm through ignorance. Before going on the river, every rafter listens to a talk about certain hazards and procedures. This "safety talk" is a by-product of the culture and the result of legal requirements designed to suggest the worst-case scenario of what could happen on a rafting trip (Cook, 1998a). Class V rafting is *defined* as hazardous. Rafting companies, to comply with the demands of insurance companies and state laws, deliver ritual safety talks and use release forms that both articulate the hazards of participation and explicitly designate responsibility to the participant and not the company. Thus, the growth of the rafting business depends on guests attracted to an adventure vacation, but many people dismiss the liability forms and safety talks as routine formalities, as if they were all part of the show. Indeed, advances in equipment and technology, guide training and experience, and safety regulation have made rafting possible for more people.

Whitewater rafting means different things to different people. Between the first-time rafter and the experienced adventurer, the real concerns for a safe and pleasant experience on the river depend on individual experience and the interpretation of the available information embedded in the literature, insurance forms, and safety talks. To better understand the potential for meaning, we must examine these phenomena in the context of the semiotic organizational structure of the culture.

CULTURE AND STRUCTURE OF THE WHITEWATER-RAFTING BUSINESS

Jerry Cook, as the president of ACE Whitewater and Adventure Center, acts as a creative leader and represents a designated role in a secondary semiotic field (Askegaard, 1991). As the history of a culture is expressed, certain "emblems" serve to identify that culture symbolically (Askegaard, 1991, p. 16). In this case, Cook's early experiences as a guide serve as emblems signifying an identity within the culture. As an entrepreneur who has helped develop the rafting business, he enters a secondary semiotic field that extends his cultural identity through a prospective view of the future of commercial outdoor recreation. Semiotically, a leader is a dynamic position that extends across a time line from the past into the future and thereby demands a broad vision of his or her field. Historically situated within the ethos of river culture, Cook must understand the limits of the appeal of outdoor adventure to those outside the culture.

Askegaard diagrams cultural identity on vertical and horizontal axes. The horizontal axis denotes time, with the past to the left and the future to the right (Askegaard, 1991). The past, or retrospective, suggests stability, whereas the future, or prospective, suggests change. The vertical axis represents the individual and "coalescence" of the cultural community below and interaction with others outside the immediate culture above (Askegaard, 1991).

This model has been adapted to demonstrate how the rafting cultural identity is structured within society. The horizontal axis is a time line that begins on the left in 1964 with the invention or idea of commercial whitewater rafting. The future advances to the right. The top of the vertical line represents all the people in the world who are not specifically involved in river culture. Across the horizontal time line, there is the river culture. At the intersection of the two cultures, first-time rafters merge with the outer perimeter of the river culture. Return rafters are located deeper within the river culture, and adventurous rafters advance even further, close to the heart of the culture. Weekend warriors and part-time guides with regular jobs are again deeper into the structure that represents river culture. The guides live at the heart of the culture.

As explained previously, a whitewater business leader is situated along the intersection of the two cultures. The leader's identity begins in the past as an adventurer or river enthusiast. Moving toward the future, the leader becomes an entrepreneur with a vision of sustaining river culture through commercial growth and development.

The entrepreneur brings the ontology of rafting into focus as a business. Thus, the leader looks to the future of the culture as a business while remaining in the area where river culture interacts with general society. Cook (personal communication, 1998), for example, expresses a retrospective history in his vision of the future because he has been involved in the development of the outdoor adventure industry for 26 years. Along the way, he has acquired the emblems of river culture through the enactment of the rituals and initiations that are essential to the cultural identity. For example, in conceiving promotional materials for his company, Cook (personal communication, 1998) suggests that video and catalog information should be organized according to popular interest rather than some categorical logic. He notes that people tend to look for action and appeal rather than practicalities until they are ready to buy (Cook, personal communication, 1998). Thus, his vision must integrate others so that consumers can visualize themselves enjoying whitewater rafting.

Staff meetings are conducted at ACE Adventure Center to discuss the business, policy, and strategy; air grievances between employees and management; and enjoy a social evening of pizza, beer, and talk. Lee Fuqua (personal communication, 1998), a manager and partner at ACE and another example of an outdoor-recreation entrepreneur, publishes a newsletter to help organize general information and the meeting. He demonstrates concern about employee satisfaction and understands the impact that employee satisfaction has on the guests' experience. According to Mark Nadler (personal communication, 1998), this exemplifies "that the people selling the product are still engaged in a lifestyle manner with the product." A guide's commitment to the lifestyle and adventure of rafting can seem extreme to guests, but it also enhances the experience. The guide embodies the culture and serves as the ritual initiator for the whitewater-rafting experience. Thus, the success of the outdoor-recreation business is strongly dependent on employee satisfaction. The guides simply would not be there if they did not love what they do.

BRACKETING THE RESEARCHER

Whitewater rafting is distinct from what is ordinarily considered a sport. The people who choose to become guides like the spontaneity and challenges of competing with nature. They want to know the river and be able to maneuver through its force. Thus, the cultural identity of experienced rafters is embodied in practice and understood as an acknowledgment of a particular concept of reality and beliefs. Along these lines, Berger and Luckmann (1967) endeavor "to define 'reality' as a quality appertaining to phenomena that we recognize as having a being independent of our own volition ('we cannot wish them away'), and to define 'knowledge' as the certainty that phenomena are real and that they possess specific characteristics" (p. 1). As in any culture, whitewater-rafting guides find (the hazards and rewards of) their lifestyle in concert with the world as they know it.

I came to this study because, after several experiences on the river, I liked rafting and had questions about the communicative processes of river navigation, the knowledge of the guides, and the nature of the business. During the summer of 1998, I officially began to train as a whitewater-rafting guide on the New River in West Virginia. As a participant observer, I became friends with my coresearchers. I camped out in a tent in a mountainous, forested area shared by other guides and visitors and usually spent five hours each day on the river. My awareness of rafting came from my occasional participation as a tourist over a 10-year period. In 1997, I became friendly with some guides who had gotten me interested in the sport and its culture. At that time, I asked several guides where they expected to be in five years. The response was generally limited to, "I'll probably be back here next season." Having evaded the question, I would persist with, "What will you do when the season is over?" Not surprisingly, most guides responded that they worked in another recreational industry, such as skiing, or went to some place like Costa Rica to guide whitewater in the winter. Most of the people were in their 20s. Those approaching 30 years of age tended to have questions and concerns about their future, but most maintained that whatever happened, they wanted to continue making their living in outdoor recreation. Survivors in their 40s and 50s generally were entrepreneurs in the recreational business, had worked their way into the management, or had alternative seasonal careers.

Living and working daily at the river, I began to adapt to the perceptions and practices of river culture. Like the habitus of any coculture such as a corporation, ethnic group, or institution, ORPs construct cultural patterns of behavior and beliefs. Habitus is a phenomenological concept that addresses the preconscious generation and organization of practices and representations (Bourdieu, 1993). With regard to the discursive elements that code the everyday lives of professional rafting people, the habitus provides the "principles which generate and organize practices and representations[,] . . . embodied history, internalized as a second nature and so forgotten as history[, and] . . . the active presence of the whole past of which it is a product" (Bourdieu, 1993, p. 483). As I began to experience my river training, my experience was a ritual reenactment of the habitus of the guides instructing me.

My participation in this research involved training to be a whitewater-rafting guide at ACE Adventure Center in Minden, West Virginia. As a participant and observer, I had to bracket my many preconceptions about the project. In the context of the culture of the ORPs, I was a beginner in my late 40s, I had a career as an academic professional, and, as I began training, I was out of shape and overweight. Considering the nature of whitewater rafting, my lack of skill and experience, my poor physical conditioning, and the guides' responsibilities for the safety of others, I began a careful process of observing the ontology and phenomenology of perception I experienced as a trainee. The balance of the data emerged through daily observations and interviews. As I lived with, observed, and recorded the words of my coresearchers, I endeavored to follow Orbe's (1998) cocultural theory and "present specific communicative behaviors as described from the standpoint(s) of co-cultural group members" (p. 14).

The notion of sport communication as a discipline fed my perceptions of daily activities on the river, of the people, and of the unique geographic conditions provided by the New and Gauley Rivers in West Virginia. The development of rafting as a commercial sport is directly connected to these conditions.

HISTORICAL GROUNDING OF RIVER CULTURE

The history and mythology of rafting is tied to early Native Americans and river explorers. As was suggested to me by the 1964 World's Fair, the invention of rafting as a sport emerged through the technological developments and economic conditions that allowed for leisure-time activity. The military and some adventurous souls had tried wooden boats on the rivers, but it was the development of vulcanized neoprene technology during World War II that first made it possible to build rafts durable enough for whitewater rafting (Cook, personal communication, 1998). Commercial rafting began around 1963 in Pennsylvania on the Youghiogheny River when Karl Kreuger and Lance Martin first started taking people out on whitewater adventure trips through their Wilderness Voyagers. By 1964, one of their associates, Jon Dragan, had arrived at the New River in Fayette County, West Virginia, and eventually started Wildwater Expeditions (Cook, personal communication, 1998; Kreuger, personal communication, 1998; Leatherman, 1998). As the company names suggest, whitewater rafting was promoted as an adventurous activity. Before the interstate highway system came to West Virginia, even getting to the remote, mountainous area near the river was a challenge. Movies such as *Deliverance* in the early 1970s and, more recently, *The River Wild*, with Meryl Streep and Kevin Bacon, helped bring rafting into popular awareness (Cook, personal communication, 1998).

Rafting companies usually were started by whitewater enthusiasts. For example, Ernie Kincaid, founder of ACE Whitewater and Adventure Center, was an avid kayaker who wanted to be on the river and capture the beauty and excitement of the sport through photography (Cook, personal communication, 1998). Cook, who had started a whitewater rafting company in 1973 in Tennessee and later joined Kincaid at ACE, had a diverse background in outdoor recreation. Noting the economic limits of his business, he sold five raft companies in Tennessee and North Carolina in 1986 and started looking at a map of the country to find where his company could establish a more diverse program of outdoor recreational activities. His vision was to expand the outdoor adventure business concept to include rafting, kayaking, mountain biking, rock climbing, caving, horseback riding and overnight camping (Cook, personal communication, 1998).

The industry developed by trial and error as equipment and knowledge of river navigation advanced. A revolutionary change came with the development of self-bailing boats in the early 1980s (B. Burgess, personal communication, 1998). Before self-bailing boats, solid-bottom "bucket boats" had to be bailed out often because they would fill up in the rapids and become too heavy to maneuver. The floor would sink, and control was minimized by the weight of the water. Guests and guides would bail the rafts by tossing out five-gallon buckets of water that weighed 40 pounds each (B. Burgess, personal communication, 1998). Self-bailing boats, which have inflated floors laced to the side tubes that allow water to drain, evolved in style and function into today's self-bailing rafts, which enable the sport to be both safer and adventurous (Cook, personal communication, 1998). Differences in design, size, and shape offer different qualities of rides with various river conditions. The first self-bailing rafts were not designed quite properly, but manufacturers worked with guides' suggestions to improve the boats (B. Burgess, personal communication, 1998). Eventually, the design was improved to provide a safer and more exciting ride. Surfing, or maneuvering the raft upstream into recirculating water below a rapid, was difficult or impossible before self-bailing rafts but now is a big part of the sport (Wanty, personal communication, 1998). In the early years, anyone could become a guide with minimal experience. Over time, guides shared their knowledge about and experience of the rivers, significant locations were identified and named, and each rapid developed a collective history. Oral narratives "celebrating noteworthy exploits" (Bourdieu, 1991, p. 359), embodied in specific rapids named to commemorate an event, stories told to the guests, and other events that circulate among guides, constructed a mythology of the river culture that grows with every commercial trip.

THE IDENTITY, COALESCENCE, AND MYTHOLOGY OF RIVER CULTURE

Whitewater-rafting guides value their culture and the lifestyle that affords them a way to make a meager living by spending time doing what they love. Knowledge of whitewater rafting as a recreational activity is located in the body of the participant. Cultural identity is thus an embodied phenomenon reinforced through experiences manifest as emblems and symbols. Physical participation marked by certain shared experiences creates communication structures "by which the intersubjective common-sense world is constructed" (Berger & Luckmann, 1967, p. 20). These experiences are culturally inclusive emblems of ritual initiation through chance events that predictably occur over time while engaging in whitewater rafting. For example, there are approximately 22 rapids in the Lower New River, and falling out of the raft at any particular rapid will emerge as a shared experience. These shared experiences evoke a historical perspective of past events and river conditions celebrated in the building of a cultural mythology of river adventure.

The training of whitewater guides is by no means standardized, yet the nature of the river—the rocks, hydraulics, waves, and so forth—provides opportunities for similar, memorable experiences to happen in particular water conditions and predictable locations. Guides recognize that accidents and injuries are inevitably part of the experience. When a guest has such an experience, guides see it as a normal possibility when on the river, an initiation, and, in a sense, a value-added dimension of the adventure.

In the early days through the 1970s, after a single trip down the river, a person could become a guide the next day (B. Burgess, personal communication, 1998). Presently, each trainee must go on at least 10 trips supervised by another guide as one of the minimum state requirements. Despite the processes initiated by individual companies, guides acknowledge that most learning really begins after officially becoming a guide. Learning how to read water takes time, and experienced guides make it a point never to follow another raft. Inexperienced guides tend to learn the "hard way" about reading water because obstacles and hazards are presented differently as the river conditions vary greatly from day to day. Without doubt, the most significant learning occurs through mistakes and surprises that produce memorable events that constitute an embodied initiation. Ritual initiation occurs in many ways. One such example is when an experienced guide notices a new guide following him or her and intentionally leads the new guide through a hazard that is beyond the ability of the novice. Learning to read the river broadens the phenomenological field of perception and is ascertained over time with careful observation and experience. Guides share a lexicon of river conditions that is beyond the perception of the uninitiated. The coalescence of the cultural identity of ORPs is built on a semantic field that articulates a history of shared events, experiences, knowledge, and mythology.

Despite the exclusivity of the river culture, the economic conditions of the ORPs necessitate interaction with others. Many guides believe they compromise their enthusiasm for rafting by being a guide. Among themselves, some guides cynically refer to guests as "tourons," a mixture of tourist and moron. An inside joke is to address a guest as "Sport," which stands for a "Stupid Person On a Raft Trip." Despite the beauty and adventure of the river, the relationships with guests, telling river stories, and answering the same questions day after day become as difficult and repetitious as the experiences found at any job. Yet, when a guest falls out of the raft in a rapid and has a radical experience in the river, guides recognize the episode as a bonding event that brings the guest deeper into the river culture.

Consider the ORPs and their clients, or guest participants, in rafting and other commercial activities as a structured relationship. The semantic field of the ORP constructs an insulated society in which coalescence is a by-product of lifestyle, activities, initiation rituals, and emblems that signify cultural identity (Askegaard, 1991, p. 22). The consumer paradigm is understood by the purchase of a particular product or service. Some guides recognize that this is the business end of their occupation and the relationship constructed by company communications. The last thing a trip leader generally does on the return bus ride after a rafting trip is thank the guests for going on the river, because, "Otherwise, we'd all have to get real jobs!" (Wanty, personal communication, 1998). This is taken as a joke, but to some extent, all the guides know this to be true, though some tend to resent the commercialization and commodification of their lifestyle.

The semantic field of the coalescence within the culture of river professionals weighs the semiotic construction of individual identity against the semiotic reading of those outside the culture (consumers and society). Manifest through the interaction with consumers as outsiders who relate to the experience of the river, the customers' perceptions of the purchased service may or may not be privileged by the ORP. Participants with more significant experience coalesce deeper into river culture.

During a safety orientation, a trip leader will explain that each raft guide will be "reading" the crew's ability to follow instructions and work together as a team. That ability will then determine whether the guide will choose the safest route through each rapid or the most exciting and challenging ride. Some guides proactively make adjustments in seating to control the distribution of power in the raft, whereas other guides simply adjust their own strategies on the basis of what they observe about the crew. The guide must recognize if the client is an active participant, responsible for his or her own success, enjoyment, and safety, or is terrified. Sometimes, clients perceive the trip as an amusement park ride. This raises the safety/adventure dichotomy and is potentially a direct assault on the cultural identity of a guide, in that it denies the expertise of the guide and the power of the river. The guide also understands the satisfaction of mastering technique and navigating safely and appreciates the chance elements and potential hazards of the river.

Regarding the chance qualities of the river, two deaths occurred on the New River during the spring of 1998 when I was training. A lone kayaker died in "Meat Grinder," a treacherous undercut rock below a Class V rapid, and a fisherman who was not wearing a personal flotation device lost his footing and was swallowed by an eddy. His body was discovered two days later. Although neither incident was directly connected with a commercial rafting trip, both events contributed to an appreciation of the power of the river and the mythology of river culture.

Ultimately, if coalescence, the semantic field, and a strong cultural identity were privileged over the quality of the interaction with customers, the river culture would be isolated. In the case of commercial outdoor recreation, this is an impossibility. Individual ORPs must adjust their attitude to preserve their own identity—that is, to maintain the viability of the business that ensures their employability. Some clients perceive rafting as an amusement park ride and expect the guide to take full responsibility for their safety and enjoyment. Others come physically fit and prepared to engage in outdoor adventure. In reality, rafters come in various groups of mixed classifications, skills, abilities, readiness, and willingness. They may be young or old, experienced or inexperienced, confident, or fearful. A good balance between the river professional and the product consumer, as well as a mutual respect for the expertise of the guide and the individuality of each paying customer, sustains the fun and adventure of whitewater rafting.

READING THE RIVER

There are substantial differences between the professional raft guide and the novice consumer. The embodied identity of the guide accesses a phenomenological field, present in the river, that lies beyond the perception of the uninitiated. When I began training to be a guide, I was aware that I could not see what I was being told to observe. All I could see was flat water and whitewater. Trainers would identify significant points along the way that remained invisible to me. Eventually, I began to read the signifiers that distinguished differences embedded in what were once, to my senses, just flat water and whitewater. Understanding that a "hydraulic" is whitewater that can be a "keeper" that holds a raft against the current or holds a person underwater, and how it is different from a "curler" or a "haystack," enables the guide to make quick decisions about how to maneuver the raft (Hyde, 1991). In the same way, it is essential to know how to follow a "tongue" into a rapid, how to use the upstream current of an "eddy" to control a raft, and what the swirling current of an "eddy wall" can do to a raft.

Because the water level changes day to day, reading water reveals subtle changes that are essential to successful navigation, but even the experienced guide will be fooled at times. A key difference between a guide and a guest who falls out of the raft in a rapid is that the guide knows when he or she is in trouble and probably knows what to do. An incident that makes the novice panic may be experienced as exhilaration by the knowing guide swept away by the powerful river currents.

There are many places on the river where falling out is to be avoided at all costs. An incident on July 1, 1998, during my training, illustrates the importance of reading water and understanding river culture. The New River was running at a brisk five feet above normal, a swift and challenging level. I was in a raft with Jack, a senior guide who was training me.

Our crew consisted of a family: mom, dad, and two sisters about 18 and 20 years of age. We came to the "Keeny Brothers," a series of three consecutive Class V rapids that require preparation and skill. A raft needs to set up before each rapid because they appear quickly, one after the other. At the bottom of "Middle Keeny" is a collection of jagged, deadly undercut rocks called the "Meat Grinder." In an undercut, a strong current pulls water under the rocks. As mentioned previously, a kayaker had died and was found stuck under Meat Grinder some weeks earlier.

As we entered "Upper Keeny," Jack tried to cut behind "Whale Rock," which is the ordinary line to take. The current was strong at five feet. We lacked paddle power from the crew and cut close to the rock. Behind Whale Rock was an eddy wall, where the swift downstream river current meets the upstream water of the eddy, that formed a wave that threw everyone out of the raft. It happened so suddenly that only experience, which told me that I would probably come up in the water right next to the raft, helped me keep my wits about me. I came up to the surface, knew what had happened, and looked for the raft. It was just in reach, and I could see Jack scrambling to get back in. I could also see the sisters floundering as I swam for the raft. Suddenly, I was pulled underwater, and I realized someone was trying to use me as a floatation device! I pushed myself free and swam hard, because I had drifted farther away from the raft in just a second or two. Having just taken a course in first aid and CPR, I did not hesitate to follow Rule #1: Get yourself out of harm's way before you try to help anyone else.

I made it back to the raft, saw Jack's paddle, and pulled it out of the water, knowing that we had to have a paddle to navigate. Then I pulled both sisters aboard. Jack had already grabbed a paddle and was trying to control the raft as we dropped into Middle Keeny, a huge, rocky, crashing wave train. I turned to paddle and saw that the sisters had their mother in tow. Although the sisters were without paddles, they should have been able to get their mother into the raft while Jack and I struggled to get control and prevent another, possibly worse crash into Meat Grinder. Mom continued to hang on but did not get into the raft. She was acting as a sea anchor and making it impossible for us to navigate away from Meat Grinder. Jack screamed at her to get in. She said she couldn't. Then, he glared and hollered, eyes bulging, "Get in or die!" She was back in the boat in seconds.

I was paddling hard for the eddy on river left when I realized Jack was yelling at me to paddle to river right. When I looked up, there was Meat Grinder, just a few feet away and coming fast. We just managed to get around the rocks, dropping between them and out of harm's way. No one runs the narrow slot through the jagged rocks behind Meat Grinder, but at the time, we had no choice.

Meanwhile, the father was heading right for Meat Grinder. He was overwhelmed by the force of the river and apparently did not see the raft and so turned the wrong way. He was sucked down in a whirlpool, came up, and swam to river left as he had been instructed, but he gave up just short of reaching the still water of the eddy. Just in time, Shane, another guide in our group who was waiting and watching from the safety of the eddy, scooped him out of the water. All this probably took approximately one minute. No one was hurt, we lost one paddle, and we managed the rest of the trip very conservatively.

In a strange way, I felt elated that everything was all right and that I had responded well under the conditions. Through events like this, shared experiences become the knowledge and emblems of cultural identity, and a new guide learns every rock and rapid in the river.

Guides know sections of the river intimately and accept their dangers with humor and respect. For example, the following event occurred on the Gauley River on July 10, 1998. A guide trainee fell and out swam "Hawaii Five-0," a section of the "Lost Paddle" rapid. I told two guides, each with more than 10 years of experience on the river, about the incident. They had not witnessed the event but responded with eloquent profanity and colloquialisms:

Woow hooow, he ha, that's funny! Bad place to swim because after Five-0, it's shallow and Six Pack is coming quickly, baby! (laugh) If you end up going right beside Six Pack, it's nasty shallow and undercut over there. Go left of Six Pack. If you don't make the swim away from the rocks on the bank, that's nasty. And then you're going into the third drop! If you ain't bearing right as you drop it, you're sunk. You're liable to be *gone!* If somebody don't bag your ass, you're goin' to fuckin' Tumble Home baby!

Tumble Home is the shittiest drop on the Lost Paddle run. It's nasty. It's rocky. It's not forgiving at all. You'll go deep, deeeep! It's tight in there. It's very tight. There's a fine line between not getting stuck, and getting stuck for a minute, or a second, and getting *stuck.* If people ain't giving you the two or three strokes you need to get away from the right bank, and then back-right, or all-back, you're screwed baby! You're going up on the rock. You're going to drop. People are going to swim. And, there's a hydraulic right there! (B. Burgess, personal communication, 1998; F. Wanty, personal communication, 1998)

The water moves so swiftly through this section of the river that it only takes about 30 seconds to get through it. If you are in the water, this can be a very long, heart-pounding 30 seconds. The kind of description these experience guides provided reveals an intimate level of embodied knowledge that is emblematic of cultural identity.

COMMUNICATION AND CULTURE IN SPORT COMMUNICATION

The structures of communication among West Virginia's whitewater-rafting professionals are representative of sport communication in general. Sports are highly organized, socially constructed, institutionalized, ritual activities. As a sport, whitewater rafting fits the category of "human against nature," which has emerged in a market of adventure activity products. Rafting skills are not generally appreciated through spectatorship or competition; rather, the sport functions through cooperative participation. Although people with no skills can participate, the popularity of rafting depends on a specific quality of embodied knowledge. The relationship between guests and guides is built on the assumed risks and the binary opposition of adventure and safety. The mythology of river culture assumes that a guide must be an expert to maintain the enjoyment and safety of participation by clients. The notion of rafting as a safe-yet-adventurous experience has enormous appeal for the outdoor sports market. Nature provides an element of chance and a need for spontaneous interaction that challenges even the "experts."

Layers of institutional structures support the technology, facilities, safety regulation, and marketing that maintain the commercial viability of whitewater rafting. The commercial appeal of rafting as a product builds on a postindustrial economy steeped in a classical alienation from the product of labor. The entrepreneur represents whitewater rafting as a tangible experience, an adventure with calculated risks that further enhance the appeal. Participants know the product of their labor as it is inscribed in their flesh.

Like a cowboy of the Old West, the cultural identity of rafting guides is embodied in their everyday lives. People within a culture assume that others recognize the same phenomena that are distinct to their way of seeing the world. The skills of rafting are developed simultaneously with the phenomenological field of perception. Just as the "accomplished surfer makes himself part of the wave" (Simon, 1998), the rafter's knowledge is embodied in a spontaneous interaction with the river.

A semiotic phenomenological study underscores the popular appeal of all sports. The expression of organized social ritual performance lives in the body. Participation is corporeal, intersubjective, spatial, and temporal. Spectatorship takes on the same caliber of experience, so that the sports fan adopts the identity of the object. Ritual organization of events unfold at a prescribed time and place. Risk is resignified through initiation to river culture, and market appeal is enhanced and perpetuated through the retelling of the adventures. Performance is embodied for the participant and the intersubjectivity of the spectator. The passion for sport is manifested through a quality of reality and a shared knowledge that possesses "specific characteristics" that define a sports event or activity (Berger & Luckmann, 1967, p. 1). Sport communication can incorporate understandings of semiotic structures of cultural identity in developing diverse perspectives and communication strategies for commercial or recreational purposes.

REFERENCE LIST

Askegaard, S. (1991). Toward a semiotic structure of cultural identity. In H. H. Larsen, D. G. Mick, & C. Alstead (Eds.), *Marketing and semiotics: Selected papers from the Copenhagen symposium*, pp. 11–30. Copenhagen: Handel-shojskolens Forlag.

Berger, P. L., & Luckmann, T. (1967). *The social construction of reality: A treatise in the sociology of knowledge*. Garden City, NY: Anchor Books.

Bourdieu, P. (1991). Sport and social class. In C. Mukerji & M. Schudson (Eds.), *Rethinking popular culture: Contemporary perspectives in cultural studies*, pp. 357–373. Berkeley: University of California Press.

Bourdieu, P. (1993). Structures, habitus, practices. In C. Lemert. (Ed.), *Social theory: The multicultural and classic readings*, pp. 479–484. Boulder, CO: Westview Press.

Cook, J. (1998). *ACE Adventure Center* [Promotional brochure]. Oak Hill, WV.

Hanson, C. (Director). (1994). *The river wild* [Motion picture]. United States: Universal Pictures.

Hyde, A. Jr. (1991). *New River: A photographic essay*. Charleston, WV: Cannon Graphics.

Leatherman, D. (1998). Wet and wild: Celebrating 30 years of whitewater. *West Virginia Outdoors, 1*, p. 2.

Orbe, Mark P. (1998). *Constructing co-cultural theory: An explication of culture, power, and communication*. London: Sage.

Schroder, K. C. (1991). Marketing and semiotics as a challenge to critical semiotics. In H. H. Larsen, D. G. Mick, & C. Alstead, (Eds.), *Marketing and semiotics: Selected papers from the Copenhagen symposium*, pp. 177–195. Copenhagen: Handelshojskolens Forlag.

Simon, S. (1998, September 12). *Weekend edition*. Washington DC: National Public Radio.

CHAPTER 8

Coachtalk: Good Reasons for Winning and Losing

John Todd Llewellyn

There is no room for second place. . . . There is a second place bowl game but it is a game for losers played by losers. It is and always has been an American zeal to be the first in anything we do and to win and to win and to win.

— Vince Lombardi (quoted in Eitzen, 1996, p. 182)

Winning has a joy and discrete purity to it that cannot be replaced by anything else. . . . Winning is not everything; but it is something powerful, indeed beautiful, in itself, something as necessary to the strong spirit as striving is necessary to the healthy character.

— A. Bartlett Giamatti (quoted in Green, 1986, p. 374)

We [Americans] worship the victors. But why? The Dutch don't especially, nor do the Swedes, neither do the Danes, the Swiss, or the English, and they all seem fairly civilized people.

— John Tunis (1958, p. 6)

Winning is a prominent concern in American life. Ironically, this preoccupation may go unnoticed precisely because we attend almost exclusively to winners; others are only furniture in the victorious scene. Nevertheless, we know that in every contest there will also be a loser. In a straightforward sense, all that the sports fan needs to know about winning and losing is shown on the scoreboard. However, the reality is that, win or lose, fans do not want dry statistics; they want a sense-making story. They are seeking more than the numbers can tell them. So it is that both winning and losing coaches are expected to account for themselves and the contest's outcome. In this sense, a coach is called on to be a rhetorician and offer a fitting response to the athletic exigence the fans have just witnessed.

In her work, "Apologia in Team Sport," Noreen Kruse (1981) pointed to the significance of sport in American society and listed a dozen aspects of sport and discourse worthy of future study. This chapter examines several of the areas suggested by Kruse for research: What do winning and losing coaches say after a contest? What features are common to winners' talk? What are the common features of losers' talk? How do these two kinds of talk work together to create the social drama of American sport?

In examining the use of apology in team sport, Kruse (1981) undertakes the study of what she posits to be a genre: "[A] classification based on the fusion and interrelation of elements in such a way that a unique kind of rhetorical act is created" (Campbell & Jamieson, 1978, p. 25). Simons (1978) defines genre as "any distinctive and recurrent pattern of rhetorical practice" (p. 36). Kruse points out the special problems, constraints, and forms that embody apologies rendered by those involved in team sports. Her analysis of these patterns of talk reveals the inner workings of the world of team sports by showing how it is driven by certain core values that often are at variance with societal norms (e.g., there is no need to apologize for breaking rules if the goal is to help the team win, an athlete or owner apologizes for racist statements not from a sense of decency but because racial tensions can harm team chemistry). Likewise, this chapter represents a genre study whose goal is to illuminate the world of men's college basketball coaches by identifying and examining recurrent patterns in their talk about winning and losing.

The talk of coaches is rhetorical action that delineates social norms pertaining to sport, competition, and the coaching profession. This "coach-talk" helps create the meanings that enthusiasts take from sports activities. An examination of the common message patterns produced by experienced coaches will offer insight into culturally prescribed themes in the drama of sport. By demonstrating how this professional group talks about its major concerns, this study should shed light on the world of collegiate coaching and the culture that shapes its world.

To analyze the talk of winning and losing coaches, newspaper accounts of postgame comments made by both coaches in the National Collegiate Athletic Association (NCAA) men's national championship basketball games were examined. In all, 14 games played across 26 years, involving 18 schools and 22 coaches, were studied.[1] From this extensive sample, the standard themes of winning and losing discourse were identified.

Burke (1954, p. 38) has pointed out the influence that the means of earning an income can have on a person's patterns of thought and action. The effect of this influence is termed "occupational psychosis." Burke notes that this pattern is not a mental illness; the pattern is the logical consequence of being occupied with a certain set of concerns. For example, there are issues that occupy members of the coaching profession—notably, winning often and losing rarely. We would not be surprised by the notion that someone would speak like the physician, professor, or police officer that he or she is. This study investigates the common patterns in coaches' talk regarding winning and losing.

PROFESSIONAL CONTEXT

Before examining the particular rhetorical choices made by coaches, it is important to establish the social and professional context in which coaches operate. In the years following World War I, team identification surpassed participation in mass recreational activities as the primary national pastime (Edwards, 1973). Americans became fans first and recreational players second, if at all. The role of a fan requires an interpreter of events; coaches and media commentators perform this function.

In modern America, sports contests have become ritual morality plays. The psychology of ritual is very different from the psychology of play. Ritual is hypnotic and has real effects in the lives of people; play is the release of emotion in a benign setting without long-term effects (Calhoun, 1981). So playfulness is not an element of sport. What these sports rituals emphasize instead are "American articles of faith: accomplishment, production, bravery, and goodness" (Lahr, 1972, p. 110). If play and release are not the payoffs of fandom, then what are? In the modern era, the benefits for the sports fan are a sense of belonging and a socially approved outlet for attitudes and behaviors that would be otherwise unacceptable (Edwards, 1973). Earl Warren, former Chief Justice of the Supreme Court, remarked on these benefits: "I always turn to the sports page first. The sport page records people's accomplishments; the front page nothing but man's failure" (Green, 1986, p. 285).

Sociologist Harry Edwards (1973) underscores the central role of the coach in sport: "In American society, it is commonly accepted that the success or failure of an athletic unit depends almost entirely upon the competence or incompetence of its coach" (p. 137). This perspective is rooted in America's Judeo-Christian heritage with its linkage of effort and reward. If you work hard enough, you will win (Tutko & Bruns, 1976). The irony in that position is that when teams led by two hard-working coaches meet, one of those coaches and one of those teams will come away the loser. By this standard, in the NCAA men's basketball championship field, 64 of the 65 coaches whose teams are invited to the tournament must come away losers, including—and perhaps most especially—the runner-up. Defeat is evidence that those 64 coaches did not work hard enough. Pennsylvania State University football coach Joe Paterno had counted the cultural costs of America's inability to understand or accept defeat: "I think our whole country has been twisted a bit because we don't know how to lose. This was basically our problem in Vietnam. Nobody had the courage to tell the American people, 'Look, we got licked. Let's get out' " (Tutko & Bruns, 1976, p. 32). As this chapter will reveal, Paterno's observation could be made without harm to his professional stature only because of his long-established record as a winning coach.

So the coach is the primary architect of the luster and meaning of the fans' sense of belonging, as well as the lightning rod for fan dissatisfaction. This role is fraught with pitfalls and inevitable defeat. To illustrate the pressures of modern collegiate coaching, one coach recounts this story: "I had a friend with a lifetime contract. After two bad years, the university president called him into his office and pronounced him dead" (Green, 1986, p. 121). The harsh realities of the coaching profession are often presented to the public through this sort of gallows humor. The public perception of total accountability puts the coach in the unenviable position of being completely liable for outcomes over which he has only limited control (Edwards, 1973). Former college basketball coach and athletic director C. M. Newton reinforced the tenuousness inherent in the profession: "When a coach is hired, he's fired. The date just hasn't been filled in yet" (Green, 1986, p. 101).

The case of University of Arkansas basketball coach Nolan Richardson illustrates all of these points. In 17 years, he took the Razorbacks to three Final Four tournaments and the 1994 national championship. Near the end of an uncharacteristically mediocre 2001–2002 season, Richardson reacted to media and public pressure by stating, "If they go ahead and pay me my money, they can take the job tomorrow" (Barnhart, 2002, p. 1E). Richardson subsequently said, "I've earned the right to have the season I've had" ("Arkansas' Richardson," 2002, p. 2D). These statements deal with real tensions in the world of sport. The comments led to Richardson's removal by the University's chancellor, variously described as a contract buyout or a firing; charges of racial inequities; a threatened lawsuit; and an unsuccessful appeal to the President of the University. A racial discrimination lawsuit is pending. The point of the Richardson case remains: Coaches who speak in ways that penetrate the veneer of sports do so at their own peril. In contrast to humorous anecdotes of coaches, it only took one bad season and one contentious news conference for Richardson to be declared metaphorically deceased.

The contests between competing teams, coaches, and universities represent "antagonistic cooperation," the circumstances in which two groups are in conflict but exist within a wider system of cooperation (Calhoun, 1981, p. 212). Like trial lawyers and political candidates, coaches must work to defeat their twins—people who act and think just like they do—to ensure their own survival. Tutko and Bruns (1976) note that professional coaches at every level are a remarkably homogenous group, due the common pressures they face to win: "If the coach is not winning or not conspicuously moving toward that goal, none of his other attributes are likely to be of any relevance" (p. 134). All these elements—the strength of fan identification, ritual morality dimensions, coach-centered understandings of victory and defeat, and antagonistic cooperation—help shape the world and the rhetoric of the coach.

MAXIMS AND QUIPS

In this world of coaching, many participants make a public demonstration of their commitment to winning. These maxims are one way of "conspicuously moving toward that goal" (Tutko & Bruns, 1976, p. 134); the maxims constitute a form of insurance against defective-attitude charges. It is important to remember that mature adults—professionals in their field—promoted the maxims that follow.

Said the late George Allen, coach of the Washington Redskins, "The winner is the only individual who is truly alive. I've said this to our ball club: 'Every time you win, you're reborn; when you lose, you die a little' " (Tutko & Bruns, 1976, p. 5). "It's only a game when you win. When you lose, it's hell," said Hank Stram, former coach of the Kansas City Chiefs (Tutko & Bruns, 1976, p. 6). Former Boston Bruins coach Bep Guidolin summed up the importance of winning: "The more you win the less you get fired" (Tutko & Bruns, 1976, p. 6). Professional coaches are not the only ones with hard-hitting slogans. The late Bill Musselman, then coach of the University of Minnesota men's basketball team, noted in a sign over the entrance to the shower room: "Defeat is Worse than Death Because You Have to Live With Defeat" (AP Sports News, 1988). According to these coaches, the antitheses of victory are death or, worse, hell and firing.

For all these fierce maxims, coaches produce an even greater number of quips—humorous commentary on the circumstances and pressures they face. Michigan State University football coach Duffy Daugherty recounted a supportive alumni telegram before a big game: "Remember, Coach, we're all behind you—win or tie" (Green, 1986, p. 8). University of Florida football coach Doug Dickey explained why it is preferable to have a 7–3 record: "The fans talk about the games you won following a 7–3 season. When you go 9–1 they talk about the one you lost" (Green, 1986, p. 108). Bud Grant, the Minnesota Vikings' coach, inventoried what a good coach needs: "a patient wife, loyal dog and a great quarterback—not necessarily in that order" (Green, 1986, p. 112). Bob Devaney described his goals when hired as the University of Nebraska's football coach: "I don't expect to win enough games to be put on NCAA probation. I just want to win enough to warrant an investigation" (Green, 1986, p. 366). Knute Rockne of Notre Dame also observed that "[o]ne loss is good for the soul. Too many losses are not good for the coach" (Green, 1986, p. 367). Finally, college football coach Red Sanders offered this observation on runner-up status: "The only thing worse than finishing second is to be lying on the desert alone with your back broke. Either way, nobody ever finds out about you" (Green, 1986, p. 372).

THEMES OF TALK

This study identifies four themes in the discourse of winning coaches: elevation, humility, value reinforcement, and suffering. For losing coaches, there were also four discourse themes: deference, justification, redefinition, and, once again, suffering.

Winners' Themes

College coaches whose teams win the national basketball championship face a scene of complete exaltation. The winning team has just proven itself the best in the nation in head-to-head competition rather than through a national media survey or coaches' poll. The spotlight and the emotional climate provide all the more reasons for winning coaches to recognize their rhetorical situation and produce a fitting response.

Winning coaches often return to the elevation theme, which elevates everyone associated with the championship game. Players and coaches point to their roots, thank supporters, make the game heroic, and praise opponents. Winners frequently note that they are representatives of a university and occasionally point out their kinship to a state or even region of the nation. A dramatic example of the kinship bonds is found in Coach John Thompson's comments to supporters after his Georgetown University team won the 1984 NCAA championship: "We're back, we've been away too long. . . . When I die, if I don't go to heaven, bring my body back to Georgetown" (Wilbon & Anderson, 1984, p. D1). Jerry Tarkanian, then-coach of the University of Nevada–Las Vegas (UNLV) Runnin' Rebels, used his team's 1990 championship as a forum to defend the reputation of his hometown. In noting that he wanted to win for the people of Las Vegas, Tarkanian added: "People don't know the real Las Vegas. There are 700,000 people who never go near a casino" (Lincicome, 1990, p. 4:3).

Former University of North Carolina coach Dean Smith provided a good example of the way winning coaches make the championship game heroic after it is over. "Sitting on the bench it seemed like just another game. But now, as you talk it back to me, it doesn't," he said to reporters (Denlinger, 1982, p. D4). Michigan State University coach Tom Izzo had a similar reaction to their 2000 championship: "This is more overwhelming than I thought it would be, if you want the truth" (Blaudschun, 2000, p. C1).

Even in a 30-point defeat, Duke University coach Mike Krzyzewski had no problem describing the UNLV effort in heroic terms: "I think it was the best a team has ever played against me. It was quite an incredible game. I'm in awe of what they did tonight" (Myslenski, 1990, p. 4:3). Denny Crum, the University of Louisville coach, praised the intensity of his opposing team this way: "UCLA played tough defense and didn't give us much at all" ("Crum's tongue-lashing," 1980, p. III:5). Duane Thomas, the former Dallas Cowboy football star, has pointed to the paradox inherent in championship hype: "If it's the ultimate, how come they're playing it again next year?" (Green, 1986, p. 168).

As a group, winning coaches express pleasure and satisfaction at their success but always in the context of humility. Georgetown's Thompson provided the clearest example when he commented, "The biggest thing that leaps out in my mind is all of the people, particularly of my race, who I felt never had an opportunity to experience what I have" (Denlinger, 1984, p. D1). After naming skilled black coaches who were never nationally recognized, Thompson said, "Those guys probably forgot more about basketball than I'll ever learn" (Denlinger, 1984, p. D1).

Similarly, UNLV's Tarkanian sounded a theme of humility and refused to take too much credit for his team's sound defeat of Duke: "I thought we played about as well as we were capable of playing. The first 10, 12 minutes of the game our man-to-man defense was excellent. I still want to give Duke a lot of credit. This game was no reflection on their team. We just played a great, great ball game; the ball came our way. It was just one of those games you dream about" (Rhoden, 1990, p. B9).

The value-reinforcement theme is clearly demonstrated by former University of Kentucky coach Joe B. Hall, who used the winner's spotlight to issue a declaration reinforcing the transcendent values of sport. Hall made this statement after noting the tremendous pressure his team had been under all season: "There are certain people who can't shoulder defeat. They can't accept it. But I'm going to say something very controversial. There's more to it than winning and losing. The relationships between players, the lasting friendships, the coach-player relationship, all these things are more important" (Harvey, 1978, p. D1).

Arkansas' Nolan Richardson also spoke of transcendent values when asked if some of his star Arkansas underclassmen would return for the next season. He replied: "I'm a today person. After I lost my daughter [Yvonne] seven years ago [to leukemia], I don't worry about what's going to happen tomorrow. I know that I'm not promised tomorrow. So, I have to enjoy everything that I can now. Right now" (Berkowitz, 1994, p. G1).

Winning coaches also acknowledge the suffering of the season and tournament once the victory is won. Kentucky's Hall noted, "We've been under constant pressure since we started practice October 15" (Harvey, 1978, p. D1). Georgetown's Thompson referred to winning the national championship with relief: "I won one, that monkey is off my back and that's very important to me" (Asher, 1984, p. D4). Rick Pitino, then the coach at the University of Kentucky, noted the pressure his players had endured all season long: "Every fan they see on campus it's 'Win it all, win it all, win it all' " (Isaacson, 1996, p. 4:5).

Losers' Themes

Losing coaches sound four themes: deference, justification, redefinition, and suffering. Whereas winners elevate their roots, their schools, and their regions, the most consistent feature about losers' discourse is the act of respectfully acknowledging the winner. The University of Michigan's former coach Johnny Orr showed deference to the Indiana University team that had beaten Michigan by 18 points in the national championship."They are a great team. There is no doubt they are No. 1. I'm not going to compare them with anybody else, but they're damn good," he said (Damer, 1976, p. IV:2). When Duke defeated the University of Michigan by 20 points in the 1992 championship, Steve Fisher, then the Wolverines' coach, did not have to search far for an explanation: "Grant Hill creates problems for everybody because he is so quick, so athletic, so intelligent" (Muscatine, 1992, p. C8). "They played a great basketball game," Billy Tubbs said in praising the Kansas Jayhawks, the 1988 NCAA champions. "You can't shoot any better than they did in the first half. This is a bitter defeat because we came here thinking we could win it all and we didn't do it" (Feinstein, 1988, p. E1). Mike Davis, Indiana University's coach, was plainspoken in acknowledging the University of Maryland as the 2002 men's champion: "The victory was won. We had a chance tonight, but Maryland is a better team than we are" ("A much better feeling," 2002, p. C1).

Losing coaches also are called on to justify tactics in not-so-subtle challenges to their judgment. When Georgetown defeated the University of Houston, losing coach Guy Lewis defended his choice of a half-court zone trap."That defense probably won us 150 games over the years. We tried several different presses, several different offenses and defenses and just couldn't get over the hump," he explained (Wilbon, 1984, p. D5). In contrast, Duke's Krzyzewski was clear about his team's problem with UNLV: "They were totally in control. . . . I don't know if you realize how good they were defensively. They were great. They were great" (Rhoden, 1990, p. B9).

At a subtler level, losing coaches are called on to offer a metaphysical rationale for the loss. Most coaches answer the "deep explanation" question by pointing to fate. Lewis noted that his team "just couldn't get over the hump" (Wilbon, 1984, p. D5). Former UCLA coach Larry Brown observed, "We had our chances and we had a lot of good shots early that wouldn't go down" (Florence, 1980, p. III:1). Only fate could explain the outcome described by Thompson in recounting how North Carolina's James Worthy intercepted a Georgetown pass in the final 17 seconds of the 1982 game to seal the win. "He [Worthy] was just where we wanted him. He was following Smith and went back the other way. But the ball went right to him. He was definitely in the wrong place," the Georgetown coach concluded (Huff & Wilbon, 1982, p. D1). Krzyzewski offered a lighter touch in accounting for the blowout by UNLV: "We were our best in March. This game was in April [April 2], huh?" (Moran, 1990, p. B12). Former Duke assistant coach Pete Gaudet seemed to reason from a what-goes-around-comes-around perspective. Gaudet philosophically accepted a desperation three-point field goal by Arkansas big man Scotty Thurman that sealed Duke's 76–72 loss: "After all the shots we've hit—Christian Laettner against Kentucky [a buzzer beater in the 1992 East Region finals] and the others, we'd be fools to complain about it happening to us" (Cotton, 1994, p. C6).

Once the game's outcome is settled, losing coaches quickly redefine the situation so that supporters and players can find positive values in it. These redefinitions focus on an alternate concept of victory, one found in the heart rather than on the scoreboard. So Thompson says, "You certainly can call North Carolina national champions, but you can't call us losers" (Huff & Wilbon, 1982, p. D1). Coach Larry Brown commented that his UCLA team had "[c]lass. These kids have more class in defeat than a lot of people have when they win. Look at James Wilkes. He could give away half his heart and still have as much heart as anybody you know" (Littwin, 1980, p. III:1). Syracuse University coach Jim Boeheim took on the issue frontally: "Too much is made about losing, but to my way of thinking we didn't lose anything tonight. They [his players] should be just as proud as Kentucky is" (Cotton, 1996, p. D6). Boeheim added, "We gave everything we had. I told my team: 'I think you're champions' " (Kornheiser, 1996, p. D1). Tubbs sounded a similar theme in 1988 when he noted that the Sooners "didn't start this season or this tournament wanting to be No. 2 in the nation, we wanted to be No. 1 . . . but I think this is a championship team" (Canfield, 1988). Indeed, Tubbs took redefinition to new heights, as perhaps he could only before a hometown crowd, when he asserted that Oklahoma had the best team in the country. "If there is any team that disputes that, they can call my office if they want to play," Tubbs added (Canfield, 1988).

Discussions of suffering by losing coaches are so frequent and intense that such talk must be the rhetorical equivalent of donning sackcloth and ashes. After the 2000 championship, Florida's Billy Donovan observed, "It's always hard for me to talk to the guys when the season comes to an end. Probably there's not a whole lot that they want to hear" (Herman, 2000). UCLA's Brown reported, "This is one of the toughest losses I've ever had. I've had some tough ones but never the magnitude of this one" (Litwinn, 1980, p. III:1). Michigan's Fisher sounded a similar theme following his team's 1992 loss to Duke: "We are crushed and you should be when you get this far and don't walk away with the championship" (Berkowitz, 1994, p. C1). The remarks by Brown and Fisher reveal the redemptive aspect of suffering. It only afflicts those with high standards.

Themes and the Culture of Coaching

There are themes in the discourse produced by winning and losing coaches. But what is the "sum" of the themes in each category? How do the themes of winners and losers interact to help create the drama of sport in society?

The discourse themes suggest that winners are true to their roots and their supporters. Winners are humble. Winners know and say that "winning is not everything" and point to the value of relationships. Winners confess the suffering involved in reaching the top. However, these themes can be broached only after the ultimate victory. In the culture of sport, the "winning is not everything" admission can be made only when the coach has a firmly established reputation as a winner. This is the irony of the victor's confession; only ultimate victors can say that victory is not the ultimate. This paradox is underscored by the consistent efforts of losing coaches to redefine winning and success, again only after the loss. To attempt to redefine victory before it is absolutely necessary would be evidence of flawed character. Similarly, only a winner can acknowledge the incredible pressure to win. In a loser, this behavior betokens a defective attitude. So, the coach is in an absurd position in which, to be temporarily above the cultural value system that drives the world of sports, he must be recognized as epitomizing that very system. To be free from the social rules of sport, he must excel in demonstrating conformance to those rules.

Losers' themes suggest that losers know who the winners are and how they are to be respected. Losers must explain their actions and the outcome in both strategic and metaphysical terms. Losers find a way to see themselves as winners. Losers suffer. These discourses by losers serve to demonstrate their total dedication to victory while subtly acknowledging the option to redefine success when absolutely necessary. Losers believe that victory may be controlled by fate, whereas winners have no trouble accepting victory as divine compensation for proper attitudes and effort. Losing hints at the presence of a moral flaw and requires redemption.

The themes of winners and losers reflect two contradictions embraced by each of these groups. Winners elevate all of the elements of the contest while remaining humble. They reinforce the traditional values of sport while acknowledging the extent of their suffering. Losers defer to the winners while subtly giving their followers an alternate definition of winning.

They justify their loss as fated at the same time that they suffer for that loss.

This pattern of talk by winners and losers serves to maintain a social system in which each party creates and maintains the other. This linkage is evident in discourse. Winners elevate vast groups and areas and receive their plaudits, whereas losers show deference to winners. Winners humbly say that winning is not everything and acknowledge how difficult winning the championship can be. Losers recount suffering and blame the fates while examining their character and attempting to "talk themselves into" a victory of some sort.

Although this pattern of talk reveals the construction and maintenance of a social system, there are exceptions in the universe of coaching. Both Bobby Knight, previously of Indiana University and now coaching at Texas Tech University, and Buddy Ryan, of several professional football teams, come to mind. Neither man engages in many of the discourse practices previously outlined because both are true believers in their system of training and strategy. Consequently, for them, a loss is a failure of the players to execute the system; in this narrow sense, these coaches are invincible. According to Feinstein (1986, p. 3), "Knight was incapable of accepting failure. Every defeat was personal; *his* team lost, a team *he* had selected and coached. None of the victories or milestones of the past mattered. . . . He always told his players, 'Follow our rules, do exactly what we tell you and you will not lose.'" When his team defeated Syracuse for the national championship in 1987 on a last-second shot, Knight told his team in the locker room, "What you did was refuse to lose. You've been that kind of team all year. I want you to know I would have been just as proud of you if you had lost" (Feinstein, 1986, p. 348). That statement, coming from this coach, could only be said in victory. Both Knight and Ryan seek no rhetorical quarter through their treatments of winning and losing, and none is given. This stance makes their teams particularly attractive targets for opponents. These message strategies, which can be summarized as "rhetorical insensitivity," serve to paint a bull's-eye on Knight- and Ryan-coached teams.

Even when his team is not involved, Knight does not sugarcoat his thoughts. In analyzing the NCAA finalists in the 1986 Louisville–Duke contest, he noted, "There are tough matchups for both teams. I think that Dawkins will be a tough matchup for Louisville. I really don't think that Louisville's guards [Milt Wagner and Jeff Hall] are as good as Duke's guards [Dawkins and Tommy Amaker]. But I also think that Billy Thompson and Pervis Ellison become a tough matchup for Duke" (Florence, 1986, p. III:8).

Knight can be brusque even in complimenting an opponent. He praised the offensive prowess of Cleveland State University. When told that many people in Cleveland did not think their team, Indiana's opponent in the opening round of the 1986 NCAA East Regionals, stood much of a chance, Knight replied, "People in Cleveland don't know anything about basketball. These kids can play" (Joyce, 1986).

Knight was less kind to the University of Michigan team that beat Indiana by 28 points (80–52) and ended its chances for a Big Ten conference title in 1986. Even thought the Wolverines manhandled the Hoosiers, Knight was not satisfied with their performance: "I don't think they play hard all the time. If they can get everything together and play hard every night, then they'll have a . . . chance to go in the NCAA tournament" (AP Sports News, 1986a).

In 1986, while researching his book on Knight, Feinstein offered his assessment of the man. "I think a lot of people misunderstand Bob Knight because you only see one side of him," Feinstein said. "I think one thing Bob Knight is not, is image-conscious. He's not going to change at this point in his life to make people who know him, like him" (AP Sports News, 1986b).

Ryan's similar approach is epitomized by a series of comments surrounding a 1990 game between his Philadelphia Eagles and the Dallas Cowboys. To the charge that his team had a reputation for taking cheap shots that served to inspire opponents to play beyond their abilities, Ryan replied, "That could be part of it." He said, "I don't think we're a cheapshot team, but we'll knock you on your butt if you give us the opportunity" (Bernstein, 1990). Ryan also had been accused of inspiring the Cowboys by guaranteeing a victory over them on his radio show. To that charge, Ryan added, "I'll guarantee one this week too, because that's the way I am. Actually I didn't guarantee it [a Dallas win]. I said Dallas hasn't beaten us [in his Eagles' tenure] and we don't plan on them beating us this week" (Bernstein, 1990). The coach went on to explain his philosophy: "We don't ever go into a game planning on someone beating us," Ryan said. "I expect to win every game from here on out. That's the way we play football. If we don't we're in the wrong . . . business" (Bernstein, 1990).

Ryan's stance does aid the opponent, as Cowboys' coach Jimmy Johnson revealed: "Considering the team we are playing, we shouldn't have any trouble getting ready for it" (Brinster, 1990). A sportswriter confirmed Johnson's assessment, noting that "[t]he Dallas players also were low-keying the game, but they already had made their feelings known immediately after a victory last Sunday against Tampa Bay. Just one word—'Eagles'—was word [sic] scribbled on a dressing room blackboard" (Brinster, 1990).

Ryan did not shake hands with Cowboys' coach Johnson after the game. Win or lose, he never shakes hands. As one sportswriter observed, "You'd love to share a beer with Ryan, and you'd love to have the former Marine on your side if you went into battle. But coaching and public relations. . . . "

(Rowe, 1990, p. D4). While acknowledging Ryan's ability, Rowe (1990) added, "It's just that outside of Philadelphia, Ryan is known more for his hot air than his coaching prowess. If the Eagles don't make the playoffs, Ryan, who's in the final year of a five-year contract, should be out. If so, don't expect any sympathy cards, Buddy. You've alienated everybody" (p. D4).

CONCLUSION

What is the rhetorical world of the college basketball coach? The interlocking messages crafted by winning and losing coaches show that forms of respect and regard reside beneath the level of competition. The ubiquitous humility may also reflect a strategic awareness that the winners of today may be the losers of tomorrow. The reality of home and away conference schedules and annual tournaments makes palpable the Golden Rule's admonition to do unto others as you would have them do unto you. Thus, a head coach ought not always display his humility too convincingly; after all, he and the administrators who hired him must believe that he can win and motivate his players to that end. The pragmatics of coaching suggest that the mantle of humility be worn lightly; nevertheless, the rhetoric of coaching requires that it be worn. An absence of pre- and postgame expressions that demonstrate humility and a suitable regard for the opposing team and coach can be interpreted as overconfidence and even disrespect. As the Buddy Ryan–Jimmy Johnson interplay suggests, such statements can also become great fodder for the opposing team. There are famous examples of such unguarded comments. Consider the response of Clemson University football coach Frank Howard, when asked at a clinic how many great coaches he thought were present: "One less than [Maryland football coach] Tom Nugent thinks there is" (Green, 1986, p. 293).

The world of the coach is one of ephemeral glory; coaches know that even those with lifetime contracts may be "declared dead." The talk of coaches suggests a belief in justice and the rewards of hard work, yet there is also a sense of fate—even fatalism—in the comments of losing coaches. In a world in which a certain amount of loss is inevitable, the coach must be able to displace the angst or risk being consumed by it.

Games, seasons, and careers for athletes are analogous to days, years, and lives for other people. The literal result of the games or the season is clearly presented on the scoreboard or in the box score. It remains for someone—usually coaches and commentators—to color the figures rhetorically to give them dramatic meaning. In the culture of sport, winning coaches ride high, and losers suffer. When a championship is decided, many respond as though that moment were the happy ending of a play. But dramas rarely end happily, and what had been taken for the entire play is revealed as only the first act. The second act is called "next season," and in that act, the winner will try to repeat his triumph while the loser seeks to redeem himself.

Sports psychologist Thomas Tutko (Tutko & Bruns, 1976) has observed: "Winning is like drinking salt water; it will never quench your thirst. It is an insatiable greed" (p. 2). Year after year, coaches, like the mythical Sisyphus, attempt to roll a stone to the top of a hill. On the rare occasions that the stone reaches the summit, the respite is brief. When Georgetown coach Thompson was asked about his 1984 championship team's chances in the future, he replied, "What do you mean the future? I want to digest the past" (Asher, 1984, p. D4).

This instant discounting of the victory by the media and fans and the blunting of the satisfaction that should flow from such a win is evidence of what Freud called a "repetition compulsion" (Tutko & Bruns, 1976, p. 3). Even when the elusive goal is reached, there is minimal satisfaction; it must be done again and again, and there is no respite from the pressure. Even former UCLA coach John Wooden, the most successful college basketball coach in history with nine NCAA titles in 10 years, was not immune. Wooden made only a dozen recruiting trips in his entire career and believed in his approach to the extent that he did not scout opponents. Nevertheless, as a 64-year-old man with heart trouble, he made three recruiting trips to Salt Lake City in pursuit of a 17 year-old, seven-foot-tall player. This uncharacteristic behavior came immediately after North Carolina State University beat his team in the NCAA semi-finals in 1974 (Tutko & Bruns, 1976, p. 10). Similarly, North Carolina coach Smith did not return to Chapel Hill with his team following their 1993 NCAA championship in New Orleans. Instead, the next morning, he was in Philadelphia recruiting the six-foot, eleven-inch, high-school prep star Rasheed Wallace.

This chapter has carried forward the work of Kruse (1981) in studying discourse related to sport in America. The way coaches talk about winning and losing can be analyzed to explain their world and elements of the larger culture. There are many other areas for research, including a comparison of winning and losing discourse by professional men's coaches, as well as professional and collegiate women's coaches. It would be interesting to determine whether professional or gender status makes a difference in approaches to winning and losing. Some of the results here may be a function of the NCAA tournament championship's finality, and other results might be attributable to college-level play. For example, whereas players' tears are the hallmark of collegiate defeat, these displays are not found in professional championships. A useful study might examine how coaches talk about winning and losing during the span of a season. Instinct suggests that coaches may work to construct "progress" across that time, but a careful study could test that view. The study presented here and the possible further investigations suggested confirm that sport is a window into cultural values. The rhetorical analysis of sport will continue to repay scholarly attention.

NOTE

1. This selection includes teams and coaches that competed in the final game for the men's Division I NCAA national basketball championship in even-numbered years from 1976 to 2000. Here is a listing of the teams, coaches and results by year during that period:

Year	Winning Team/Coach/	Losing Team/Coach/	Score
1976	Indiana/Bobby Knight	Michigan/Johnny Orr	86–68
1978	Kentucky/Joe B. Hall	Duke/Bill Foster	94–88
1980	Louisville/Denny Crum	UCLA/Larry Brown	59–54
1982	North Carolina/Dean Smith	Georgetown/John Thompson	63–62
1984	Georgetown/John Thompson	Houston/Guy Lewis	84–75
1986	Louisville/Denny Crum	Duke/Mike Krzyzewski	72–69
1988	Kansas/Larry Brown	Oklahoma/Billy Tubbs	83–79
1990	UNLV/Jerry Tarkanian	Duke/Mike Krzyzewski	103–73
1992	Duke/Mike Krzyzewski	Michigan/Steve Fisher	71–51
1994	Arkansas/Nolan Richardson	Duke/Mike Krzyzewski	76–72
1996	Kentucky/Rick Pitino	Syracuse/Jim Boeheim	76–67
2000	Michigan State/Tom Izzo	Florida/Billy Donovan	89–76
2002	Maryland/Gary Williams	Indiana/Mike Davis	64–52

REFERENCE LIST

A much better feeling. (2002, April 3). *Winston-Salem Journal*, p. C1.

AP Sports News. (1986a, March 10). PM cycle.

AP Sports News. (1986b, March 14). BC cycle.

AP Sports News. (1988, August 23). AM cycle. Arkansas' Richardson says he has earned right to "average" season. (2002, February 26). *The Advocate* (Baton Rouge, LA), p. 2D.

Asher, Mark. (1984, April 4). The best of the Hoyas may be yet to come. *The Washington Post*, p. D4.

Barnhart, Tony. (2002, March 2). Richardson out; An era ends at Arkansas with contract buyout. *Atlanta Constitution*, p. 1E.

Berkowitz, Steve. (1994, April 6). Razorbacks get a grip on championship feeling. *The Washington Post*, p. G1+.

Bernstein, Ralph. (1990, October 30). AP Sports News, AM cycle.

Blaudschun, Mark. (2000, April 4). Men's final; The Spartans accomplish their mission. *Boston Globe*, p. C1.

Brinster, Dick. (1990, October 26). AP Sports News, PM cycle.

Burke, Kenneth. (1954). *Permanence and change* (3d ed.). Berkeley: University of California.

Calhoun, Don. (1981). *Sports, culture and personality*. West Point, NY: Leisure Press.

Campbell, Karlyn K., & Jamieson, Kathleen. (1978). Form and genre in rhetorical criticism: An introduction. In K. K. Campbell & K. H. Jamieson (Eds.), *Form and genre: Shaping rhetorical action* (pp. 9–32). Falls Church, VA: Speech Communication Association.

Canfield, Owen. (1988, April 5). AP Sports News, AM cycle.

Cotton, Anthony. (1994, April 5). Razorbacks find renewed focus. *The Washington Post*, p. C6.

Cotton, Anthony. (1996, April 2). Syracuse has upset feeling. *The Washington Post*, p. D6.

Crum's tongue-lashing got Louisville moving. (1980, March 25). *The Los Angeles Times*, Sec. III, p. 5.

Damer, Roy. (1976, March 30). Unbeaten Hoosiers prove unbeatable. *Chicago Tribune*, Sec. IV, p. 2.

Denlinger, Ken. (1982, March 30). Powerful game of heartbreak and class. *The Washington Post*, p. D4.

Denlinger, Ken. (1984, April 4). Thompson wants to divvy up the pride. *The Washington Post*, p. D1.

Edwards, Harry. (1973). *Sociology of sport*. Homewood, IL: Dorsey Press.

Eitzen, D. Stanley. (1996, January 1). Ethical dilemmas in American sport. *Vital Speeches of the Day*, pp. 182–185.

Feinstein, John. (1986). *A season on the brink*. New York: Fireside.

Feinstein, John. (1988, April 5). Manning the man, Kansas the champion; Oklahoma defeated 83–79. *The Washington Post*, p. E1.

Florence, Mal. (1980, March 25). Crum calls them chokers; NCAA calls them champs. *The Los Angeles Times*, Sec. III, p. 1+.

Florence, Mal. (1986, March 31). NCAA men's championship. *The Los Angeles Times*, Sec. III, p. 8.

Green, Lee. (1986). *Sportswit*. New York: Ballentine Books.

Harvey, Randy. (1978, March 28). It's serious at Kentucky. *Atlanta Constitution*, p. D1+.

Herman, Steve. (2000, April 4). Magic's '79 team recedes in Spartan lore? AP Sports News, BC cycle.

Huff, Donald, & Wilbon, Michael. (1982, March 30). Thompson would play it again as he did. *The Washington Post*, p. D1.

Isaacson, Melissa. (1996, April 2). Waiting to exhale is over for Pitino. *Chicago Tribune*, Sec. 4, p. 5.

Joyce, Dick. (1986, March 13). AP Sports News, AM cycle.

Kornheiser, Tony. (1996, April 2). A title page for Pitino. *The Washington Post*, p. D1+.

Kruse, Noreen. (1981). Apologia in team sport. *Quarterly Journal of Speech, 67*, 270–283.

Lahr, John. (1972). The theatre of sports. In M. Marie Hart (Ed.), *Sport in the sociocultural process* (pp. 105–115). Dubuque, IA: Wm. C. Brown.

Lincicome, Bernie. (1990, April 3). So, the Shark gets the NCAA before it gets him. *Chicago Tribune*, Sec. 4, p. 3.

Littwin, Mike. (1980, March 25). Tears fell but Bruins held heads up. *The Los Angeles Times*, Sec. III, p. 1+.

Moran, Malcolm. (1990, April 3). Blue Devils struggle to find a meaning. *New York Times*, p. B12.

Muscatine, Alison. (1992, April 7). Grant Hill responds as 1-man rescue squad. *The Washington Post*, p. C8.

Myslenski, Skip. (1990, April 3). UNLV leaves no doubt. *Chicago Tribune*, Sec. 4, p. 3.

Rhoden, William. (1990, April 3). Las Vegas hits jackpot in a record runaway. *New York Times*, p. B9+.

Rowe, John. (1990, Oct. 29). Eagles might be better off if Buddy took a hike. *Bergen Record*, p. D4.

Simons, Herbert. (1978). Genre-alizing about rhetoric: A scientific approach. In K. K. Campbell & K. H. Jamieson (Eds.), *Form and genre: Shaping rhetorical action* (pp. 33–50). Falls Church, VA: Speech Communication Association.

Tunis, John. (1958). *The American way in sport.* New York: Duell, Sloan & Pearce.

Tutko, Thomas, & Bruns, William. (1976). *Winning is everything and other American myths.* New York: Macmillan.

Wilbon, Michael. (1984, April 4). Cougars study tactics after loss in final. *The Washington Post*, p. D5.

Wilbon, Michael, & Anderson, John W. (1984, April 4). Hoyas return home in the midnight hour. *The Washington Post*, p. D1.

CHAPTER 9

Metaphor in Sport Policy Debate: Parliament and British Soccer Violence

Robert S. Brown

The use of metaphor in the rhetoric of war has received a significant amount of attention by communication scholars. What is often overlooked is the tactic of turning the war metaphor around to handle domestic social issues. Critics need to examine the way politicians employ dehumanizing metaphors to initiate actions against their own citizens. This chapter, for example, examines how the British Parliament dealt with soccer-related violence in its country, possibly at the expense of the human rights of its own people.

In 1974, Robert Ivie began to examine the justifications for war, centering his analysis on Burke's notion of the victimage cycle. According to this notion, a country aims at perfection, falls short, and then looks to blame others for its failure. In a sense, the country is relieved of any blame by becoming the victim and placing fault on an outside force. Ivie's (1974, p. 339) methodology employs Burke's pentad, focusing on the use of god terms to describe the victim and devil terms to describe the enemy as part of a larger drama. In a later study, Ivie (1980) would describe this process as a justification of war through images of savagery, in which the United States was the victim and depicted using terms of logic and peace, whereas North Vietnam became the savage, irrational enemy.

This contrast between good and savage images enables a government to justify warring actions. The government makes itself the victim of a group of inhuman savages, which demands a defensive reaction. War against other humans may not be accepted, but fighting against aggressive monsters is justified and requires that any means possible be used to stop them.

Instances of acts of war are clear to the most casual observer of history, and the dangers involved are obvious. More insidious is when warlike rhetoric is turned against a segment of the local population. Perry (1983) examines just such an occurrence in Hitler's anti-Jewish rhetoric. Metaphors of cancer and infestation were used to depict Jews as less than human and to establish a national mindset that could foster the Holocaust. The rhetoric is just as effective as if it were being used against an outside people and perhaps more dangerous because it can be more subtle than most war propaganda. Rather than an outside enemy, the danger comes from your own neighbor, yet the results are the same as with an outside enemy—annihilation.

A similar, though far less cataclysmic, pattern was followed in Great Britain, resulting not in war, but in the loss of rights for British citizens. Over a two-day period, July 3 and 4, 1985, the House of Commons hastily debated and passed the *Sporting Events (Control of Alcohol etc.) Bill*. The bill, aggressively pushed through by Prime Minister Margaret Thatcher (Taylor 1987, pp. 172–173), was a direct reaction to the incident-marred 1984–85 football season and the culmination of a debate over a societal issue that had been ongoing since the late 1960s. Although this debate may have been brief, the dialogue produced provides an interesting means to study reactionary government and the use of metaphor to hasten decision making, even at the expense of human rights.

This chapter analyzes the first day of the debates, which focused on the bill as a whole, rather than the second day, which dealt with the details of the provisions. I first present a brief history of English football to frame its cultural significance and the violence that led to government action. I then focus on the debate over policy initiatives aimed at ending the violence by emphasizing the use of metaphor in defining the problem and identifying the group that was causing the problem. This analysis develops the argument that members of Parliament used god and devil terms to construct and differentiate a civilized, victimized populace from a dehumanized, aggressive minority present in the same society. This construction then allowed the debate about soccer disruptions to be treated as a military situation, which expedited the passing of legislation without the need for time-consuming discussions of human rights.

A BRIEF HISTORY OF BRITISH FOOTBALL

According to Stephen Wagg (1984), British sociologist and football historian, the roots of football can be traced to English feudal villages. During the Industrial Revolution, football moved into the cities, and the "modern" form of football, developed in school leagues during the 1840s, became professional in 1885 (Wagg, 1984, pp. 3–5). During subsequent decades, the number of football clubs and leagues grew, hitting a popularity zenith by drawing 77 million spectators for the 1949–50 season (Dunning, 1988, p. 132).

From this high point, the popularity of football, at least as measured by attendance, began to fall. The average seasonal attendance dropped every decade: 33 million during the 1950s, 25–29 million during the 1960s, 24–25 million in the 1970s, and less than 20 million in the 1980s (Dunning, 1988, p. 132). There have been many reasons offered for this decline, including fans' ability to watch the game on television rather than attend the game in person (Wagg, 1984, p. 220), the growth of other forms of leisure activities, and the lack of competitive games due to the number of weak teams (Dunning, 1988, p. 133). The increasing violence at games is also a factor in the decline of attendance (Dunning, 1988, p. 133), a factor that was a major issue in the Parliamentary debate examined later in this chapter.

According to the book *The Roots of Football Hooliganism*, there have been recorded incidents of fan violence at football matches since the earliest stages of the professional sport (Dunning, 1988). During the period 1894–1914, the *Leicester Daily Mercury* reported 159 incidents of "spectator misconduct" (Dunning, 1988, p. 48). This figure doubled during the years after World War I (Dunning, 1988, p. 95) but still was minor and received little attention. The number of incidents of fan violence continued to grow, however, and by the "middle of the 1960s a major escalation started to occur" (Dunning, 1988, p. 234). England hosted the World Cup in 1966, and all of the hype and media attention brought on by this event gave fan violence a lot of exposure. After this, fan violence became a topic of conversation as a pressing social problem (Dunning, 1988, p. 148).

It was during this time that the problem of violence at football matches became known as "hooliganism." Although the origin of the term is not exactly known, it is "generally thought to have been derived from the reputation of an especially rowdy Irish family in the East End of London during the nineteenth century" (Wagg, 1984, p. 195). Descriptions of hooliganism include verbal abuse of players, referees, and rival fans; throwing objects and physical assaults among these same groups; and destruction of property and physical assaults in riot-like conditions outside of stadiums before and after matches. This hooliganism was taken to matches on mainland Europe by British fans, which led to the banning of English football fans from the mainland by the United European Football Association in 1985,[1] a subject that also became a factor in the Parliamentary debates.

THE IMPORTANCE OF FOOTBALL IN ENGLAND

In America, though baseball is commonly recognized as the national pastime, it is highly unlikely for the U.S. government to become involved in the operations of the sport. This is not to say that there is no connection; the President throws out the first pitch every season, and state governments are often called on to fund the building of new stadiums. Yet, government rarely gets involved in the rules and operations of sport. When this kind of federal interference does occur, such as with debates over the antitrust status of baseball, there is usually a separation between government regulation and sport.

This is not the case in England. In England, a government official, appropriately titled the Minister of Sport, oversees game playing and administration. The government also receives significant income from the taxing of sport and betting placed on sport. As Gerald Kaufman, a representative from Manchester, Gorton, said in the debate, "The Government obtain hundreds of millions of pounds annually in taxation from football" (*Hansard Parliamentary Debates*, 1985, p. 347). This financial gain was a matter of some controversy during the debate, as some members argued that the government should use some of this money to pay for the clubs' security improvements, whereas other members believed that club security was not the government's responsibility.

The importance of the sport of football to England is evident in the arguments used during the debate. Joseph Ashton, the representative of Bassetlaw, pointed out that football teams give the residents of cities a sense of identification and pride. In talking about the teamless town of Croydon, a big city of which few have heard, Ashton said, "If there had been a Croydon United [football team], everybody would have heard of the town . . . that is the value of a team to a town" (*Hansard Parliamentary Debates*, 1985, p. 384). In reference to another town that has a team of its own, Ashton reported, "Apart from elections, it [scores and highlights on the news] is the only time that Darlington gets a mention on television. Quite rightly, Darlington is proud of that" (*Hansard Parliamentary Debates*, 1985, p. 383).[2] Many other members of Parliament also emphasized the importance of football as the national leisure activity. Robert Hicks of Cornwall, South-East, stated that "it is important to remember that football is our national sport. It is watched on average by 500,000 spectators every Saturday . . . the very structure of our football league system is important to perhaps 20 to 25 percent of the population. That is why the Government must be careful before introducing legislation that could harm the fabric of our national game" (*Hansard Parliamentary Debates*, 1985, p. 404).

Unfortunately, the national game was already damaged by the problem of hooliganism. The Minister of State Giles Shaw responded to Hicks's warning by arguing that Parliament must pass legislation because "the events of the last season have undoubtedly harmed the fabric of the national game" (*Hansard Parliamentary Debates*, 1985, pp. 414–415). The Secretary of State for the Home Department Leon Brittan, reiterated this claim, declaring that "[f]ootball is a great national game which gives pleasure to millions. We cannot tolerate the mindless violence and hooliganism that now disfigures it" (*Hansard Parliamentary Debates*, 1985, p. 341). Football is not trivial entertainment but an important part of England's society and a popular issue among the voting public. For this reason, the disruptions of 1985 demanded attention, lest, from Parliament's perspective, the very fiber of England be torn further.

1985: THE IMPETUS FOR THE BILL

If, as mentioned previously, the problem of hooliganism was first widely identified in the 1960s, why did the Parliament wait so long to take action?[3] The answer was provided during the debate by Shaw, who pointed out that the bill was a reaction to an accumulation of events from the previous football season. "It was not just the enormous tragedy in the Heysel stadium at the end of May," Shaw pointed out, "but a season of ghastly tragedies" (*Hansard Parliamentary Debates*, 1985, p. 414).

The tragedies that Shaw brought up are of great importance. They created unrest that forced the government to take strong action. The first event, May 11, 1985, occurred at a match in Bradford. During a fight, a fire was started that burned down a wooden stand and killed 57 people (Taylor, 1987, p. 171). The next month, at a match held on the Continent in Brussels, English fans started a riot outside of Heysel Stadium, which resulted in the death of 39 fans, mostly Italians (Dunning, 1988, p. 181). After the Heysel incident, the European governing soccer body banned English fans from following their teams to the mainland.

It is perhaps this final insult that inspired the legislation, more so than the damage to the national game. With the banning of English citizens from the mainland, all of England had been shamed. Shaw stated, "The general mood on the morrow of the Brussels tragedy was that the good name of English football was at an internationally low level and that the good name of the British had been badly affected" (*Hansard Parliamentary Debates*, 1985, p. 414). Peter Bruinvels of Leicester, East, stated, "[T]he behavior of those so-called fans in Brussels was a discredit to the whole country. It brought shame to people no matter where they lived or what views they held" (*Hansard Parliamentary Debates*, 1985, p. 409).

It was Prime Minister Thatcher who, on seeing the violence and the banning of fans from Europe, pushed Parliament to create the bill and pass it before the start of the next season. This meant the government had to complete the whole bill in four months (*Hansard Parliamentary Debates*, 1985, p. 342). Some, such as John Carlisle of Luton, North, expressed concern about moving so hastily. "I understand the Government's anxiety to get the measure on the statute book," said Carlisle, "but the subject is so important that to steamroller the Bill through the House . . . is unfortunate" (*Hansard Parliamentary Debates*, 1985, p. 376). Such opposition was slight, however, and the debate was completed in two days with the passage of the bill.

THE *SPORTING EVENTS (CONTROL OF ALCOHOL ETC.) BILL*

The need to pass the bill through the Parliament quickly is an important aspect of this analysis. Because of pressure from above, the representatives could not spend a lot of time going over the issues raised by the new law. A few members, raising possibly the most important issue, expressed fears that the new law ignored some basic human rights. For example, Sir Elden Griffiths pointed out that the bill allowed police to search fans entering a stadium and seize weapons or alcohol found on that person, which runs against Britain's protection of private property (*Hansard Parliamentary Debates*, 1985, p. 374).

Kaufman, speaking for the opposition, stated that they would support the bill, even though some of the proposals "are profoundly disturbing to many people because of their limitations on free speech and orderly public assembly" (*Hansard Parliamentary Debates*, 1985, p. 344). Kaufman and the membership he spoke for thus stated their support for the bill even with clear apprehensions.

Some members also expressed their fear that the bill gave too much power to authorities outside of Parliament. Griffiths was "doubtful whether it is right in principle to place upon the police officer the onus and authority to override the decision of a magistrates' court. As far as I am aware, that is a serious innovation in our public law" (*Hansard Parliamentary Debates*, 1985, p. 388). Douglas Hogg of Grantham believed that the Secretary of State was being given powers beyond those traditionally granted to the office. Hogg argued, "We are giving the Secretary of State power to enlarge the ambit of the criminal law. We are giving him power to impose penalties, sanctions, and prohibitions where presently there are none" (*Hansard Parliamentary Debates*, 1985, p. 402).[4]

These arguments, however, were quickly dispelled or ignored completely. With both the government and the opposition voicing support, and with pressure from the Prime Minister, the bill passed in two days despite the fears that were expressed about the damage being done to human rights. This speedy passage was made easier because the terminology used during the course of the debate removed any concerns about the rights of individual English citizens. First, the disruptive British football fan was dehumanized, in comparison with the "good" fan, so that the bill was no longer about humans and their rights. Second, the problem was spoken about in military terms so that the bill became a military action, which allowed for a swift, strong reaction and a suspension of individual human-rights concerns.

THE DEHUMANIZATION OF THE FAN

As long as Parliament was not dealing with humans, it did not have to spend time concerning itself with human-rights issues. Through the descriptive language used when speaking about the football violence, human involvement was removed and replaced with images of savagery that demanded strict regulation.

To begin with, there was the idea of the terms "hooligan" and "hooliganism." This terminology helped differentiate between two groups involved in football violence. Sir Peter Emory pointed out the distinction when he said that the new law would help football clubs "receive the support not of hooligans but of ordinary decent people" (*Hansard Parliamentary Debates*, 1985, p. 367). Kaufman further reinforced this idea by arguing that "when the legislation is drafted, a careful distinction must be drawn between action against hooliganism, which action we all support, and attempted and unacceptable restrictions on open-air meetings" (*Hansard Parliamentary Debates*, 1985, p. 344). Brittan also pointed out this distinction when he offered that "trouble inside grounds deters peaceful, genuine supporters, especially families, from going to matches" (*Hansard Parliamentary Debates*, 1985, p. 333). The hooligan is not a person with a family doing human things, but rather some kind of awful force creating a negative atmosphere for humans. By using the hooligan terminology, especially when contrasted with normal human terminology, Parliament made it easier to pass laws that help stop such things from occurring, even though some basic rights may get sidestepped.

Because the hooligans and their actions are not human, they must be described using another set of terms. Like the term "hooligan," other words, which had no specific referent, carried a very negative connotation. "Thugs" was a common term, as used by Michael Colvin in supporting "the Bill and tougher sentences for football thugs . . . which will prevent further drunken football thuggery" (*Hansard Parliamentary Debates*, 1985, p. 361). Michael Lord of Suffolk, Central, blamed society for "allowing this kind of marauding thuggery to develop and create havoc and death at events designed for pleasure and relaxation" (*Hansard Parliamentary Debates*, 1985, p. 371). Lord also combined thugs with bullies when he argued that "to be weak with the bullies and thugs is to be uncaring about the gentle and law-abiding people whose enjoyment and not infrequently lives may be ruined" (*Hansard Parliamentary Debates*, 1985, p. 372). Again, note how the contrast of the bad with the good makes the thuggery appear that much worse and increases the likelihood of support for actions to stop it.

Other interesting dehumanizing terms from the dialogue included Bruinvels's description of "football traveling nasties" (*Hansard Parliamentary Debates*, 1985, p. 408) and Denis Howell's use of the well-known cancer metaphor to describe the problem of hooliganism (*Hansard Parliamentary Debates*, 1985, p. 411). All of these terms allowed people to regard the problem of football violence as not being perpetrated by humans.

There is also a consistent use of animal terminology that dehumanized the participants in football violence. For example, one of the methods to discourage football violence was to keep the visiting fans separate from the home fans, commonly known as segregation. Segregation took two forms, "the use of lines of policemen to keep rival fans apart" and "the erection of dividing fences on terraces" (Dunning, 1988, p. 167). These methods acted to funnel fans in certain directions. Segregation techniques also provided the largest body of animal metaphors. Ken Weetch of Ipswich referred to visiting fans being "herded off the terraces like cattle" (*Hansard Parliamentary Debates*, 1985, p. 392). Weetch furthered this description when he described how "the citizens of Ipswich are very glad that visiting fans are met at the railway station and escorted to the ground. . . . In effect, a large crocodile from the train is taken under escort to the turnstiles and then put into a cage" (*Hansard Parliamentary Debates*, 1985, p. 393). Bruinvels described a similar situation in his town, though instead of a crocodile being controlled, he saw "an orderly snake" (*Hansard Parliamentary Debates*, 1985, p. 407).

When segregation failed, however, the animals got out of control. Kaufman described the violence being led by "the leader of the pack" (*Hansard Parliamentary Debates*, 1985, p. 349), a reference to wolves. These groups then went out "rampaging" (*Hansard Parliamentary Debates*, 1985, p. 333) and "running loose through the streets of many town centres" (*Hansard Parliamentary Debates*, 1985, p. 419). When animals get out, society is threatened, and the new laws would help control them. By using animal terms, the actions lost more of their connection to humanity and again became easier to legislate against.

There was one voice during the debate that recognized the symbolic action occurring in dehumanizing the spectators. Robert N. Wareing of Liverpool, West Derby, whose main interest appeared to be fighting class-distinction bias, voiced his concern about the negative depictions of football fans. "If they were all public schoolboys, they would be described as high-spirited," Wareing posited, "but when working-class youngsters engage in boisterous behavior it becomes hooliganism" (*Hansard Parliamentary Debates*, 1985, p. 398). This lone appeal was ignored by the rest of Parliament, but Wareing should be saluted for his attempt to break through the metaphorically induced haze.

FOOTBALL VIOLENCE AS MILITARY ACTION

Although government legislation can, and usually does, develop slowly, there is a certain amount of urgency that accompanies military actions. The use of military terminology to describe football violence in this debate acted as a justification for moving quickly on the bill. Also, by describing football violence as a war situation, members of Parliament could dispel human-rights concerns, as is the case under martial law. Similar to the dehumanizing terminology, military descriptions further removed concern for English citizens from the debate and left issues that could be dealt with quickly and decisively, without requiring lengthy debate about human rights.

The first step in a military engagement is often an invasion, a term used many times in the debate. Kaufman recounted stories of football hooligans at a match who participated in a "violent invasion of the pitch [English word for playing field]" (Hansard Parliamentary Debates, 1985, p. 348). Fans traveling overseas were described as invading other countries. David Ashby described one such tour as a military campaign in which "there were frightening episodes. They [fans] were not too bad in Turin, but along the whole of the Ligurian coast three or four coach loads of British supporters beat up the towns. They started in the town of Celle and moved on to Savona" (Hansard Parliamentary Debates, 1985, p. 396). Ashby referred to a leader who "can marshal his forces very well" (Hansard Parliamentary Debates, 1985, p. 395), as well as followers that "get together on the Thursday or Friday before a match to plan how they will 'take' the other end [the rival fan's side of the stadium]" (Hansard Parliamentary Debates, 1985, p. 394). Ashby also described how these groups "make certain signs to one another, and they dress in certain ways" (Hansard Parliamentary Debates, 1985, p. 394), suggesting codes and uniforms. Bruinvels was "sure that the Bill will reassure those who worry about offensive weapons being taken into the grounds. The Bill will also cover empty containers, which can become missiles" (Hansard Parliamentary Debates, 1985, p. 410).

With all of this description of invasion and missiles, it should be no surprise that the tone of the debate became one of retaliation with military aggressiveness. Shaw urged that "the spread of the problem, its duration and complexity require action to be taken across a broad front" (Hansard Parliamentary Debates, 1985, p. 416). Weetch argued that "the problem is one of social terrorism . . . and the solution requires a parallel with military intelligence (Hansard Parliamentary Debates, 1985, p. 392). When war terms are used, war reactions can be taken, which includes working fast at the expense of some basic rights.

Again, some voices spoke out against the notion of military action. Ashton claimed that, many times, the problem of spectator violence was caused not by martial thoughts by the fans, but by the militaristic treatment of the fans by the security force. Ashton described how visiting fans "are met at the station and escorted through the streets like prisoners of war. It is not unusual to see a copper give an away fan a cuff because he does not like the look of him or because he has stepped off the sidewalk" (*Hansard Parliamentary Debates*, 1985, p. 382). Here we not only see the military metaphor, but also the suggestion of lost rights caused by the military action. Griffiths also attempted to reign in the militaristic approach being taken by the Parliament by reminding his listeners that "[w]e are not going to war; we are simply trying to deal with the problems of football matches" (*Hansard Parliamentary Debates*, 1985, p. 390). Again, these are lonely voices in Parliament that failed to garner much notice.

CONCLUSIONS

After less than two days of debate (on the first day, debate did not even start until 3:39 P.M.), the *Sporting Events (Control of Alcohol etc.) Bill* passed through the House of Commons. It was hailed as a significant step in solving the problem of hooliganism that had been spoiling football in England since the 1960s. The law aimed to limit alcohol consumption at football games and strengthen policing powers, which would keep fans sober and nonviolent.

The bill, despite its supposed ability to limit violent outbursts, has failed to stop football violence. One of the worst incidents since the bill passed was the Hillsborough disaster of April 15, 1989. One report on this incident detailed how "[n]inety-five Liverpool supporters died whilst penned into a human cage at the Leppings Lane end" (Taylor, 1991, p. 3). The animal metaphors stemming from segregation tactics had come back to haunt Parliament. The *Sporting Events Bill* was a quick-fix reaction to an unusually violent football season, which was further marked by declining attendance and the disgrace of being barred from mainland travel. The Prime Minister and her government, out of both good intentions and the need for good public relations, created the new legislation and got it passed in four months' time.

Much of the credit for the speedy passage of the law is due to the language used to discuss the bill. To work as quickly as it did, Parliament needed to get through the debate about the bill without spending a lot of time debating issues of human-rights infringements, or any other time-consuming, bill-jeopardizing issues. A fast-paced debate was achieved through two rhetorical tactics: dehumanizing metaphors and military terminology.

These tactics must be watched carefully by critics. The use of such devil terms and military language can steer the debate and silence voices that offer other, less violent alternatives. When the human element is removed, concern for human rights can also be removed from debate. Since Vietnam, critics have been very aware of how killing can be made more acceptable if the enemy is described with inhuman terms. Equal attention must be given to the use of dehumanizing terminology in all policy debates. According to the example of the *Sporting Events (Control of Alcohol etc.) Bill*, any government debate can lead to human-rights abuses if the human element is removed from the terminology of the debate.

NOTES

1. The book *Hooligans Abroad* (Williams 1984), written before the events studied in this chapter, gives a good description of violence by British fans, especially at the 1982 World Cup in Spain. The book also predicts that more disturbances by English fans will lead to their banishment from the continent, a prediction that came true after the Brussels incident.

2. The idea of identity through sport is not limited to small towns. Williams and Wagg (1991) argue that football and its decline represent England and its decline.

3. Although a few minor football bills had been discussed in the past, and were brought up during this debate, they were treated as insignificant by Parliament. According to Geoffrey Dickens, "For 20 years the country has been waiting for a Government to do something about the football problem in the United Kingdom" (*Hansard Parliamentary Debates*, 1985, p. 346).

4. A Reuter textline press release dated October 12, 1985, reports the creation of a new Public Order Bill to provide "the police with more effective means of controlling all forms of hooligan and anti-social behavior which cause alarm, harassment or distress." Fifteen years later, the August 29, 2000, issue of the *World Socialist* Web site criticized another attempt to stop soccer violence as undermining civil liberties. The Football (Disorder) Act 2000, hurriedly pushed through by the Blair government after British fans were at the center of violent clashes at the Euro 2000 football tournament in Belgium, was accused of overturning "the presumption of innocence" and allowing "police the right to search, arrest, and impose a travel ban on anyone they suspect to be potential "football hooligans."

REFERENCE LIST

Dunning, Eric (with Murphy, Patrick, & Williams, John). (1988). *The roots of football hooliganism*. London: Routledge & Kegan Paul.

Hansard Parliamentary Debates. (1985). London: Cornelius Buck.

Hyland, Julie. (2000, August 29). New measures against football hooligans undermine civil liberties in Britain. *World Socialist* Web site. Retrieved from http://www.wsws.org/articles/2000/aug2000/act-a29.shtml.

Ivie, Robert L. (1974). Presidential motives for war. *Quarterly Journal of Speech, 60*, 337–345.

Ivie, Robert L. (1980). Images of savagery in American justifications for war. *Communication Monographs, 47*, 279–294.

Perry, Steven. (1983). Rhetorical functions of the infestation metaphor in Hitler's rhetoric. *Central States Speech Journal, 34,* 229–235.

Taylor, Ian. (1987). Putting the boot into a working-class sport: British soccer after Bradford and Brussels. *Sociology of Sport Journal, 4,* 171–191.

Taylor, Ian. (1991). English football in the 1990s: Taking Hillsborough seriously? In J. Williams & Stephen Wagg (Eds.), *British football and social change* (pp. 3–24). Great Britain: Leicester University Press.

Wagg, Stephen. (1984). *The football world.* Sussex, England: The Harvester Press.

Williams, John, & Wagg, Stephen. (1991). *British football and social change.* Great Britain: Leicester University Press.

Williams, John (with Dunning, Eric, & Murphy, Patrick). (1984). Hooligans abroad: Behaviour and control of English fans at Continental football matches. London: Routledge & Kegan Paul.

CHAPTER 10

Fifty-Eight American Dreams: The NBA Draft as Mediated Ritual

Richard Olsen

Studio executives know that basketball is a box office draw. Several film-makers have successfully used the game of "hoop" as a central plot or key subplot on the silver screen. Films such as *He Got Game, Space Jam, Eddie, Blue Chips, Celtic Pride, Basketball Diaries, Hoop Dreams, Heaven is a Playground, White Men Can't Jump,* and *Hoosiers* are just a few examples. We can also find a plethora of basketball stars profiled on video, such as Michael Jordan in *Come Fly With Me* and others in *Legends of the Game.* As the popularity of basketball may explain the draw of audience members into movie theaters or rental stores, perhaps film theory can explain the draw of audience members to the televised draft coverage of National Basketball Association (NBA) basketball.

This analysis will draw from the film theory of David Bordwell (1989) and the phenomenon of ritual to analyze the live media event of the NBA draft and use the 1995 and 1996 broadcasts as text. The nature of the analysis offered here is best defined as a rhetorical close reading (Leff, 1980); however, because the televised draft coverage is highly visual and sequential in nature, many of the tools Bordwell offers will facilitate a close reading. This close reading reveals that, by framing the NBA draft as a mediated ritual, its popularity can be explained.

First, I begin with a brief discussion of Bordwell's (1989) neo-formalist approach to film and his tools for analysis. Second, I present a brief de-scription of the NBA draft and discuss its place in the NBA year. Third, I identify significant elements of the draft coverage and their functions within the coverage and discuss them using key excerpts from the drafts. Fourth, I identify some central semantic fields to begin to interpret the popularity of the draft.[1] Fifth, I discuss the genres that shape the coverage, using the work of Victor Turner (1974) and others to suggest the dominant element in the draft coverage that explains its popularity is ritual.

BORDWELL'S NEO-FORMALIST APPROACH

Adapting Bordwell's (1989) tools to the analysis of a highly visual, mediated, nonfilm artifact is hardly difficult because his assumptions and critical concepts are closely tied to rhetorical theory.[2] A key assumption of Bordwell's approach is the primacy of the text. The text is the primary locus of meaning and should have discreetness to it. The text means something; we do not simply bring our meanings to the text. That assumption has clear implications, the foremost being that textual features have functions and effects that the critic should describe and then attempt to explain.

The method Bordwell (1989) offers can be summarized in the following steps: First, take the text on its own terms and describe what the actual features are and how they function in that text. Second, attempt to identify the central semantic fields operating in the text to give it form and substance. Third, search for the dominant element that best explains the meaning of the artifact.

According to Bordwell's (1989) definition of a semantic field, various structural relationships among concepts can provide meaning for a film. Some fundamental structures that underlie common semantic fields will be discussed here, including clusters, doublets, proportional series, and hierarchies. Clusters in the NBA could include point guards, rookies, or even athletes as groups. Bordwell's doublets refer to meaning often found in binary opposites, such as night and day. The New York Knicks and the Miami Heat are often thought of in doublet fashion because of their similarities (both coached by Pat Riley, both known for tough defense) and their intense rivalry. The Clippers and the Lakers would be another doublet example, in that they share the home city of Los Angeles yet are rivals. Bordwell illustrates proportional series in the progression from hamlet to village and from town to city. Within the context of the NBA, we find a progression from Philadelphia to New York to Chicago to Boston to Los Angeles in terms of franchises. Of course, Knicks' fans—or any true believer in any of the other franchises—might disagree with the order offered here! Finally, hierarchal series are more clear-cut: high school, college, and professional. There are also a variety of proportional series. For basketball, the hierarchical series would be meaningful relations implied by semantic fields such as opposition, inclusion, and scale, among others.

These semantic fields help unpack the various levels of meaning offered in a film. For Bordwell (1989), there are four levels of meaning: referential, explicit, implicit, and symptomatic. Two levels deal with comprehension, whereas two deal with interpretation. *Referential* meaning is the most basic level of meaning. Issues such as causality, space, and references to concrete information ("The Bulls are looking for help at every position") are referential. When the meaning of an artifact is discussed directly in the film and is comprehended by the viewer, there is *explicit* meaning. When a father turns to his son and says "Killing is wrong, son," he is providing explicit meaning. However, when meaning is derived indirectly through symbolism, we move into *implicit* meaning, which is the first level of interpretation. In the first three types of meaning, we "assume the film 'knows' more or less what it is doing" (p. 9). However, if we take the interpretation beyond that constraint and examine the masked motives of the author, or the ways in which cultural ideology may have shaped the artifact, we are uncovering *symptomatic* meanings. For example, if, in examining the draft, we find significant use of red, white, and blue coloring, we may determine that there is an implicit but intentional desire by the NBA to promote basketball as an American game. Or, we may consider the time limits set for first-round versus second-round draft picks (five minutes and two minutes, respectively) and note that this is consistent with our American orientation toward time; time is money. The more money a player stands to make, for himself and for his team, the more time he is given in the draft coverage. This is an example of symptomatic meaning.

We can find numerous semantic fields and meaningful relations in any significant artifact. How then does the critic focus the analysis? The work of Bordwell (1989) seeks to uncover the "dominant element" of a film.[3] The dominant element is the key semantic field, key meaning, or framing device that helps the reader make the most sense of the artifact. How do we best explain the cultural attraction of the driver's license? Maturation? Responsibility? Neither of these terms typically causes a teenager's pulse to quicken. However, the dependent/independent and the immobile/mobile doublets probably focus our attention on the core issues. On receiving a driver's license, a teenager moves from dependent and immobile to independent and mobile. Although the license may be taken as a sign of maturation and require responsibility, neither of these function as the dominant factor in understanding the meaning of "driver's license."

As mentioned previously, the first step in a neo-formalist analysis is to take the artifact on its own terms. This involves a thorough description of the key elements and their functions. The next section of this chapter offers a thorough description of the draft and its coverage to provide the background necessary for identifying key semantic fields and the dominant element.

THE NBA DRAFT

Both the NBA game and the draft itself have changed over the years. Many of these changes have been initiated as explicit attempts to make the game and the draft more accessible to television viewers. Two of the most noticeable changes to the game have been the additions of the 24-second clock and the three-point shot. The 24-second clock requires the team with the ball to attempt a shot that at least touches the rim within 24 seconds of gaining possession of the ball. This keeps the action moving for most of the game. The three-point shot has been instrumental in increasing scoring and encouraging longer jump shots that are visually dramatic.

The draft itself has become a spectacle during the past several years. Once held at a small venue in New York, it is now held in a stadium of one of the NBA teams. The 1995 draft, held at the arena of the then-new Toronto Raptors, had a live attendance of approximately 21,000 fans. The 1996 draft, held in the Continental Airlines Arena in New Jersey, had a similar turnout.

Since the draft began in 1966, it has undergone several modifications to pique fan interest in late-season games and in the draft itself. To discourage weaker teams from "tanking" (playing to lose) during the last part of the season to secure the best pick in the draft, the league instituted a lottery system in 1985. (In traditional drafts, the team with the worst record during the preceding season receives the first draft pick.) The lottery system has been modified and refined over the years since its introduction. Top picks are determined using Ping-Pong balls placed in a giant drum. For weaker teams, more Ping-Pong balls are placed inside the drum to encourage, but not ensure, that they will draw top picks. The better teams (a relative term because only the worst teams participate in the lottery) have fewer Ping-Pong balls placed in the drum on their behalf. This drawing then determines the picking order. The announcement of the draft picking order is often used as a key segment of half-time programming for one of the NBA playoff games.

In a typical lottery, a representative from each team (a coach, general manager, owner, key player, etc.) is present—often with good luck charms or other such items that might help secure a good pick in the lottery. Hope of securing the best player seems to override any apparent shame of being one of the worst teams in the league. The commissioner then reveals the draft order for these lottery teams. As with a beauty contest, when the second pick is announced, by default, the top pick has also been revealed, and this team has "won" the lottery. Determining the draft order roughly a month before the actual draft allows time for intrigue to develop. Speculation regarding which college player the team with the first selection in the draft will choose usually follows. For the non-lottery teams, their regular-season records determine the draft order, with the more successful teams drafting later. Intrigue and speculation is further enhanced as teams and fans wonder if any college underclassmen will declare they are coming out for the professional league early. Many of the best college players elect to come out early—a situation that often means a change in the likely order of top picks.

Since 1989, the NBA drafts have been limited to two rounds. In the first round, each team has five minutes to make its selection. Commissioner David Stern announces each choice from a podium located at center stage. Many of the top candidates wait in a designated area with their families and friends. On being selected, the draftee is given a baseball cap-style hat bearing the logo and/or name of the team that drafted him. He puts on the hat as he is led to the stage to shake the Commissioner's hand while pictures are taken. This waiting area is closed off from the fans in live attendance, and thus, there is a "coming out" of sorts as the draftee proceeds to the stage. He is then led to another location where a broadcaster conducts a short interview. The second round is similar in format, except that each team is given only two minutes to make a selection, and the Deputy Commissioner, rather than the Commissioner, announces the choices. In addition, these second-round players are seldom present at the draft, so there is no coming out or postselection interview.

The Turner Network Television (TNT) coverage of the 1995 and 1996 drafts featured two analysts and an announcer assessing team needs, making predictions about the likely pick, and then reacting to the pick while video of the chosen player was shown. Typical live video coverage shows the draftee coming to the stage, his statistics, and highlight footage from his college career. All trades announced during the draft are analyzed in a similar manner: by focusing on how the trade met the team's needs.

With this thumbnail sketch of the draft as a backdrop, we can now examine specific elements of the draft coverage in more detail.

ELEMENTS OF THE DRAFT COVERAGE

A frequent cry of sports-program hawkers is "Program! Get your program! You can't tell the players without a program!" This section of the chapter is like the "program" for the artifact of the NBA draft. This program focuses on elements specific to the TNT live coverage of the draft. This limitation is necessary because most sports media outlets offer some predraft feature, so the entire body of media discussion and analysis is quite extensive. It may also be surprising for non-fans to learn that TNT devoted more than four hours of live, prime-time coverage to the selection of 58 basketball players. This live coverage was preceded the night before by a one-hour, predraft special in which viewers "met" many of the top players on a "personal" level. Biographical sketches—similar to those used in Olympic coverage—showed viewers the players' unique skills and attributes, their triumphs over injuries or hardships, and their favorite activities outside the game of basketball.

In analyzing the live draft coverage, we have our own "starting five": characters, dialogue, plot, graphics, and video. Like any good basketball team, we also have a great "sixth man": setting. Each offers distinct contributions, or functions, within the draft coverage.[4]

Characters

The first key element in the draft coverage is the characters. There are six major groups of characters in the coverage: the players, their families, the announcers, the "correspondents," the commissioner, and the live audience.

The players are obviously central to the draft. The plot centers around what happens to them and how they react to it. The other elements function largely to bring about their character development and story. Although there is no casting in the traditional sense, human nature being what it is, there is a natural diversity in the draftees as characters. They vary in physical stature (albeit from tall to very tall), disposition, background, race, and nationality.[5] There are players who went to college solely to play ball, with the primary hope of getting into the NBA, and there are others, such as Todd Fuller and Roy Rogers, who focused on earning high grade point averages and never thought they would wind up playing in the NBA. Rogers discussed his priorities during his postselection interview with TNT's Craig Sager (CS):

CS: . . . When did you think you'd be sitting here?

RR: Well, to be honest Craig, I never thought I'd have this opportunity. You know, my dream was to go to college and get my degree. I fulfilled that dream by graduating last year with a degree in marketing. . . . I just have to say congrats and thank you to all my people back at the University of Alabama for working so hard with me, all the fans for their support. It was tremendously hard on me waiting back there in the green room, but I'm just glad to be selected here in the draft. (TNT, 1996)

Sager asked him where he'd like to be five to ten years from now. He responded that he hoped to be in the front office of an NBA team making decisions on who will be hired and fired. Clearly, a key to the success of the draft coverage is exposure to a variety of characters, even in the seemingly one-dimensional world of "jocks." One draftee was even asked to sing during his interview, because he plays two musical instruments and is a big fan of Stevie Wonder.

Another facet of the characters is the way the draftees dress on draft night. Variety and flash seem to be the unofficial dress code for the draft.

The players wear bold, distinctive suits, and the announcers often comment on their sartorial splendor. For example, in the 1995 draft, draftee Gary Trent wore a green suit and was drafted by the Milwaukee Bucks. Because the Bucks' team colors are green and purple, his suit became an item for discussion with broadcaster Sager. The flashy suits simultaneously express the players' common distinction as NBA draftees, while also expressing their individuality and style.

The primary function the players serve is to be the objects or catalysts for events to which others—family, fans, viewers, and commentators—can react. They are the reason for this event. All the coverage, the commentary, the edited video clips, and so forth are in anticipation of and, ultimately, reaction to what will happen to them. In the draft, as in the game they play, the players are to do things and be the initiators of "events" so that others—commentators and fans—can ascribe significance to those events.[6] However, in the draft itself, what they actually do is a bit more passive: They get selected. Yet they are still the catalysts for an event that must now be interpreted.

The families of the top picks also become central characters in the draft. As noted, there is a waiting room for the top picks and their families. On selection, the reaction of the families—who are rarely wealthy prior to the draft—is a key component of the coverage. For these top picks, the notion of "lottery" takes on a double meaning. Prior to the introduction of the modern salary cap in 1984, rookies occasionally signed contracts in excess of $40 million over seven years. Even with the pay scale for rookies now determined by the players' union, salaries for top picks are in the millions. The 1999 minimum player salary in the NBA, for example, was just over $300,000.

The drama of the draft is heightened by the families' reactions. Family friends gathered at the players' table in the "green room" are expected to exhibit appropriate reactions of joy and relief when that player is selected. Particularly tearful or emotional reactions are both shown during video coverage and noted by the broadcasters. Family members are usually dressed in a manner consistent with the new status of their young draftee. The focus is typically on the mother, who is often shown thanking God and crying openly. The families help the TNT coverage provide the emotional, nonverbal reaction so the audience can better identify with what it must be like to undergo such a sudden transformation in social and economic status.

The broadcasters, however, are just as crucial to the draft coverage as the players. They interpret the events for the television audience and must exhibit the appropriate ethos to do so effectively. Typically, sporting events are covered by a play-by-play and a color commentator. The play-by-play person is responsible for offering basic description of events and questioning the color commentators. Color commentators are often former players and coaches that offer analysis of the events as they unfold. The play-by-play commentator for the 1995 and 1996 draft was Ernie Johnson, well-known to fans that follow TNT's coverage of the NBA as the anchor of half-time reports and other related coverage. The two color commentators, Hubie Brown and Rick Pitino, were both former NBA coaches. Hubie Brown is known as a "lifer" in the NBA who seems to have always been there and loves the game. He is also a color commentator for TNT NBA game coverage. The much-traveled Rick Pitino was a successful NBA coach with the Knicks before moving back into the college ranks as the coach for the 1996 NCAA Champion Kentucky Wildcats. He later moved back to the NBA to be the coach and general manager of the Boston Celtics. The Celtics had hit bottom, and Pitino was able to secure complete authority regarding personnel. Many big-name coaches seek to become general managers as well because that position reasserts their authority over players.

The TNT commentator who interviewed the top players selected at the draft site was Craig Sager. He is also familiar to those who follow TNT coverage through his feature stories on various players and issues in the NBA. In addition, he has occasionally substituted for Johnson on TNT or hosted half-time reports when another of Turner's stations covers an NBA game. The 1996 draft added one more commentator at the draft site: Peter Vescey, a sports columnist known for his analysis of various events in the NBA and for having the hard-to-get information. He is syndicated nationally, has a regular feature in *USA Today*, and appears as an analyst during NBC's coverage of the NBA. These five characters clearly are "regular cast." The individual ethos of the former coaches and Vescey is particularly important, as will be demonstrated subsequently. At the draft, their dress is credible and not nearly as flashy as the players'. Viewers' familiarity with the cast offers a heightened sense of continuity to the draft coverage and helps frame it as a natural installment in the sequence of the NBA season. This cast of regulars also functions to interpret the draft. Johnson offers little in the way of analysis but must set up the others and offer transitional material as attention shifts from video shots of the commissioner announcing a selection to family reactions to interviews with Sager to more analysis and reaction from the experts. The experts' (Brown, Pitino, Vescey) role is to offer more rational assessments of the pick, such as answering questions about how the player will fit in, what his strengths and weaknesses are, and so forth. For example, before the first pick in the draft, the Philadelphia '76ers were anticipated to pick one of two point guards. Johnson (EJ) set the scene for the experts Brown (HB) and Pitino (RP):

EJ: Quickly, guys, if you had to make a choice between Stephon Marbury and Allen Iverson, where do you go?

HB: Well, it comes down to style. You have a new coach, a new general manager. How are you going to play? . . . It will come down to your philosophy. Here in New York, it's unanimous—it should be [New Yorker] Stephon Marbury. (Laughter)

RP: From where I sit, I like Marcus Camby. Because of the style of play of having to wait for [current '76er player] Derrick Coleman to get down the floor. [He's] The X-Factor. Derrick Coleman gets in shape, and you have three wonderful players with Iverson, Stackhouse, and Derrick Coleman. (TNT, 1996)[7]

Each of the experts working with Johnson is able to offer, though somewhat indirectly, his opinion about which player the '76ers should pick. Johnson then offers a transition into the next segment: a graphic that outlines the recent instability the '76ers have had at the point guard position. This clip is followed by an immediate switch back to the experts for more analysis. Finally, there is a shift to the commissioner for the pick. All of this occurs in about one minute of airtime.

Vescey functions much like the informant in a fictional police show. He gets the "word on the street." He is not seen much until he has a vital piece of information to add to the puzzle. Thus, whenever Johnson makes the transition to Vescey, viewers' heartbeats quicken because his comments should be an "inside scoop" about a trade or other such happenings:

EJ: The number-three spot belongs to the Vancouver Grizzlies, Let's see what's going on in the number 3, 4, 5, area right now. Let's check in with Peter Vescey. Peter, whatcha got?

PV: Well, there's been some talk that the Vancouver Grizzlies might take Stephon Marbury at this spot. But they're going to take Sharif Abdur-Rahim—and they're going to keep him. They love this guy. . . . The [Milwaukee] Bucks are then going to go for Stephon Marbury. [General Manager of the Bucks] Mike Dunleavy loves him but could also be talked into trading him. The [Minnesota] Timberwolves are already offering Andrew Lang and a flip-flop of picks. . . .

The very phrase "whatcha got?" confirms Vescey's role in advancing the plot. In this sense, Vescey brings back information that viewers can react to and interpret.

Sager's role is to push players to articulate emotions and gently probe their character. The interview may focus on the often-inane query, "How do you feel right now?" but more often is geared toward revealing the players' off-court personal characteristics. These functions were particularly clear when Sager exploited the overwhelming emotion a young Stephon Marbury (who declared himself eligible after an exceptional freshman year at Georgia Tech University) felt in reaction to his selection:

CS: Well, Stephon, it is always an emotional scene in the back room when you get drafted, but I'll tell ya', when we saw your family hugging everybody, the tears coming to your mother Mabel's eyes, tears coming down your face ... did anyone in your family sleep last night? What was it like?

SM: [Shakes his head, team baseball-style cap covering his face and eyes. He slowly looks up] I can't even explain the way I feel right now. [Pause] It's been 20 years, 20 long years I've waited for this day [breaks up], and it's here, it's here, it's here now.

CS: Can I take off your hat for a second [removes hat]? What has been talked about in your family? What has it been like?

SM: We'd sit around a long time at night just thinking about when this day was gonna come. And for it to be here now, it just feels so good. I could put a permanent smile on my mother's face.

CS: Also buy her that nice greenhouse for her plants.

SM: Oh, yeah. She's gonna have a nice big greenhouse. (TNT, 1996)

The reference to the greenhouse is a call back to the predraft show, in which a feature on Marbury showed him and his family anticipating how their lives might change. On his mother's wish list was a greenhouse. Dreams come true in the draft, and Sager's role is to ensure that the human and emotionally laden side of the draft is brought to the coverage—even if that means taking a draftee's hat off so viewers can see his tears.

As is typical of live coverage of news or sporting events, there are additional TNT broadcasters at key locations throughout the country reporting on news from that region. Each of these characters would be somewhat familiar to regular TNT NBA viewers. The decision to refer to the four broadcasters as "correspondents" certainly suggests a particular ethos normally reserved for hard news organizations and political convention or campaign coverage. Typically, the correspondents offer rumors and/or substantiation of rumors, as well as interviews with coaches fresh from the "war room." The "war room" is the term often given to the boardroom in which the staff of each team gathers to decide on their selection and entertain trade offers from other clubs. Much of this discussion takes place prior to the draft, but an unanticipated pick by an early team or a top player sliding down farther than expected can lead to significant activity during the draft itself. Thus, there is potential for these correspondents to contribute meaningful coverage of key subplots.

The function of these correspondents is to reinforce the national and local significance of the draft and to provide, as Vescey does, information that fuels the sense-making activities of Johnson, Brown, Pitino, and the audience. The geographic dispersion of the correspondents helps them position the draft as an event of national significance. By being strategically placed to represent each of the four divisions in the NBA, they also bring the coverage "home" to fans of teams in their respective divisions.

A highly symbolic character in the draft is Commissioner David Stern, almost unanimously considered a marketing genius. He brought the NBA from a marginal, drug-tainted league in the 1970s to a highly successful international sports conglomerate. He is a dedicated marketer, a fact not lost to the no-nonsense local New Jersey and New York hoop nuts in live attendance at the 1996 draft. When Stern's welcome began to run long as he thanked national, Canadian, and, finally, international audiences, a small smattering of boos and other such reactions arose. The never-flustered Stern simply thanked the fans for their "strong and enthusiastic turnout," quickly smiled, and said, "Let's get started. The first pick in the 1996 NBA draft will be made by the Philadelphia '76ers who have five minutes to make their selection" (TNT, 1996).

His function, like that of the queen at a ship christening or the mayor who cuts the ribbon and takes the ceremonial first shovel full of earth at a groundbreaking, is to add pomp to the circumstance. He is the living symbol of "officialness" for the NBA. The stage is dominated by the NBA logo and official NBA draft signage. But this is an event that is happening in time, not a still life, and so he must be that symbol that can also participate in the event of the draft. By announcing picks in a manner clearly designed to be "for the record," he officiates the rite of passage. After calling out a draftee's name, the draftee greets Stern on the platform in a manner similar to the graduation of the college senior that most players never became, and it is official.

The live audience becomes a mass of undifferentiated characters with a nevertheless clear role to play. The New Jersey setting allowed three groups of fans to be within driving distance: Philadelphia '76ers' fans, New Jersey Nets' fans, and New York Knicks' fans. The attendees in 1996 were dominated by long-time hoop nuts and young kids whose cities have always had an NBA team. In recent years, a new or expansion team in the league often hosts the draft. For the fans in that city, it is all new and exciting.

The fans serve several functions. First, they add to the "eventness" of the draft and reinforce that this is a live event. Sometimes they cheer louder than expected; sometimes they disagree with a pick. Second, they function to model what constitutes the ideal fan. Given that the NBA and TNT prosper when the intensity of fandom increases, those who exhibit ideal fan behavior—purchasing hats, jerseys, and shoes; making signs declaring allegiance to particular players or teams; participating in NBA-sponsored activities, such as filling out the official draft card—are more likely to get on the air (and become part of the coverage). Third, they offer, like the families, emotional reactions to the events taking place. For example, when Joe Smith was selected by the Golden State Warriors, a young fan was shown wearing a Golden State cap and cheering. When Jerry Stackhouse was picked, footage appeared of a fan in University of North Carolina garb—Stackhouse's college for two years. Thus, two plotlines are evidenced and shown to advance through the footage of the fans: the professional team plotline (acquiring Joe Smith to strengthen their roster) and the college player moving up to the professional level.

Dialogue

The importance of dialogue in the draft has already been partly illustrated in the previous section: Each character is distinguished by his or her dialogue. Dialogue is critical in the draft because, as with marriage vows, the critical act takes place symbolically or verbally rather than physically. It is a deed done with words. The gravity of the dialogue is underscored by the uniformity of the commissioner's words. For every pick, the commissioner (or in the second round, the deputy commissioner) begins his sentence the same way. For example, "With the 18th pick of the 1996 NBA Draft, the New York Knicks select John Wallace of Syracuse University" (TNT, 1996). It is a formula that will allow the pick to be replayed years later with the same significance and specificity, should the selection prove to be a momentous occasion for the franchise. The very rare exception sometimes involves the home team. During the1995 draft held in Toronto, the commissioner varied the script slightly because it was the first pick the Raptors had made. Ever the showman, Stern reminded the audience of this as the fervor surrounding the pick continued to rise until its announcement.

In addition, a key to the draft is the verbal reaction to selections by the commentators. Plot twists often emerge from insider information or dialogue from the correspondents and Vescey's and Sager's interviews. Despite this significance, the dialogue is largely a function of character. That is, we expect certain dialogue from certain people, and the roles are fairly clearly defined. We expect transitions from Johnson and analysis from Brown and Pitino. In addition, we expect platitudes from team executives and coaches who are interviewed, and we expect inexperienced—perhaps refreshing, perhaps disappointing—answers to Sager's questions from the novice draftees. As an example of the platitudes offered by coaches, consider the following by the new Dallas Mavericks coach, who inherited a team with three star players who had not gotten along well during the previous season:

Jim Durham (TNT correspondent): Can we expect a trade?

Dallas Coach: The Dallas Mavericks will do what we feel is necessary to maintain competitiveness in the marketplace. (TNT, 1996)

Such a vague response has little do with basketball in general, never mind the specific question, but this kind of dialogue is what makes the correspondents and Vescey so valuable. Perhaps not this time, but in the future, if they are persistent, they will uncover the inside information and report back to viewers. They are on the viewers' side as fellow interpreters of the events being covered.

Plot

Plot is clearly a significant element of the draft coverage. Parallels in the various plotlines of the draft can be found in other culturally relevant arenas. The opening segment of the 1995 draft placed the draft within the narrative of the NBA year. It began with footage of the NBA Champion Houston Rockets and the role that various players had in winning the championship: "Stardom may not have been forecast for them, but there was something about their talents that turned heads and helped turn Houston into champions for two years running" (TNT, 1995). The plot of players being chosen and undergoing a transformation is certainly key for viewers who identify with the draftees. For those viewers who identify with the team, there is a clear plot of trying to build a dynasty and ac-quiring a piece in that building process. The images of these two types of fans are indicative of both of these plotlines. More will be said about the various plotlines in an upcoming section on the dominant element. It is sufficient at this point to make clear that plot is alive and well in the draft. The draft is an open text because it allows for multiple readings and frames of reference, or what Fiske (1993) has called polysemy. This poly-semic characteristic of the plot is important for the draft's appeal to casual fans, as well as to hard-core hoop nuts. Those who follow the NBA and the draft will also see plots that originated during the regular season or continued from previous drafts. These plots include such issues as trades, decisions to overhaul the team ("start over"), and the loss of key players to free agency,[8] as well as plots that tie back to the college game, as the following excerpt illustrates:

PV: Well, every year somebody drops in the draft. A couple of years ago it was Wesley Person. Last year it was Michael Finley. This year, it's John Wallace. We all praised him for going back to school, and he did everything he was sup-posed to do. He took Syracuse to the final two. He worked on his game. He's fiercely competitive. But for whatever reason, he's dropped. Maybe the [Phoe-nix] Suns are supposed to get him as he drops. Or maybe the [Sacramento] Kings will take him at this slot. (TNT, 1996)

There are several active layers of plot in this analysis. First, the comment is clearly about John Wallace, who has not been picked as early as the analysts thought he might be. Second, there is a mini-morality play im-bedded in his slide. Wallace is unique in that he had made himself eligible for the draft the previous year as a junior, then changed his mind and completed his senior year. Will this decision to "do the right thing" be rewarded by the "powers that be"? Third, what is happening to John

Wallace has happened to other players that have gone on to do well in the NBA, such as Finley. who was considered one of the best rookies by the end of his first season. Fourth, the Phoenix Suns were able to draft both Person and Finley in previous drafts when they slid. Thus, Vescey is suggesting a possible "fitting" resolution to the Wallace saga: He will go where the other sliders have gone and prosper as they have.[9] Other commentators contribute to this subplot as well. When the Kings (who have the 14th pick) do not pick Wallace, the following exchange occurs:

HB: It is interesting that they would go with this pick over John Wallace.

RP: I'm a little surprised at that. But you know you can't take it away . . . John Wallace was going to be a 17 or 18 pick last year. This year maybe a little higher, but he still has the memory of a final four, so hopefully it will all work out for him.[10] (TNT, 1996)

In this installment of the storyline, Pitino is clearly picking up on the justice/morality theme. Wallace's decision to stay in school was worth it because of the memories he now has—memories that supersede the economic issues at stake. Dialogue continues about Wallace until he is finally picked by New York with the 18th pick. He played for Syracuse University, so there is a nice resolution in that he stays in New York and will play for a team with legitimate championship potential. Vescey also makes another appeal to coherence and continuity:

PV: Let's not forget, they [the Knicks] got Mark Jackson at number 18 once upon a time. They do well at number 18. (TNT, 1996)

Mark Jackson went on to become rookie of the year, one of the lowest picks ever to achieve this honor in the NBA. In this exchange, Vescey launches a new subplot even as he attempts to provide coherence and resolve the current one—will Wallace get rookie of the year? We also see a clear reference to superstition in this commentary by Vescey. The numbers know nothing of the players who are drafted under them or who eventually wear them on their jerseys. However, this use of numbers helps unveil the ritual nature of the draft that will be elaborated on later.

This example of some of the dialogue surrounding key emergent subplots is indicative of how plot functions in the NBA draft. It provides a satisfying level of predictability, along with enough unpredictability and potential for new stories, to maintain audience interest.[11]

Graphics

Graphics play a significant role in the informational coverage of the draft, as well as in its aesthetic presence on television. The opening of draft coverage is dominated by music and graphics consistent with TNT coverage of the NBA and sports coverage in general. In addition, there are graphics throughout the coverage that help transition to the correspondents on location and video clips of the draftees. Finally, there are graphics that provide information about the draftees and issues being discussed.

These graphics can be seen in light of the four motivations offered by Thompson (1988). Clearly they serve an *artistic* motivation; they are stimulating in and of themselves. They are also *compositionally* motivated in that they advance the plot by providing information about the draftees or problems or needs the team is facing. Finally, graphics are consistent with sports coverage and thus add a sense of realism or verisimilitude to the coverage by being consistent with "real-life" coverage of other sporting events. Thompson calls this motivation *realistic* motivation. This element might also be seen as a *transtextual* motivation because it is derived from other sporting texts.

One example of the way graphics reinforce the transformational aspects of the draft occurred in the 1996 draft. A graphic of a basketball would pass over the word "draftee" that appeared to the left of a picture of the most recent pick. As the basketball passed over the "draftee," it was transformed into the team logo. The graphic—along with a swoosh sound—illustrated the change in identity for the player. I take up this change in identity more fully when discussing the specific ritual aspects of the draft.

Video Clips

The graphics work closely with video clips. When discussing video as a distinct element, I am referring to the prepared video clips used within the overall coverage. These video clips include highlights of a draftee's basketball skills and interviews with outside experts, such as college coaches, who can provide additional plot material about the draftee. For example, when Marcus Camby of the University of Massachusetts was drafted in the first round, the coverage included a video clip of basketball legend Julius Erving ("Dr. J") commenting on Camby's skills. The commentary by Erving was important because Camby was the first University of Massachusetts player since Erving to be drafted in the first round, which revived for a moment the storyline that posed the question, "Will Camby be like Dr. J?" It also served to legitimize the NBA by highlighting its history and drawing attention to the continuity between past greatness and the present game.

Video also functions as evidence for the arguments being made in the dialogue. For example, after the Vancouver Grizzlies picked Sharif Abdur-Rahim, Johnson set up Brown to discuss the pick:

EJ: ... and his skills [are] obvious, Hubie.

HB: Yeah, they needed a power forward to play with Reeves [the center]. They have a number of players that can play small forward. Their guards are adequate. But what they need is a dominant guy who can board [rebound], block shots, get out on the [fast] break, fill the lane. He has all those qualities. Plus, he's excellent with the dribble facing [the basket]. (TNT, 1996)

During this dialogue, video highlights supported most of Brown's claims. Viewers saw blocks and dunks and Abdur-Rahim running hard. More important to the general storyline of the draft, viewers saw him succeeding. Brummett (1991, p. 14) has argued that television logic is visual and that video functions to provide visual support to the claims offered by the commentators.

Setting

The setting, like the presence of the commissioner, functions symbolically as much as it does pragmatically. The increased fan interest in attending the draft moved it out of the small venue in New York, where it had been hosted for many years. However, this meant that the spectacle of the draft needed to increase to symbolically fill the huge arenas. The TNT coverage does not focus on any of the activities that occupy the attention of those attending the draft. Coming back from commercial breaks, viewers can catch only glimpses of the cheerleaders and audience participation contests taking place. The Sager interviews are broadcast to the live audience as well.

The arena is a symbolic setting because that is where big-time sports events take place. But then, so do other major events. Recent political conventions have been held in large arenas, as are some rock concerts, large trade shows, and other entertainment events. Thus, the arena itself is a site of legitimation beyond sport. However, all the arenas that host the draft are primarily sports arenas and, most often, basketball arenas. Consequently, they are linked most closely with this form of symbolic activity. Within this context, the fans function as part of the setting, as well as characters in their own right.

Consistent with Sage's analysis (1996), the colors that dominate the setting are red, white, and blue. The NBA logo is a combination of these colors, so these choices are not inconsistent with the league. However, the overall effect is strikingly similar to a political convention. The podium is substantial and displays the NBA draft logo prominently. In addition, as the commissioner announces the picks, he is flanked in the background by two large NBA logos. Viewers also see the banks of tables where team representatives sit near their team phones and prepare for last-minute negotiations.

As noted, the green room is a big part of the setting. The round tables around which each of the players and their chosen few gather is much less a symbol of sport than of civilian life, perhaps at a prom or a dinner banquet. Thus, the players move from a civilian/familial setting, up a long ramp, to the red, white, and blue stage to meet the commissioner. They are not in Kansas anymore. This segment functions to portray the draft as a significant turning point for the player, his family, and the team that has drafted him.[12]

This sequence of events also offers transtextual motivations. Thompson (1988) notes that transtextual motivations "appeal to conventions of other artworks" (p. 18). We can make sense of the configuration and sequence of devices because we recognize them from prior experience. We are able to draw on political conventions, beauty pageants, and perhaps even the senior prom to understand the coverage. Later in this chapter, I will explore the implications for several of these interpretive frames.

SEMANTIC FIELDS

In this section, I briefly identify key semantic fields that are manifest in the coverage of the draft. First and most obviously, there is hierarchy. The NBA is at the top of the basketball hierarchy, both nationally and internationally. It is the most talented and competitive league in the world. This semantic field manifests itself in all the dialogue that entails what it will take for these players to succeed "at the next level." Dialogue pertaining to this hierarchy occurs with international players who are drafted, as well as with those coming out of colleges in the United States. In the 1995 draft, Johnson expressed concern about the fact that there were "a lot of undergraduates in the field this year" (TNT, 1995). In the 1996 draft, he explored the transition more directly while talking with Brown:

EJ: When a kid first comes into the NBA, what's the first thing you've got to teach them?

HB: To play under duress. Over here you have high school basketball and college basketball. And over here you have the game played at the top of the box, which is at eleven feet! (TNT, 1996)

The "top of the box" refers to the square on the backboard directly behind the hoop. It helps players see the angles necessary for bank shots and lay-ups. It is one foot above a rim that is ten feet high. Many current NBA players can jump high enough to touch the top of the box. Banks uses that aspect of the game to position the NBA and its players at the top of the hierarchy.

Second, there are several doublets, or binary opposites, at work that offer the building blocks for some of the themes discussed previously.

Boy/man, amateur/professional, and poor/rich are but a few of these doublets that are played out in the visual images and the dialogue of the draft coverage.

These young men, who ultimately will make their living playing a game in shorts, are dressed in suits for the draft. Once selected, they literally leave their family to assume their position on stage. In these acts, they directly engage the doublet of boy/man, especially those who have come out of college early and those increasingly more common draftees that make themselves eligible immediately after high school. Dressed in a tailored suit and meeting with Sager for their "first professional interview," as Johnson calls it, they engage the doublet of amateur/professional. Finally, by implication and even explicit commentary, they move from poor to rich. In addition, the draft is framed with at least some recognition of these doublets. The opening segment of the draft is a voiceover of former Lakers' point guard Earvin "Magic" Johnson reflecting on the day he was drafted:

Magic: . . . You wait for that moment all your life to have your name called. Don't think that every basketball player does not watch the draft and one day say, "Hey, I want my name to be called. I want to walk across that stage." I don't think there is one guy who ever has forgotten when he was drafted. You'll always remember that. You'll always have that because you've always dreamed of being in the NBA. So when that moment comes and your name is called, you have finally arrived.

EJ: And tonight you've arrived at a place where childhood dreams will come true. With the city of New York as a backdrop, some of the best young players in the world stand at the doorstep to the big time: the NBA. (TNT, 1996)

The video during Magic's voiceover consists of NBA footage of former and current NBA players who were drafted first, and slowly there is a shift to the current selection of draftees that might go first. This review serves not only to address the doublets, but also to frame the draft as a historic event.

In the preceding dialogue, several fields can be identified. Clearly, the hierarchy of the NBA as it relates to all other forms of basketball is imbedded throughout. In addition, both Magic and Johnson recognize the childhood origins of the dream and the transition into something different from childhood. Later in the introductions, Johnson further addresses the youth element in the draft by saying there are a ". . . lot of kids coming out. Childhood a not too distant memory for some of these guys. What is the risk you take if you draft one of them?" (TNT, 1996). In this example, the relationship between semantic fields and the larger plot is evident. The tension between boy and man offers a catalyst for the plot theme of risk in the selection of younger players. Johnson's phrase, "doorstep to the big time," signifies the shift from amateur to professional, as well as from poor to rich.

THE SEARCH FOR THE DOMINANT ELEMENT

The search for the dominant element seems almost redundant in an event that is about the search for the dominant, namely, the best player. Yet this search poses some interesting problems. The draft borrows from many genres and is marketed as many things. It borrows from the sporting-event genre with its use of highlights and graphics and in the relationship between the players and the commentators. A strong case also can be made that the compositional decisions orient around the sporting-event genre and that therefore the dominant is located there as well.[13]

However, the draft is not a contest as such, and the players can do nothing at this point to alter the outcome. We might argue, then, that the coverage draws from election coverage or political convention coverage. From this perspective, the draft relates to the peaceful transfer of power and inspires a certain level of hope that comes with change. Those who have been most out of power (weaker teams) typically have the higher picks and therefore the most hope of getting back in to power. In this sense, the selection process of the draft may be seen as more fair than current systems of "democratic" elections. In addition, TNT, like CNN, is a Turner company, and the compositional choices made in CNN election coverage may be imported to TNT draft coverage. Certainly, the term "correspondents" and subplots about character issues, leadership skills, and whether the player will fit into that team are similar to election issues of character, leadership skills, and whether the candidate can galvanize his or her constituents or "balance a ticket." The dramatic use of red, white, and blue is also suggestive of the political election/convention genre. Yet elections are not dominated by the physical attributes of the candidates.[14] Nor can they be said to be as transformational for those elected as the selection of draftees is framed to be. The draftees are transformed and will transform their team. Many Americans have long since lost this expectation for political candidates.

Another interpretive option is the dominant analogue of a beauty pageant. There is a secretive panel of judges that makes a selection, and viewers have their personal favorites. These favorites may be a particular college player, a particular NBA team, or a combination of both. There are even short interviews with the "contestants." However, this perspective also falls short because there is no competition during the draft. The contestants in a beauty competition are interviewing as part of the competition, not as a result of having been selected. Furthermore, even the players selected late in the draft are generally considered winners, which is not typically the case in beauty pageants.

The draft might also be framed as a more generic news event that involves a merger or acquisition (a selection) and subsequent attempts to personalize the event by showing real people (the families) react to the unfolding scene. This business news genre is further augmented by the constantly rolling graphic of already made selections moving from right to left at the bottom of the screen, which looks very similar to the electronic stock reports shown on some cable stations. In addition, viewers hear from expert commentators and civilians "live on the scene" and around the nation about the impact of this event.

There is also the more literary narrative analogue of the gambler/mystery/detective genre, in which the brains and "guts" of the protagonist are key to the outcome of the plot. From this perspective, the war room deals and bold trades become central. Vescey, as the informant, becomes the key player. And though each of these frameworks speak to many of the structural decisions present in the draft coverage, they fail to capture the structure and theme succinctly in the way asked for in Bordwell's (1989) notion of the dominant.

Clearly, TNT tries to project both informational and human-interest dimensions in the draft. The desire to increase the size of the audience beyond those specifically interested in the NBA as sport or sport in general seems a key motivation for this approach. The spokesman for the human-interest side in the coverage is Sager, just as Vescey is the informational guru. We need only contrast their summaries of the significant outcomes of the 1996 draft after the 58th player had been chosen to find the distinct focus for each:

CS: Well, as we've seen tonight, kids think of the NBA on playgrounds all over the world. And I think that happened on the concrete just outside of the housing project in the Bronx where the three older brothers of Stephon Marbury dreamed of playing professional basketball. And tonight I think Stephon fulfilled the dream for all of them. The thoughts of Mabel, his proud mother, and the sights of her crying, overwhelmed with emotion, probably brought a tear to some of us as well. I thought the kids did a great job, and it was a very emotional scene because it's a dream for an entire family. (TNT, 1996)

Vescey's reaction to that summary is one of barely restrained mockery. He lets out a mild laugh and is clearly underwhelmed by Sager's emotional reporting. He gathers himself and proceeds. His "OK" is almost uttered as a question:

PV: OK. My thoughts: It occurs to me that the Suns getting Steve Nash might kill the deal they have with the Rockets. They don't need Sam Cassell anymore, and I'm told that that deal is dead. So there will be no Charles Barkley going to the Rockets. What I think we might look for at this point is for Charles to go to the Hornets. They're reshuffling there. They're going big-time. So let's look for that in the next couple of weeks. (TNT, 1996)

In these two summations, the commentators focus on markedly different elements: one dramatic and evoking the rags-to-riches and beauty pageant storylines, the other focusing on the business news of the draft and the transfer of power. Rather than trying to find a dominant explanation that merely reconciles these contrasting themes and dimensions, it seems more fruitful to offer a dominant analogue that transcends them.

THE DRAFT AS RITUAL

What seems most consistently to unite the structural and thematic elements in the draft is the idea of ritual. From this perspective, the elements function as a coordinated whole. Bordwell (1989, p. 107) notes that the identification of semantic fields should take into account the film's specificity and cover the entire film. Ritual fulfills both of these obligations well.[15]

In saying that the draft functions as ritual, I am arguing, as Michael Novak (1976) has, that sport functions similarly to religion. He notes that "the ceremonies of sport overlap those of the state on one side, and those of the church on the other" (p. 19). Thus, this position incorporates the insights offered by viewing the draft as election/convention coverage, as well as those gained by viewing it as a sporting event. Novak also notes that this perspective on sports will not resonate with everyone: "Sports is, somehow, a religion. You either see or you don't see what the excitement is" (p. xi).

Joseph Bastian and Anson Shupe (1980) state that the three important functions of ritual are to provide continuity or movement, enhance solidarity, and provide occasion for the mystery and majesty that are part of human social life. The draft satisfies many of these functions in ways accessible to casual viewers, but even more so for NBA fans. The dominant explanation of ritual functions effectively in the opening segment that used Magic Johnson's comments about the significance of the draft. It is also present in the music that attempts to create a mood of impending climax and in the video that shows each draftee at his peak. The use of interviews with former NBA greats and the draftees' coaches, which typically convey themes supporting the idea that "this kid is ready," function to project the draft as a ritual of transformation and a rite of passage and provide continuity as well. The draft is a ritual because it is a deed done with words and other symbols. The initiates are dressed in unique costume. They put on the team hat as a symbol of their new identity. They move from the civilian setting of the green room to the professional setting of the podium and interview chair. Each element of the coverage re-inforces the dominant notion of a ritual of transformation.

Ronald Grimes (1985) argues that mapping rituals involves addressing questions related to ritual space, ritual objects, ritual time, ritual sounds and language, and ritual identity (pp. 21 ff.). The preceding analysis ad-dresses many of these areas explicitly. His categories also offer an oppor-tunity to review and highlight the ritual elements of the draft.

The draft takes place in one of the NBA arenas, which can be seen as sacred space within the context of sport. There are also attempts through color, the ramp up to the stage, the podium, and the prominence of the NBA logo to further transform the setting into sacred space. David Chidester and Edward Linenthal (1995) note in the introduction to their edited volume *American Sacred Space* that "we can identify sacred space as ritual space, a location for formalized, repeatable symbolic perfor-mances. As sacred space, a ritual site is set apart from or carved out of 'ordinary' environment to provide an arena for performance of controlled 'extraordinary' patterns of action" (p. 9). We find this dimension in No-vak's (1985) claim that arenas themselves are sacred spaces, as well as in the efforts to set the draft apart through changes to the hosting arena. Elevated platforms; red, white, and blue as dominant colors; and the board that contains the names of the selected draftees function to desig-nate the arena as sacred space. There are also sacred objects, the most obvious being the team hat that succinctly symbolizes the draftee's new allegiance. The basketball graphic is also positioned as a sacred object to the extent that it is seen to literally and graphically transform the draftees.

There are two ways in which sacred time is invoked. First, the draft functions as a transformational ritual in its position in the NBA year. It is simultaneously the end of one season and the start of the next. It is the end of one year because the order of selection has been determined by the success—or lack thereof—of that team during the prior season. It is also the start of the next season because the selection, for many teams, is a source of hope for the *future* seasons. In this sense. it is what Victor Turner (1974) has called a seasonal ritual.

Second, time is sacred in how it is used during the draft. The explicit use of five minutes and two minutes between picks is sacred time. Prag-matically, it allows discussion and analysis, but for teams and fans, it also becomes the penultimate moment before the selection is announced. In addition, the use of five and two minutes makes a clear distinction be-tween the first and second rounds. In a culture in which time is money, there is a value statement here. First-rounders are worth more, and the decisions surrounding them are more consequential. Such explicit use of time is not critical to all rituals but may reflect the values of Western culture, which have a heightened orientation toward time.

Ritual sounds and language also occur during the draft. Stern's (and

later Assistant Commissioner Rod Thorn's) repetitive phrasing when announcing the picks is one indication of the ritual language of the draft. A
less obvious example is the draft logo and music used to establish the
location and activity after most commercial breaks. In each case, repetition
is key to function. Only after knowing that Stern will say the same phrase
each time does it take on its ritual function and speak "history" into
being.[16]

Finally, Grimes (1985) notes the importance of ritual identity. The draft's
allure hinges on ritual identity, or rather, the transformation of identity
from boy to man, from amateur to professional, from college kid to mil-
lionaire, and so forth. There also is significant ritual identity with the
teams and other players. Many teams and players function both metaphorically and literally within the draft coverage, and their symbolic identities enrich the NBA fans' understanding of the draft as ritual.

The draft is clearly a ritual, but what kind of ritual is it? Turner's (1974)
work leads to the conclusion that the draft is a rite of passage for the
individual players, as well as for the teams. Borrowing from the work of
Arnold van Gennep on rites of passage, Turner notes that van Gennep
originally meant for the term "rites of passage" to stand for both changes
in a person's social status and changes associated with seasonal altera-
tions. He also uses van Gennep's stages for the basis of his own work:
separation, transition, and incorporation. Separation and incorporation
are fairly clear—the setting apart and then reintegration of the initiates,
respectively. Turner's contribution extends and refines the transition
phase and the implications of this threshold, or marginal status of the
participants, which is given the name "liminal." Turner summarizes it as
follows: "[T]he ritual subjects pass through a period of ambiguity, a sort
of social limbo which has few (though sometimes these are most crucial)
of the attributes of either the preceding or subsequent profane social stat-
uses or cultural states" (p. 24).

Turner (1974) also offers an insightful contrast between the two forms
of rites of passage identified by van Gennep:

I have argued that intitiatory passage rites tend to "put people down" while some
seasonal rites tend to "set people up," i.e., initiations humble people before permanently elevating them, while some seasonal rites (whose residues are carnivals
and festivals) elevate those of low status transiently before returning them to their
permanent humbleness. (p. 25)

He also suggests that the "passage from one social status to another is
often accompanied by a parallel passage in space, a geographic movement
from one place to another" (p. 25). Each of these insights is exemplified
in the form and coverage of the NBA draft.

The draftees are clearly in a liminal state during the draft. Turner (1974) suggests that initiates in such a state are temporarily undefined. That is not quite the case here. They are defined, as draftees. However, consistent with Turner's work, they are defined in terms of their weakest state. They were outstanding college players—the BMOC (Big Men On Campus) who will later become NBA players. But for now, temporarily, they are simply draftees. Even after their symbolic transformation and union with their new teams, they cannot practice with their new team until their contracts are officially signed. The draft is about the transitional moment when they move symbolically, if not literally, to their elevated status. But first they must be humbled. This humbling appears in the waiting to be picked (for all but the first pick), the donning of the team cap (not something traditionally worn with a suit), and the interview with Sager.

Fortunately, from the standpoint of television coverage, many of these markers are visual and incorporate the movement Turner (1974) suggests is necessary in a rite of passage. The green room is a distinct location that may represent the epicenter of their liminality. It is not a place for civilians, and it is not a place for players. It is only a place for draftees (and family and agents). After selection, they must begin the transition: Leave family and agent to be briefly guided by a team representative but then ultimately to venture alone to the commissioner. Following that official greeting, the draftee usually faces Sager for an interview. Again there is movement, and the initiate's first real test begins. It is not a test that will determine whether he is accepted by the NBA, but rather a test in the court (no pun intended) of public opinion. The draftee is under scrutiny to meet implicit standards, one of which is humility, or at least recognition of his draftee-turned-rookie status. This transformation underlies Sager's conversation in 1995 with Antonio McDyess:

CS: Well, Antonio, just two years ago you were playing high school basketball in Mississippi, now you're up on the podium before a world-wide audience [the] second pick in the draft. How surprised are you [that] all this has happened so quickly?

AM: I'm real surprised. I mean I never thought I'd be in this position so quick, but it came and it's a great honor for me and I'm happy and my family is too.

CS: You go from Quipmen to Tuscaloosa, now to LA—*Lifestyles of the Rich and Famous*. Is it a scary thought to go out there?

AM: Yeah, but I'm ready to take the challenge and I've got good people behind me and I'm ready to take that challenge. (TNT, 1995)

The interview continues with references to values instilled in him during his childhood and what McDyess will bring to the team. Sager concludes the interview with the following:

CS: Enjoy LA but don't forget those values you were taught back in Quipmen. (TNT, 1995)

For the draftees who are going through a liminal state that ultimately leads to an elevated status, the rite of passage is one of humbling before exalting. Consistent with Turner's (1974) scheme, the draft also functions as a seasonal rite that elevates those who are traditionally humbled throughout the year. For bad teams, the draft may be the highpoint of the year and the time they feel best about themselves and most hopeful about their abilities. The right to top talent is secured through a lack of ability (and subsequent status) throughout the year. Now these same teams have the top picks. The pecking order is in reverse. Better teams are calling them about trading for that pick because they finally have something of value. Fans of these poor teams are able to hope that "this is the year" that their team picks the right player or makes the right trade to redefine the exercise from a seasonal rite (in which the poor teams return to their lowly status) to a rite of passage (in which the poor team emerges as a good team). A brief article from wire service reports illustrates this dynamic well:

It's called "Clippers Time" [sic] around the NBA. It's the NBA draft, and it's the one time in the season when the worst teams get all the attention because they have the highest draft picks. It's one of the few times the NBA recognizes Canada. (NBA Notes)

It is important to note how the Clippers' image as a perpetually inept team is maintained in this coverage. The Canadian reference includes Vancouver and Toronto, both homes to two expansion teams. These teams typically do poorly their first years in the league and secure high draft picks.

The various storylines and other elements of the draft frame it as a rite of passage for the initiates and a seasonal rite for many of the teams. Throughout the coverage, viewers are able to witness draftees confronting and passing through their liminal state and then emerging as sources of hope for the teams that pick them. Each player is given a positive spin. Any pick or player that the commentators disagree with is typically qualified by a statement such as, "We don't know what is going on behind the scenes," a reference to possible trades set up prior to or during the draft. This discourse pattern preserves the expectations of hope and transformation for the fans of that team, expectations that come with a rite of passage and a seasonal rite of hope and transformation. Examine the dialogue surrounding pick 58, the last pick of the 1996 draft:

EJ: We are down to the final pick of the night, 58 for the Dallas Mavericks. One more time for Rod Thorn.

RT: With the 58th and final selection of the 1996 NBA Draft, the Dallas Mavericks select Darnell Robinson from the University of Arkansas.

RP: If I'm Darnell Robinson, what I do right now is go out and hire myself a trainer and every single day [he] works me out for three hours, because this young man can make it if he comes in in great shape and just concentrates on his body, his conditioning. This man has a future in the NBA, if not he's going to Europe.

HB: Rick, when he came out of high school he was the leading scorer in the history of the state of California. Everyone thought he had tremendous potential. But he just seemed to stay at a certain level. But you're right, the body is there and he's going to a team that he could make. . . .

RP: No question.

HB: . . . you see, and make a contribution.

RP: And that's all he has to do is dedicate himself. When he came back from the injury, he got in great shape. He helped Arkansas play well in the NCAA tournament. Then, as soon as the season ended, he got back out of shape.

EJ: We hearken back to what we said earlier in the night. The last pick of the draft last year was Don Reid of Georgetown going to the Detroit Pistons. He proved that, yes indeed, you can be the last pick in the draft and you can have an impact in the NBA, as he did for Doug Collins's bunch. Darnell Robinson of Arkansas, the final pick in the 1996 NBA draft. (TNT, 1996)

Robinson is clearly a long shot. All initial signs suggest that he peaked in high school and has failed to develop. Yet his selection is framed as hopeful for the Dallas Mavericks and transformational for him. He has been selected; he can make it. In addition, a recap of each team's draft picks brings forth almost universally positive remarks. The objectivity of hard news gives way to an explicit recognition that the draft is a ritual of hope as well as transformation. Thus, each team is given a reason to be hopeful due to their participation.[17]

The ties of ritual with the history of a particular community are also evident here. Seen through the dominant lens of ritual, Robinson can make it because someone in the past has done it. Moreover, history is a significant theme that frames the draft as ritual. Magic Johnson is intentionally used in the opener because it is likely that a point guard will be drafted first in the 1996 draft. He was the last point guard to be taken first in the draft. Julius Erving is asked to comment on Marcus Camby because they are linked through their common history as players for the University of Massachusetts. Video highlights of great players from the past are used to set up videos of the draftees. The commissioner's constant repetition of the phrase "With the ____ pick of the 1996 NBA Draft. . . ." is a reminder of the historicity of the event.

CONCLUSION

Are there elements that this dominant analogue does not capture as well as some of the possible alternative perspectives? Yes, but the dominant explanation of ritual best reconciles the majority of the structural and thematic elements in the draft coverage. There is little precedent in contemporary media for covering rituals, so I drew on techniques and templates from other genres. The fundamental and basic nature of ritual provides the grounds for these other genres to be brought up when relevant. The draft is a business transaction that is now "in the books," as Johnson concluded at the end of coverage. It is an election, which is why Allen Iverson must be questioned about his character and leadership in his first interview and why the 1995 draftees are referred to as candidates. It is a sporting event, which is why Johnson says we are about to "tip off" the draft in both the 1995 and 1996 draft coverage and why highlights and extensive graphics appear. Yet underneath all of these surface structures, the draft is projected as ritual, and that is why Johnson concludes the coverage with the following dialogue that is followed by upbeat music, not unlike that of a contemporary church benediction, and video of draft-night highlights:

EJ: And the 1996 NBA draft is in the books as they file out of Continental Arena, here in New Jersey. Thank you so much for joining us. The draft began with the number one pick, Allen Iverson of Georgetown, and ended with the 58th pick, Darnell Robinson of Arkansas. In between, a lot of tears, a lot of happy parents, a lot of proud coaches, a lot of proud universities and colleges happy to see their guys go. That's the story of the NBA draft. We're happy we could bring it to you, thanks for joining us in New Jersey. (TNT, 1996)

It is the story of the draft indeed, a story best understood as ritual.

NOTES

1. Bordwell (1989) defines semantic fields as a "set of relations of meaning between conceptual or linguistic units" (p. 106). There are a variety of meaningful relations, including opposition, inclusion, scale, and others.

2. Rhetorical scholars would find great affinity between Bordwell's (1989) program in film and Michael Leff and Andrew Sachs's (1990) efforts toward a "close reading" in rhetorical studies. Both agree on the primacy of the text and the shortcomings of theory-driven criticism.

3. This search is not unlike Burke's discussion of pentadic ratios. Kenneth Burke (1969/1945) argues that the human drama can be better understood by identifying how five elements interact: act (what), scene (where), agent (who), agency (how), and purpose (why). Key to his system is identifying the key ratio: the two pentadic elements whose interaction best explains the nature of or success or failure of an event. Several insightful ratios may exist, yet one ratio—scene-act for example—will provide the most explanatory power for the rhetorical situation under investigation.

4. Kristen Thompson (1988) has noted that "[f]unction is the crucial factor to understanding the unique qualities of a given artwork, for, while many works

may use the same device, that device's function may be different in each work" (p. 15). Consequently, the discussion of these five devices will focus on their function within the artifact of the draft.

5. One of the more endearing moments of the 1994 draft involved an international player (Georghe Muresan). The seven-foot, seven-inch draftee, who spoke very little English, wanted to say at least a few words in English during the interview. He attempted the NBA slogan, "I love this game!" but it came out "I love you, this game." His broad smile and obvious joy combined with the ironically more intimate version of the slogan was a highlight.

6. The work of John Fiske (1993) is relevant here. Fiske argues that, for humans, the making of meaning is pleasurable. This tendency provides the basis for polysemy in his system. His concept offers some insight into why the relationship between players and observers works on some level and is not seen as one-sided by either party.

7. Pitino tends to prefer fast teams that try to outrun their opponents. His comments on waiting for Derrick Coleman to get down the floor refer to Coleman's lack of speed and effort to run on the court.

8. Free agency is the most recent plot twist to enter the NBA. After a player has completed one contract, he is a "restricted free agent," which means the team that currently has him can keep him simply by outbidding other teams. Once a player has fulfilled a second contract, he becomes an "unrestricted free agent," which means he can go anywhere he wants to, regardless of the money offered by his current team. Thus, a team could be forced to trade a good player, and get someone in return for losing the player, because it are fearful of losing him to free agency, in which case the team would have no return for his loss. Notice how quickly the free agency plotline can intertwine with the trading plotline.

9. Walter Fisher, in *Human Communication as Narration* (1989/1987), has suggested that we assess stories on the basis of coherence (does it hang together?), and fidelity (does it ring true?) (pp. 105 ff.). Vescey is clearly appealing to a sense of coherence that will ring true with the audience's ideal that there is order and justice in the sport universe.

10. That is, Wallace's Syracuse Orangemen went to the National Collegiate Athletic Association tournament and beat enough teams to make it to among the final four teams playing for the college national title.

11. Narrative continuity is expressed to link drafts with one another as well. For example, after Allen Iverson was selected first, Ernie Johnson commented: "That means that the last two picks of the draft have both been from Georgetown. Don Reid was the last pick last year and now Allen Iverson, the first pick of the '96 draft" (TNT, 1996).

12. The significance of going up on the way to greet the commissioner is significant as well. It more dramatically illustrates the transition hinted at here and that will be discussed later. The upward direction also functions metaphorically: Journeying upward is good, as Lakoff and Johnson (1981) have illustrated.

13. See Edgarton and Ostroff (1985).

14. A case could be made, of course, that physical attributes often influence political campaigns: Taller candidates frequently win over shorter opponents, very few candidates with beards have won, and so forth. However, the operative word here is "dominate," with the implication of physical confrontation or an explicit

assessment of physical attributes, neither of which is the case in a political campaign . . .; at least, not yet.

15. A variety of definitions for ritual exist. Kendall Blanchard and Alyce Cheska (1985) argue that ritual is "a facet of culture and can be viewed as the symbolic dimension of social activities that are not specifically technical in nature" (p. 53). David Kertzer (1988) offers another broad definition by defining ritual as "symbolic behavior that is socially standardized and repetitive" (p. 9). Rothenbuhler (1998) defines ritual as "the voluntary performance of appropriately patterned behavior to symbolically effect or participate in the serious life" (p. 27). This final definition highlights the communicative dimensions of rituals, which are, at their core, symbolic.

16. See Connerton (1991/1989).

17. This theme of hope even spills over to those college players left undrafted. Brown recognizes various undrafted players who spent time in the Continental Basketball Association or Europe and then have come back to be successful at the NBA level. This example also illustrates the hierarchy issue and the way in which this annual ritual is framed as a source of hope.

REFERENCE LIST

Bastian, Joseph W., & Shupe, Anson D. Jr. (1980). Metaphor in the rituals of restorative and transformational groups. In Ray B. Brown (Ed.), *Rituals and ceremonies in popular culture* (pp. 48–60). Bowling Green, OH: Bowling Green University.

Blanchard, Kendall, & Cheska, Alyce. (1985). *The anthropology of sport: An introduction*. South Hadley, MA: Bergin & Garvey.

Bordwell, David. (1989). *Making meaning: Inferences and rhetoric in the interpretation of cinema*. Cambridge, MA: Harvard.

Brummett, Barry. (1991). *Rhetorical dimensions of popular culture*. Tuscaloosa: University of Alabama.

Burke, Kenneth. (1969/1945). *A grammar of motives*. Berkeley: University of California.

Chidester, David, & Linenthal, Edward T. (1995). Introduction. In David Chidester & Edward T. Linenthal (Eds.), *American sacred space* (pp. 1–42). Bloomington, IN: Indiana University.

Connerton, Paul. (1991/1989). *How societies remember*. Cambridge, England: Cambridge University.

Edgarton, Gary, & Ostroff, David. (1985). Sports telecasting. In Brian G. Rose (Ed.), *TV genres: A handbook and reference guide* (pp. 257–286). Westport, CT: Greenwood.

Fisher, Walter R. (1989/1987). *Human communication as narration: Toward a philosophy of reason, value, and action*. Columbia: University of South Carolina.

Fiske, John. (1993). *Television culture*. London: Routledge.

Grimes, Ronald L. (1985). *Research in ritual studies: A programmatic essay and bibliography*. Metuchen, NJ: Scarecrow Press.

Kertzer, David I. (1988). *Rituals, politics, and power*. New Haven, CT: Yale University Press.

Lakoff, George, & Johnson, Mark. (1981). Conceptual metaphor in everyday lan-
    guage. In Mark Johnson (Ed.), *Philosophical perspectives on metaphor* (pp. 286–
    325). Minneapolis: University of Minnesota.
Leff, Michael. (1980). Interpretation and the art of the rhetorical critic. *Western
    Journal of Speech Communication, 44,* 337–349.
Leff, Michael, & Sachs, Andrew. (1990). Words the most like things: Iconicity and
    the rhetorical text. *Western Journal Speech Communication, 54,* 252–273.
"NBA notes." (1998). *Wilmington Star-News* 21, June: B-2.
Novak, Michael. (1976). The joy of sports: End zones, bases, baskets, balls and the
    consecration of the American spirit. New York: Basic Books.
Novak, Michael. (1985). American sports, American virtues. In Wiley Lee Um-
    phlett (Ed.), *American sports culture* (pp. 34–49). Toronto: Associated Uni-
    versity.
Rothenbuhler, Eric W. (1998). *Ritual communication: From everyday conversation to
    mediated ceremony.* Thousand Oaks, CA: Sage.
Sage, George H. (1996). Patriotic images and capitalist profit: Contradictons of
    professional team sports licensed merchandise. *Sociology of Sport Journal, 13:*
    1–11.
Thompson, Kristin. (1988). *Breaking the glass armor: Neo formalist film analysis.*
    Princeton, NJ: Princeton University.
Turner Network Television. (1995, June 22). *NBA Draft, 1995* [Television broadcast].
    Atlanta, GA: Tuner Network.
Turner Network Television. (1996, June 26). *NBA Draft, 1996* [Television broadcast].
    Atlanta, GA: Turner Network.
Turner, Victor. (1974). *Dramas, fields, and metaphors: Symbolic action in human society.*
    Ithaca, NY: Cornell University.

Index

About the Contributors

ANDREW C. BILLINGS is an assistant professor at Clemson University, Clemson, South Carolina. His research interests include the intersection of issues of gender, ethnic, and nationality within televised media content. His sports communication work has appeared in journals such as *Mass Communication & Society, Journal of Communication, Journal of Sport and Social Issues,* and *Sociology of Sport Journal.*

ROBERT S. BROWN is Associate Professor of Communication, Chair of the Communication Arts Department, and Director of the Sport Communication major at Ashland University, Ashland, Ohio. He has presented more than 30 papers focusing on the study of sport communication at both communication- and sport-oriented conferences. His work on sport communication has been published in the *Journal of Sport and Social Issues, Women's Studies,* and the recently published book *Take Me Out To the Ballgame: Communicating Baseball.* He can be contacted at rbrown2@ashland.edu.

JAMES L. CHERNEY is Instructor of Speech Communication in the Communication Studies, Theatre, and Art Department at Westminster College, New Wilmington, Pennsylvania. Current chair of the Disability Issues Caucus of the National Communication Association, he has published reviews and essays that engage disability and rhetoric in such journals as *Argumentation and Advocacy* and the *Quarterly Journal of Speech.*

ELLIOT GAINES is a professor of communication at Wright State University, Dayton, Ohio. He has lectured internationally about semiotics and communication, and his research focuses on semiotics, identity, culture, and media.

JOHN TODD LLEWELLYN is Associate Professor of Communication at Wake Forest University, Winston-Salem, North Carolina. He taught previously at Purdue University and the University of North Carolina at Greensboro and as an adjunct at UNC-Chapel Hill, where, as an undergraduate, he honed his affection for basketball and coachtalk. His area of specialty is organizational rhetoric, the examination of public relations and organizational communication. He has published in the areas of political communication, corporate social responsibility, public relations, and urban legends. Prior to academia, he worked as a media relation's specialist and speechwriter in government.

TODD F. McDORMAN is an assistant professor of speech at Wabash College, Crawfordsville, Indiana. His work has been published previously in the *Quarterly Journal of Speech* and *Women's Studies in Communication*, and he contributed to *Counterpublics and the State*. His primary research interest is the study of legal discourse and the ways various discourse communities engage the law with respect to social and political change. He has also explored issues of sport and society, as in this volume and other forthcoming work. He has further examined the area of sport communication through a freshman seminar he teaches entitled "Sport and Society."

RICHARD OLSEN is a professor in the Department of Communication Studies at the University of North Carolina at Wilmington. His work on the NBA draft is featured in *Big Game, Small World,* by *Sports Illustrated* senior writer, Alex Wolff. His broader research interests focus on the rhetorical analysis of contemporary popular culture. Other projects include analyses of sport-utility vehicle advertisements and MTV's hit program *Total Request Live.*

DANIEL J. O'ROURKE III is an associate professor of communication at Ashland University, Ashland, Ohio. He has presented numerous papers at national and regional communication conferences on the subjects of popular culture and political issues. A former chair of the Department of Communication Arts at Ashland University, O'Rourke was instrumental in seeking faculty support for the area of sport communication as field of study within the department. This is his first scholarly effort in the area of sport communication.

SARAH PROJANSKY is an associate professor in the Women's Studies Program at the Unit for Cinema Studies at the University of Illinois,

Urbana-Champaign. She is a coeditor of *Enterprise Zones: Critical Positions on Star Trek* (1996) and author of *Watching Rape: Film, Television, and Postfeminist Culture* (2001) and has published in *Cinema Journal, Signs*, and various anthologies. She is currently writing a book on high-profile, disruptive girls in twentieth and twenty-first century popular culture.

NICK TRUJILLO is Professor of Communication Studies at California State University, Sacramento, and previously held appointments at Southern Methodist, Michigan State, and Purdue Universities. He has published three books, including *The Meaning of Nolan Ryan*, and numerous articles. He is currently working on a book about dog culture in California. He can be contacted at nickt@csus.edu.

LEAH R. VANDE BERG is Professor of Communication Studies at California State University, Sacramento, and previously held appointments at Northwestern University and Southern Methodist University. She is the author of numerous articles and book chapters on television, gender, sports, and cultural values and is a coauthor and editor of four books, including *Critical Approaches to Television, Organizational Life on Television*, and *Television Criticism: Approaches and Applications*.

THOMAS VAUGHN is an assistant professor at Arkansas Tech University, Russellville. His research revolves around the study of subaltern communities.

Breinigsville, PA USA
30 July 2010
242701BV00001B/59/P